Teachers, Teaching, and Media

Transgressions: Cultural Studies and Education

Series Editor

Shirley R. Steinberg (*University of Calgary, Canada*)

Founding Editor

Joe L. Kincheloe (1950–2008) (*The Paulo and Nita Freire International Project for Critical Pedagogy*)

Editorial Board

Rochelle Brock (*University of North Carolina, Greensboro, USA*)
Annette Coburn (*University of the West of Scotland, UK*)
Kenneth Fasching-Varner (*Louisiana State University, USA*)
Luis Huerta-Charles (*New Mexico State University, USA*)
Christine Quail (*McMaster University, Canada*)
Jackie Seidel (*University of Calgary, Canada*)
Cathryn Teasley (*University of A Coruña, Spain*)
Sandra Vega (*IPEC Instituto de Pedagogía Crítica, Mexico*)
Mark Vicars (*Victoria University, Queensland, Australia*)

This book series is dedicated to the radical love and actions of Paulo Freire, Jesus "Pato" Gomez, and Joe L. Kincheloe.

VOLUME 132

The titles published in this series are listed at *brill.com/tcse*

Teachers, Teaching, and Media

Original Essays about Educators in Popular Culture

Edited by

Mary M. Dalton and Laura R. Linder

BRILL
SENSE

LEIDEN | BOSTON

All chapters in this book have undergone peer review.

Library of Congress Cataloging-in-Publication Data

Names: Dalton, Mary M., 1962- editor. | Linder, Laura R., editor.
Title: Teachers, teaching, and media : original essays about educators in
  popular culture / edited by Mary M. Dalton and Laura R. Linder.
Description: Leiden ; Boston : Brill Sense, [2019] | Series: Transgressions :
  cultural studies and education, ISSN 2214-9732 ; volume 132 | Includes
  bibliographical references and index.
Identifiers: LCCN 2019010444 (print) | LCCN 2019016810 (ebook) | ISBN
  9789004398092 (ebook) | ISBN 9789004390409 (hardback : alk. paper) | ISBN
  9789004398085 (pbk. : alk. paper)
Subjects: LCSH: Education in popular culture. | Education in mass media. |
  Teachers in motion pictures. | Teachers on television.
Classification: LCC LC191 (ebook) | LCC LC191 .T44 2019 (print) | DDC
  371.102--dc23
LC record available at https://lccn.loc.gov/2019010444

ISSN 2214-9732
ISBN 978-90-04-39808-5 (paperback)
ISBN 978-90-04-39040-9 (hardback)
ISBN 978-90-04-39809-2 (e-book)

Copyright 2019 by Koninklijke Brill NV, Leiden, The Netherlands.
Koninklijke Brill NV incorporates the imprints Brill, Brill Hes & De Graaf,
Brill Nijhoff, Brill Rodopi, Brill Sense, Hotei Publishing, mentis Verlag,
Verlag Ferdinand Schöningh and Wilhelm Fink Verlag.
All rights reserved. No part of this publication may be reproduced, translated,
stored in a retrieval system, or transmitted in any form or by any means, electronic,
mechanical, photocopying, recording or otherwise, without prior written
permission from the publisher.
Authorization to photocopy items for internal or personal use is granted by
Koninklijke Brill NV provided that the appropriate fees are paid directly to The
Copyright Clearance Center, 222 Rosewood Drive, Suite 910, Danvers, MA 01923,
USA. Fees are subject to change.

This book is printed on acid-free paper and produced in a sustainable manner.

For my parents, Hilda and Steve Dalton
– M.M.D.

For my brother, Stephen B. McLean
– L.R.L.

CONTENTS

Preface	ix
Acknowledgements	xi
List of Figures	xiii
Notes on Contributors	xv

1. A Loyalty Test for the American Educator, from Ichabod Crane to Erin Gruwell   1
   Steve Benton

2. Schooling the State: Teachers and Democratic Dispositions on *The West Wing*   13
   Stephanie Schroeder

3. Rethinking Student-Teacher Relationship Intimacy as Attachment   23
   Andrew Wirth

4. Mr. Miller Goes to War: *Saving Private Ryan* and the Children Left Behind   33
   Jeff Spanke

5. *In Loco Parentis Redux*: Bob and Linda Belcher at Wagstaff School   47
   Elizabeth Currin

6. What's a Nice White Lady to Do?: A Critical Literacy Lens on Teaching and Learning in Pop Culture Portrayals   57
   Jill Ewing Flynn

7. The Dis-Education of Rock 'n' Roll   67
   Gary Kenton

8. Promoted to Control?: School Office Culture in HBO's *Vice Principals*   81
   Chad E. Harris

9. The *Insecure* Teacher: How Issa Rae Has Normalized the Black Woman to Create TV Magic   97
   Naeemah Clark

CONTENTS

10. Contrasting the Archetypal Sage with the Mentor Coach in Young
    Adult Literature: Insights for Teacher Reflection
    Ian Parker Renga and Mark A. Lewis   107

11. *Saved by the Belle*s: Gender Roles in the Quintessential Teen Comedy
    Elizabeth Currin and Stephanie Schroeder   119

12. "Good" Teacher on Her Own Terms: Miss Shaw in ABC's
    The Wonder Years
    Chad E. Harris   133

13. Liberatory Pedagogy in Action: The Embodied Performance of
    Community College Instructors in Film and Television
    Kristy Liles Crawley   147

14. Q the Teacher—TV Lessons from the 24th Century: You Do Not Have
    to Be an Omniscient Teacher, But It Helps
    Roslin Smith   161

15. Speechless to *Speechless*: Nontraditional Teacher Characters in
    Recent Sitcoms
    Mary M. Dalton   169

Film Sources   181

Television Sources   183

Index   185

viii

PREFACE

We have written about depictions of educators in popular culture for nearly 25 years, and there have been enormous changes in the literature since then. During the mid-1990s, many of these publications focused on Hollywood films and explored tropes related to Good Teachers presented as heroes and saviors. While scholarship on these iconic teachers remains a staple in the field, critical approaches have expanded as some of the films produced have become more complex. Also, more and more scholars have begun researching other narrative media depicting educators. This is a positive development because, as we have long argued, popular depictions of teachers and administrators have an effect on how real educators are viewed and valued. This being the case, it is important to broaden our scope to consider various types of meaningful texts.

In this collection of original essays, authors write about literary classics, young adult literature, popular music, television, and—yes—movies. These are all forms that permeate our daily lives and become part of our individual routines. Our contributors write about iconic teachers, unconventional teachers, teachers in revisionist texts, deplorable administrators, and teachers who might more typically be characterized as mentors, coaches, or nontraditional educators. The range of representations considered on these pages is a strength of this volume, and the new ways readers are instructed to think about education in terms of form, function, and cultural context is illuminating.

Popular representations of teachers and teaching are easy to take for granted precisely because they are so accessible and pervasive. Our lives are intertextual in the way lived experiences overlap with the stories of others presented to us through mass media. It is this set of connected narratives that we bring into classrooms and into discussions of educational policy. In this day and time—with public education under siege by forces eager to deprofessionalize teaching and transfer public funds to benefit private enterprises—we ignore the dominant discourse about education and the patterns of representation that typify educator characters at our peril.

ACKNOWLEDGEMENTS

We wish to acknowledge the support of the organizers, presenters, and participants of the Teachers, Teaching, and Media Conference held at Wake Forest University in March 2017. This conference reflected a variety of critical and theoretical perspectives emphasizing the examination of representations of educators in popular culture and the use of technology and media in the classroom, and many of the chapters in this volume began as papers presented at the conference.

Many thanks to the conference coordinator and organizer, Kimberly Scholl; conference planning committee, Mary M. Dalton, Adam Friedman, Woody Hood, and Allan Louden; conference program committee, Alan Brown, Robert C. Bulman, Mary M. Dalton, Laura R. Linder, and Ali Sakkal; technical support, Jo Lowe, Scott Claybrook, and Tyler Pruitt; social media director, Leah Haynes; conference support staff, Candice Burris and Holly Stearne; and conference assistant Erin McGinnis. In addition, many thanks to keynote speakers, Robert C. Bulman and Kristen Eshleman; authors panel speakers, Jacqueline Bach, Mary M. Dalton, Laura R. Linder, and Jeremy Stoddard; and workshop leader, Georgia Terjaje.

We also want to thank our colleagues, especially the ever-helpful staff at ZSR Library at Wake Forest University. We cannot thank enough our family and friends who support us every step of the way. All those long hours, days, and months of work would have been much harder without your love and understanding. Finally, to all our teachers and students over the years from whom we have learned, we are grateful for the privilege of sharing your knowledge and experiences in the classroom.

FIGURES

1.1.	Mr. Davis and Amy March from *Little Women* by Louisa May Alcott (1896). Illustration by Frank Merrill. Courtesy Project Gutenberg	6
1.2.	Erin Gruwell (Hilary Swank) and Mrs. Campbell (Imelda Staunton) in *Freedom Writers* (2007)	10
2.1.	Sam Seaborn (Rob Lowe) and Mallory O'Brien (Allison Smith) on *The West Wing* (NBC 1999–2006)	16
2.2.	Rep. Joe Willis (Al Frann) on *The West Wing* (NBC 1999–2006)	18
3.1.	Henry Barthes (Adrien Brody) in *Detachment* (2011)	29
4.1.	Private Jackson (Barry Pepper), Corporal Upham (Jeremy Davies), Private Mellish (Adam Goldberg), Sergeant Horvath (Tom Sizemore), Medic Wade (Giovanni Ribisi), and Private Reiben (Ed Burns) in *Saving Private Ryan* (1998)	37
4.2.	Captain Miller (Tom Hanks) and Private Ryan (Matt Damon) in *Saving Private Ryan* (1998)	41
5.1.	Linda Belcher (voiced by John Roberts) on *Bob's Burgers* (Fox 2011–)	52
5.2.	Bob Belcher (voiced by H. Jon Benjamin) on *Bob's Burgers* (Fox 2011–)	54
6.1.	Jason Sherwood (Michael Angarano) and Ms. Sinclair (Julianne Moore) in *The English Teacher* (2013)	61
7.1.	Grandfather (Wilfred Brambell) and Ringo (Ringo Starr) in *A Hard Day's Night* (1964)	68
7.2.	Chuck Berry performing "School Days" on *The Dick Clark Saturday Night Beechnut Show*, August 23, 1958	71
7.3.	John Lennon (center) at Quarry Bank High School, Liverpool, England, May 1957	73
8.1.	Lee Russell (Walton Goggins) and Neal Gamby (Danny McBride) on *Vice Principals* (HBO 2016–18)	82
8.2.	Dr. Belinda Brown (Kimberly Hébert Gregory) on *Vice Principals* (HBO 2016–18)	84
9.1.	We Got Y'all logo on *Insecure* (HBO 2016–)	99
9.2.	Issa Dee (Issa Rae) on *Insecure* (HBO 2016–)	101
10.1.	Albus Dumbledore (Richard Harris) and Harry Potter (Daniel Radcliffe) in *Harry Potter and the Sorcerer's Stone* (2001)	111
11.1.	Miss Carrie Bliss (Hayley Mills) on *Good Morning, Miss Bliss* (Disney 1987–89)	120
11.2.	Kelly as "Miss Kapowski" (Tiffani-Amber Thiessen), Zack as "Principal Morris" (Mark-Paul Gosselaar), and Slater (Mario Lopez) on *Good Morning, Miss Bliss* (Disney 1987–89)	126

xiii

FIGURES

12.1. Miss Shaw (Lanei Chapman) and Kevin Arnold (Fred Savage) on
The Wonder Years (ABC 1988–93) 135
12.2. Miss Shaw (Lanei Chapman) on *The Wonder Years* (ABC 1988–93) 141
13.1. Professor Bauer (Betty White) on *Community* (NBC and Yahoo!
Screen 2009–15) 153
13.2. Mercedes Tainot (Julia Roberts) in *Larry Crowne* (2011) 156
14.1. Q (John de Lancie) on *Star Trek: The Next Generation*
(Syndicated 1987–94) 163
14.2. Q (John de Lancie) on *Star Trek: The Next Generation*
(Syndicated 1987–94) 164
15.1. JJ DiMeo (Micah Fowler) and Kenneth (Cedric Yarbrough)
on *Speechless* (ABC 2016–19) 172

NOTES ON CONTRIBUTORS

Steve Benton is director of the University Honors Program and an associate professor in the Department of English and Languages at East Central University in Ada, Oklahoma. His most recent essays on pedagogy and depictions of educators in popular fiction and film have appeared in *The Journal of Popular Film and Television*, *The Atlantic*, *The Philosophy of Tim Burton*, and *Screen Lessons*.

Naeemah Clark is an associate professor in the School of Communications at Elon University. She teaches courses focused on the entertainment media and industry practices. Along with conducting academic scholarship, her writing has also been published by *The Huffington Post*, *The New Republic*, and *The Atlanta Journal Constitution*.

Kristy Liles Crawley is a doctoral candidate at the University of North Carolina at Greensboro and a full-time member of the English faculty at Forsyth Technical Community College. Her teaching and research interests include feminist theory, composition theory and pedagogy, nineteenth-century American literature and culture, material rhetoric, and spatial theory. Her research on ethnography and pedagogy has appeared in *Prose Studies* and *Teaching English in the Two-Year College*.

Elizabeth Currin is a doctoral candidate in curriculum and instruction at the University of Florida. Her research interests include practitioner inquiry, the history of education, and pop culture representations of schools. Before pursuing a doctorate, Elizabeth was a high school English teacher.

Mary M. Dalton is professor of communication at Wake Forest University where she teaches courses in critical media studies. Her scholarly writing includes *The Hollywood Curriculum: Teachers in the Movies*, and she is a documentary filmmaker.

Jill Ewing Flynn is an associate professor who teaches undergraduate methods courses and coordinates student teaching for the English Education Program at the University of Delaware. Her research and teaching interests center on critical multicultural education, primarily on how teachers can engage with students in productive discussions about race.

Chad E. Harris is a PhD student and graduate assistant in Cultural Foundations at the University of North Carolina at Greensboro. In addition to critical media studies and educators in popular culture, Harris's work delves into philosophical approaches to film and literature to offer new dimensions to what phenomenology can offer cinematic and literary experiences.

Gary Kenton earned his BA in Special Education from Greensboro College and his Master's Degree in Communications from Fordham University and has taught

NOTES ON CONTRIBUTORS

at every level from Head Start to college. In addition to his scholarly publications, Gary has also been elected to public office on three out of four tries.

Mark A. Lewis is associate professor of literacy education at Loyola University Maryland. His scholarship examines and critiques representations of adolescence and youth in young adult and adult literature, explores the multifaceted literary competence of secondary students, and identifies effective ways to support linguistically diverse learners.

Laura R. Linder is a retired professor of media arts. She earned her Ph.D. from the University of North Carolina at Chapel Hill in Mass Communication. Her other publications (with Mary M. Dalton) include *Teacher TV: Seventy Years of Teachers on Television* (Peter Lang, 2019), *Screen Lessons: What We Have Learned from Teachers in the Movies and on Television* (Peter Lang, 2017), *The Sitcom Reader: America Re-Viewed, Still Skewed* (SUNY Press, 2016). Her first book was *Public Access Television: America's Electronic Soapbox* (Praeger, 1999).

Ian Parker Renga is assistant professor of education at Western Colorado University. His work examines the intersection of practice, identity, and community in teacher development. He has published essays exploring archetypal depictions of teachers, and recently coedited a book on education in popular film titled *Teaching, Learning, and Schooling in Film: Reel Education.*

Stephanie Schroeder is Assistant Professor of Social Studies Education at the Pennsylvania State University-University Park. Her research interests include democratic and citizenship education, elementary pre-service teacher education, and education activism.

Jeff Spanke is an assistant professor of English at Ball State University where he teaches courses in introductory composition, young adult literature, and English teaching methods. His current scholarship focuses on multimodal social constructions of teachers, teaching, students, and learning. He is also interested in the intersections of vulnerability and resistance in teacher education programs, particularly in regard to the narrative and theatrical elements of the teaching profession.

Roslin Smith, Assistant Professor, is in her fifth year of teaching in the Communication Department at SUNY Fredonia NY. During this time, her creative work has been shown nationally and internationally including the UK, Italy, Egypt, South Africa and Quebec. Over the past two years, she has won three Broadcast Education Association awards, and is currently creating an historical documentary *Among the Hemlocks,* with financial assistance from an Artist in the Community Decentralization Grant, NY.

Andrew Wirth is a graduate of the Master's in Communication program at Wake Forest University.

xvi

STEVE BENTON

1. A LOYALTY TEST FOR THE AMERICAN EDUCATOR

From Ichabod Crane to Erin Gruwell

ABSTRACT

During the early years of the American Republic, an important strain of American popular culture helped establish the idea that there was something fundamentally un-American about those who put too high a value on intellectual community, book smarts, and cultural sophistication. Popular texts like Washington Irving's "The Legend of Sleepy Hollow" (1820) depicted schoolteachers in particular as arrogant, untrustworthy, undemocratic, and at some level, disloyal to fundamental American values.

Today, too many Americans have bought into the notion that schools are morally suspicious and ill-equipped to introduce students to complex ideological and intellectual issues. These suspicions of intellectual community are surprisingly—and ironically—reinforced in popular films that celebrate educator heroes. The formula for many of these films—such as *Dead Poets Society* (1989), *Dangerous Minds* (1995), and *Freedom Writers* (2007)—is to celebrate an educator-hero as an American icon while disparaging intellectual community more generally, a formula that they inherited from Louisa May Alcott's *Little Women* novels. These texts affirm the stereotype of *most* schoolteachers as arrogant, undemocratic, Ichabod-like tyrants while celebrating the rare alternative to the norm as the real American hero. At one level, such narratives celebrate the possibility that truly motivated educators can thrive in oppressive institutional environments, but on another level, they reinforce the dangerous belief that educational institutions and the intellectual communities they support are instinctively hostile to freedom and learning.

Keywords: anti-intellectualism, Washington Irving, "The Legend of Sleepy Hollow," Louisa May Alcott, *Little Women, Freedom Writers*, acculturation, educator-hero, American identity narrative, democratic education, intellectual community

***

It is common that we have learned not to trust "grand narratives" in postmodern cultural criticism. Too often, we have seen how such broad stroke renderings

© KONINKLIJKE BRILL NV, LEIDEN, 2019 | DOI:10.1163/9789004398092_001

S. BENTON

serve the fantasies of their authors more than they offer an unbiased account of the complex historical domains that are their subject. I believe postmodern skepticism of this kind is wise. So, it is with a reasonable degree of self-consciousness that I offer the following, *modestly* grand narrative of the way educators have been depicted in popular American culture and film. I confess at the outset that my modestly grand narrative serves an unapologetically grand pedagogical fantasy.

A MODESTLY GRAND NARRATIVE AND
AN UNAPOLOGETICALLY GRAND FANTASY

The narrative goes like this. During the early years of the American Republic, when the nation was forming a new identity narrative, an important strain of American popular culture helped establish the idea that there was something fundamentally un-American about those who put too high a value on intellectual community, book smarts, and cultural sophistication. These anti-intellectual sentiments are evident in popular texts like Susanna Rowson's *Charlotte Temple* (1791), Mason Locke Weems's *The Life of Washington* (1800), James K. Paulding's *Davy Crockett's Own Story* (1833), Timothy Flint's *Biographical Memoir of Daniel Boone* (1833), and, most notably, Washington Irving's short story "The Legend of Sleepy Hollow" (1820). Such texts depict schoolteachers in particular as arrogant, untrustworthy, undemocratic, and at some fundamental level, disloyal to basic American values.

Suspicion of intellectual community remains strong in popular American culture, and it is surprisingly—and ironically—powerful in popular films that celebrate educator heroes. The formula for many of these films—such as *Dead Poets Society* (1989), *Dangerous Minds* (1995), and *Freedom Writers* (2007)—is to celebrate an educator-hero as an American icon while disparaging intellectual community more generally, a formula inherited from Louisa May Alcott's *Little Women* novels, published between 1868 and 1876. The key is to affirm the stereotype of *most* schoolteachers as arrogant, undemocratic, Ichabod-like tyrants while celebrating the rare alternative to the norm as the real American hero. Thus, though on one level such narratives celebrate the possibility that truly motivated educators can thrive in oppressive institutional environments, on another level they reinforce the dangerous belief that educational institutions and the intellectual communities they support are—and must always be—oppressive.

This suspicion of intellectual community is poisonous, and it is a suspicion that is supported not only by popular culture. It is embedded into the very structure of our schools where educators are isolated from each other in closed-door classrooms and students are deprived from ever seeing the school as an integrated intellectual community where the lifeblood is conversation, disagreement, discussion, and debate among peers. Imagining an alternative educational structure that foregrounds the school as a showcase for intellectual community is the grand pedagogical fantasy served by the historical narrative that follows.

EDUCATOR AS ALIEN

In *Love and Death in the American Novel*, Leslie Fiedler famously described Washington Irving's "Rip Van Winkle" as the ur-text of American literature because the kind of character it celebrated ("a man on the run, harried into the forest and out to sea, down the river or into combat—anywhere to avoid 'civilization'") has become the "typical male protagonist of our fiction" (1966, p. 26). Irving's other contribution to the American literary canon provides us with an equally influential national fantasy in which the *civilizing* educator, like Ichabod Crane, is transformed (like the proud Redcoat army) into the "man on the run." The role of national hero in this drama is played not by civilization's sleepy resistor but by the virile horseman who runs a civilizing alien out of town. That the horseman is *headless*, and therefore literally impervious to the life of the mind, is almost too perfect.

In "The Legend of Sleepy Hollow," the itinerant schoolmaster is an ambitious seducer, and a vain, unattractive one at that, who journeys into the Hudson River Valley to enlighten the locals. The antipathy some in Sleepy Hollow feel for Ichabod Crane's civilizing mission is embodied in Brom Bones, the "hero of the country round," who is the hero of Irving's story as well (1820, p. 303). After Brom runs Ichabod out of town, the community burns the books Ichabod leaves behind, and the decision of one local, Hans Van Ripper, "to send his children no more to school," is apparently emulated widely, as "the deserted schoolhouse soon fell to decay, and was reported to be haunted by the ghost of the unfortunate pedagogue; …" (1820, p. 319). Though Ichabod's mysterious exit becomes a source of much speculation, the story's narrator reports that it is not much lamented.

Brom's resentment of Ichabod is spurred by the unlikely successes the schoolmaster has enjoyed in his efforts to seduce Katrina Van Tassel, the belle of Sleepy Hollow, whom Brom has long had his eye on, and it is through her that the story's ambivalence about the value of education and intellectual culture is channeled. Despite the fact that Ichabod has a head that is "small, and flat at top, with huge ears, large green glassy eyes, and a long snipe nose" (1820, p. 295), his tentative successes with Katrina move him to fantasize that under cover of singing lessons he will be able to woo Katrina, marry her, and take possession of some of her father's wealth, thereby improving the miserable living conditions he endures as the Sleepy Hollow schoolmaster.

Ichabod's poverty does not win him any compassion from the community, however. Though everything Ichabod owns can be "tied up in a cotton handkerchief," the people of Sleepy Hollow see no reason it should be otherwise (1820, p. 297). As Irving's narrator explains, they "understand nothing of the labour of headwork" and believe Ichabod has a "wonderfully easy time of it" as a professional schoolteacher, his extracurricular labors notwithstanding. Far from thinking of the educator as a noble crusader against ignorance, most of Sleepy Hollow's citizens consider Ichabod to be like all schoolteachers: "mere drones" who are "grievous burdens" to the community (1820, p. 297).

S. BENTON

Though Irving's narrator plays up the Headless Horseman as the tale's central mysterious element, the emotional drama that unlocks the narrative is rooted in the mystery that surrounds Katrina Van Tassel's feelings toward Ichabod and Brom. Katrina must choose whether to respond favorably to the schoolmaster's courting campaign or to accept instead a romantic alliance with Brom Bones, the local hero who torments the schoolmaster. Without this drama, the Headless Horseman would never have appeared in the Sleepy Hollow forest because the only reason Brom Bones dons the ghoul's disguise is that he suspects the schoolteacher threatens the traditional social order of Sleepy Hollow, an order in which the "hero of the country round" (Brom) is supposed to marry the girl with "the prettiest foot and ankle in the country round" (1820, pp. 303, 300). The question that Brom must puzzle over (as do readers) is this: What could Katrina possibly see in an ungainly figure like Ichabod that might make her choose the schoolteacher over his Herculean rival?

The cynical (and misleadingly simple) answer—hinted at by the narrator—is that Katrina didn't see anything at all in Ichabod: she was simply using the schoolmaster to make Brom jealous. Such an explanation is implied when the narrator wonders aloud whether Katrina's "encouragement of the poor pedagogue [was] all a mere sham to secure her conquest of his only rival?" (1820, p. 313). To some extent, this cynical reading of Katrina's motives seems sufficient, especially since the ruse seems to have worked by the tale's end when Katrina and Brom are happily wed.

Yet, this explanation fails to account for the fundamental dramatic logic of the story because even if Katrina's attraction to Ichabod is nothing more than a ploy to pique Brom's interest, the ploy's success depends on Brom's ability to *believe* its sincerity. Whether Katrina does or does not feel genuinely ambivalent about the choice between Brom and Ichabod, her power over Brom is rooted in his belief in the possibility of such ambivalence. In other words, Brom's vulnerability to Katrina's machinations turn on his belief that an educated character like Ichabod might bring certain virtues to the table that Brom himself does not have.

What is the sole apparent positive quality that Ichabod has? It is the sophistication that his education has given him. This educational polish—even if it does cloud Ichabod's common sense—gives him a degree of cosmopolitanism that country roughs like Brom might envy. For Ichabod is "esteemed by the women as a man of great erudition" (1820, p. 298), erudition that he displays by "instructing the young folks in psalmody" (1820, p. 297) and "reciting for ... the amusement [of the country damsels] all the epitaphs on the tombstones" (1820, p. 298). In his function as a kind of "traveling gazette," Ichabod is a civilizer who promises connection between the local community and the wider world on the basis of a shared knowledge of sophisticated cultural practices that provincial Americans, and residents of Sleepy Hollow in particular, are assumed to lack (1820, p. 298).

It is important to note that Ichabod's interaction with the younger males in Sleepy Hollow gives him an opportunity to extend his popular base for "when school hours were over, [Ichabod] was even the companion and playmate of the larger boys" (1820, p. 296). As such, Ichabod's education does not merely make him a threat to

Brom's pursuit of Katrina Van Tassel. It also threatens Brom's status as the "hero of the country round," and, in a larger sense, his status as a national icon. If these larger boys and their younger siblings were to learn to share Ichabod's intellectual interests, they might very well become a gang of scholars who could supplant Brom's "gang of rough riders" (1820, p. 305). For Brom, then, the most threatening element of Katrina's attraction to Ichabod is the attraction she—and the other citizens of Sleepy Hollow—may feel for the model of the cultivated and worldly intellectual community the schoolteacher promises to bring to Sleepy Hollow. To accept such a community as ideal would be to accept a paradigm in which the United States was, presumably, inferior to its European counterparts. The patriotic overtones of this conflict are reinforced by the fact that Brom's final face-off with the schoolteacher occurs near the very spot where Benedict Arnold's British liaison, Major John André, was captured during the Revolutionary War. The implication is that Ichabod—like Benedict Arnold—is a kind of traitor to the model of American masculinity represented by Brom. In Irving's narrative, Ichabod's humiliation, Brom's marriage to Katrina, and the restoration of his anti-intellectual authority in America's Sleepy Hollow is a happy ending.

THE ALCOTT REVERSAL: INSTITUTION AS ICHABOD, ISOLATED EDUCATOR AS HERO

In one sense, the March family novels that Louisa May Alcott published 46 years after Irving finished "Sleepy Hollow" serve as an antidote to Irving's mocking depiction of the educator as an American traitor. While Irving's short story celebrates the schoolteacher's nemesis as an American hero, Louisa May Alcott's novels recommend the selfless educator as democracy's true champion. The Alcott template for the American pedagogical drama has been beneficial to American pedagogical imagination for many reasons, not the least of which is the way it helped rescue the popular image of the American educator from its damning association with the negative aspects of the Ichabod Crane stereotype. In its own way, however, the Alcott template has been as harmful to the American pedagogical imagination as the Ichabod Crane caricatures it ostensibly challenges. By championing isolated educator-heroes whose primary pedagogical focus is moral uplift rather than acculturation into intellectual community, these books have introduced familiar, American, anti-intellectual prejudices into a new model of educational success.

Alcott affirms Irving's contempt for Ichabod-like figures and uses it as leverage for the promotion of a heroic alternative. In *Little Women*, the role of the awful Ichabod surrogate is given to Mr. Davis, a cruel, petty man who runs the school attended by Amy March, the youngest of the March sisters. Davis, a character who could easily be transplanted into any number of novels by Charles Dickens, is one of those "nervous gentlemen with tyrannical tempers and no more talent for teaching than Dr. Blimber," Alcott writes (1868, p. 68). Though he is considered by some to be "a fine teacher" because he "knew any quantity of Greek, Latin, algebra, and ologies of all sorts," Alcott encourages readers to regard Davis's sophistication with skepticism (1868, p. 68). As Amy's mother, Marmee, observes, "Conceit spoils the finest genius," and those who support an arrogant intellectual like Davis are misguided fools (1868, p. 71). For however knowledgeable an intellectual like Davis may be about "ologies of all sorts," his very intellectual seriousnessmakes him a poor instructor. In Davis's educational world, "manners, morals, feelings, and examples were not considered of any particular importance," but in the March family, they are given the highest educational priority (1868, p. 68).

The patriotic subtext that sets democratic virtue on one side and intellect on the other is echoed in the way Alcott likens the conflict between Amy and Davis to the conflict between a tyrannical British monarch and his rebellious American subjects. Borrowing familiar tropes from patriotic narratives of the American Revolution, Alcott describes Davis's efforts to banish chewing gum from the schoolhouse as a "long and stormy war" and reports that Amy's teacher has, like a jealous monarch, "made a bonfire of the confiscated novels and newspapers, had suppressed a private post-office, had forbidden distortions of the face, nicknames, and caricatures, and done all that one man could do to keep half a hundred rebellious girls in order" (1868, p. 68). When Davis declares that he will henceforth consider pickled limes to be "a contraband article" and solemnly vows "to publicly ferule the first person who was found breaking the law," a showdown with the lime-loving, American patriot, Amy, is inevitable. Davis eventually catches the youngest of the March daughters lime-handed and declines to offer her the equivalent of a royal pardon (1868, p. 68).

In the best tradition of a long line of freedom-loving American icons, Amy submits to Davis's discipline with a stoicism worthy of Patrick Henry and, as Alcott puts it, "set her teeth, threw back her head defiantly, and bore without flinching several tingling blows on her little palm" (1868, p. 69). Just as the Crown had failed to subdue the will of the American colonists, Davis's efforts to exert his will on the young Ms. March end up backfiring; when Marmee hears that Davis has whipped Amy in front of the class, she promptly denounces him and his intellectual arrogance

Figure 1.1. Mr. Davis and Amy March from Little Women *by Louisa May Alcott (1896). Illustration by Frank Merrill. Courtesy Project Gutenberg*

and removes her daughter from the school, issuing the March family's Declaration of Independence from the American school.

The March family's disdain for those who are expert in "ologies of all sorts" is later affirmed when Jo makes her first trip to New York City and is invited to "a select symposium" held in honor of several intellectual celebrities. Though she "went prepared to bow down and adore the mighty ones," when she begins to take note of their various moral flaws, "her reverence for genius received a severe shock" (1868, p. 340). A poet, who is among those in attendance, devoured his supper with an unseemly "ardor which flushed his intellectual countenance," she tells us; a novelist "vibrated between two decanters with the regularity of a pendulum"; a profound philosopher "imbibed tea Johnsonianly and appeared to slumber"; the "Madame de Staels of the age" satirized each other; and, the scientists "gossiped about art, while devoting themselves to oysters and ices" (1868, p. 340). Worst of all, however, when the intellectual colloquium finally turns to more cerebral concerns, Jo gradually realizes that "the world was being picked to pieces," that religion is being "reasoned into nothingness," and "intellect was to be the only God" (1868, p. 341). Fortunately for Jo, her escort, Professor Bhaer, is as troubled as she is by the immodest and immoral behavior of the intellectuals. Just as Marmee whisks Amy out of Mr. Davis's classroom, Bhaer adopts "the grimmest expression she had ever seen him wear. He shook his head and beckoned [Jo] to come away" from the discussion (1868, p. 341). In expressing his disdain for the intellectual assembly, he wins Jo's heart and, eventually, her hand in marriage.

Bhaer's heroism in his confrontation with the intellectual crowd at the New York soirée is depicted in terms that appeal to a familiar, nationalist paradigm in which virtue and sophistication are radically opposed. Though Bhaer, a German immigrant, speaks a "broken English" that contrasts sharply with "the brilliancy of the philosophic pyrotechnics" of his sophisticated interlocutors, he "stood to his colors like a man," insisting that "God was not a blind force and immortality was not a pretty fable but a blessed fact." Although "the wise men argued well" and "outtalked" the Professor, Jo notes that Bhaer remains "not one whit convinced" by their reasoning, and as a result, Jo "wanted to clap her hands and thank him" (1868, p. 341).

Alcott was by no means the first popular writer to express suspicion of "reasoning," good arguments, and "philosophical pyrotechnics," nor was she the first educator to emphasize the importance of moral instruction and the pedagogical value of humility and patience, but what makes her advocacy of moral education worth examining more closely is the success she enjoyed in popularizing the idea that such an education could be provided by a school teacher. The traditional alternative to turning over your children to the moral instruction provided by the Ichabods of the world was to send them to church and teach them at home, as Mrs. March does with her daughter Amy. This approach is implicitly recommended in Weems's biography of George Washington in which Weems assures readers that the future President's father knew that implanting "virtues" was the job of a parent, not a teacher, and that confusing the roles of each would be a form of neglect (1962, p. 20).

S. BENTON

Alcott's novels would have done little more than reinforce this home-schooling impulse if they had concluded with the successful education Marmee provides Amy and her other daughters within the confines of the March home. It becomes easier to see the importance Alcott gives to the classroom teacher in the moral formation of American youth, as well as in the nation's identity narrative, when *Little Women* is read as just the first installment in the larger narrative arc that follows the whole career of Jo March and her family portrayed in Alcott's subsequent novels *Little Men* (1871) and *Jo's Boys* (1886).

As we have seen, Alcott's account of Amy's encounter with Mr. Davis resembles the standard account of the brave American school scorner versus the tyrannical educators bent on disciplining him. Unlike James K. Paulding's *Davy Crockett's Own Story* (1833) or Timothy Flint's *Biographical Memoir of Daniel Boone* (1833), which depict educators in a disparaging light and celebrate the learner's liberation from the classroom, the negative pedagogical encounters in Alcott's *Little Women* function as a springboard for future, positive pedagogical experiences in *Little Women* and its sequels. Having conceded the reality of the Ichabod stereotype, Alcott's narrative quickly disabuses Amy March of the notion that her negative educational experience has liberated her from further schooling. Amy is rescued from Mr. Davis's classroom, but her education continues at home under the tutelage of her sister Beth, whom Marmee immediately drafts for the position. Similarly, though Jo and Professor Bhaer feel scorn for the community of intellectuals that they encounter in New York City, when they eventually get married, they dedicate their lives to establishing two educational institutions: the Plumfield Academy boarding school (described in *Little Men*) and, later, Laurence College (described in *Jo's Boys*), which she and Bhaer open when the Plumfield graduates are ready for higher education. In both cases, educational disappointment with traditional teaching is but a prelude to a celebration of a pedagogical alternative.

Many critics have seen Jo's marriage to Bhaer as a disappointing retreat from the proto-feminist independence she had flirted with to that point in the narrative. Alcott herself describes Bhaer as "neither rich nor great, nor handsome,—in no respect what is called fascinating, imposing, or brilliant" (1868, p. 339). Yet, by choosing to marry the "queer looking" Professor Bhaer rather than her more dashing neighbor, Theodore "Laurie" Laurence, Jo symbolically reverses the decision Irving's Katrina Van Tassel makes to reject her own odd-looking suitor, Ichabod Crane, and link her fortunes with Brom Bones (1868, p. 323). Laurie, like Brom, is a "universal favorite" with a streak of braggadocio and an animus toward schools and teachers. He "more than once came perilously near suspension and expulsion" from school, and he "liked to thrill the girls with graphic accounts of his triumphs over wrathful tutors, dignified professors, and vanquished enemies" (1868, p. 233). Whereas Irving presents Ichabod's tormenter Brom as a clever and irreverent American hero worthy of winning the romantic heroine, Alcott depicts the similarly school-scorning Laurie as a charming but immature figure who "though nearly through college, was as much of a boy as ever" (1868, p. 235). In rejecting Laurie, Jo rejects the kind of immature, responsibility-shirking boy that, as Fiedler notes, American literature has traditionally glorified. In Alcott's world, Laurie's irreverent attitude toward schools and learning is less subversive than it is shallow.

The contrast between Laurie and the Professor is immediately evident in the differing feelings the two men have toward the value of artistic and intellectual acclaim and the communities that produce such acclaim. In a scene in which Laurie and each of the March sisters reveal their dreams for the future, their "castles in the air," Laurie and Jo both speak of a desire to become famous artists. Laurie wants to become a famous musician and Jo a writer (1868, p. 140). When Bhaer meets Jo, however, he convinces her to abandon her desire for fame and popularity as a literary artist, a desire he sees has been realized in her "plunge into the frothy sea of sensational literature," and encourages her to turn instead to a more pedagogically-inclined vocation: writing didactic works that will contribute to the moral development of her readers, especially the youngest of them (1868, p. 337).

Professor Bhaer's own life choices are guided by just such a pedagogical instinct, as evidenced by his decision to leave Berlin where he was "honored and esteemed for learning and integrity" to come to America and educate the orphaned sons of his late sister (1868, p. 340). Whereas Laurie dreams of leaving America, establishing his musical fame abroad, and settling in Germany to "just enjoy myself and live for what I like" (1868, p. 140), Bhaer has left Germany to come to America where he was "as poor as a church mouse" and almost as anonymous so that he can teach his sister's children and, essentially, live for them (1868, p. 323).

In this juxtaposition—frivolous Laurie looking east across the Atlantic in a selfish search for recognition and reward versus serious Bhaer traveling west in a selfless effort to teach and to serve—Alcott reverses the associations American popular culture had to that point attributed to the school scorner and the educator. Previously, the educator has often been an impractical elitist with an un-American fondness for intellectual tradition and hierarchical power, and the educator is now a down-to-earth democrat with a very American commitment to moral idealism and practical service. At the same time, the school scorner is reframed as an irresponsible, morally immature adolescent with a suspicious interest in European approbation. In short, Alcott's novels help make it possible for an educator not only to be a hero but to be an iconic, American one.

ALCOTT REDUX

The power of the Alcott formula for educator-hero dramas that champion the freedom-loving outsider while disparaging larger educational institutions remains evident in a wide array of popular films. As noted at the beginning of this chapter, popular films such as *Dead Poets Society* (1989), *Dangerous Minds* (1995), and *Freedom Writers* (2007) celebrate an educator-hero as an American icon in ways that loom large in cultural consciousness and endure as narrative tropes. *Freedom Writers* provides one particularly useful example. Like Alcott's novels, *Freedom*

Writers glorifies an educator whose students come to think of her as a loving parent. Erin Gruwell, the hero of the story played by Hilary Swank in this biopic, is an idealistic, rookie English teacher assigned to teach a class of remedial sophomores at Wilson High School, one of the roughest schools in a gang-ridden area of Los Angeles. For anyone who has ever seen an educator-hero film, it will not surprise you to find out that Gruwell clashes with her supervisor, Mrs. Campbell (Imelda Staunton), a cynical, veteran department head. Though Gruwell initially struggles to connect with her students, she eventually manages to reach them by convincing them that she really cares. She does this by giving them new books (purchased with money she earns from extra jobs outside of school), by showing compassion for the scars they have received in the gang wars, and, as Mrs. Campbell complains, by eating and playing games in class.

Figure 1.2. Erin Gruwell (Hillary Swank) and Mrs. Campbell (Imelda Staunton) in Freedom Writers *(2007)*

Freedom Writers encourages teachers to ask themselves a number of valuable questions: Am I challenging my students to perform to their full potential? Do my assignments connect to their lives in a meaningful way? Have I shown that I have a genuine interest in the quality of their lives? Still, *Freedom Writers*, like Alcott's novels and Irving's "Sleepy Hollow," also offers a dismal take on intellectual community. This dark view is nowhere more obvious than in a showdown that takes place among Gruwell, Ms. Campbell, and Campbell's veteran ally, Mr. Gelford (John Benjamin Hickey) in the school principal's office. The issue at hand is whether or not Gruwell will be granted her request to continue teaching the students she has bonded with during the next school year after they have moved up a grade level. The scene has the feeling of a custody battle in a divorce proceeding, a point that is emphasized by Gelford's comment that Gruwell and her husband are getting a divorce.

Campbell is the villain in this scene. She is older and less attractive than Gruwell; she appears to be on the edge of nervous breakdown; and, she ends with the ungenerous suggestion that if any of Gruwell's students fail, it will be Gruwell's fault. Nevertheless, there is some wisdom in these words Campbell speaks, "Believe it or not, Ms. Gruwell, there are other capable teachers in this school. If you've made the progress you say you have, your students should be ready to move on." Campbell is right to challenge the suggestion made by Gruwell, by *Freedom Writers*, and by most educator-hero films, that good teachers are the rarest of creatures. It is a credit to *Freedom Writers* that the film allows Campbell to make this sensible observation, though the plot of the film works to undermine the claim.

The crucial question that Campbell poses, but which *Freedom Writers* does not encourage teachers to consider with much seriousness, is this: am I helping socialize my students into a broader intellectual community, or am I suggesting the only truly valuable community is the one that exists within these walls with me as the parent/center? *Freedom Writers* gives Campbell the opportunity to sneak a version of this question into her speech about how Gruwell's students need to be able to move into someone else's classroom. By depicting the struggle between them as a struggle between estranged parents over who loves the kids more, whom the kids love more, and who should have sole custody over them, *Freedom Writers* discourages us from imagining an alternative notion of what we can and should hope for from teacher-student encounters and encounters between teachers in an American school.

IMAGINING A PEDAGOGICAL ALTERNATIVE

We are still waiting for a meaningful turn in the American identity narrative in which readers and film viewers are encouraged to visualize the school as a valuable intellectual community in which a love of learning is modeled by more than one educator, teaching is not always done in isolation, and loyalty to intellectual community is not associated with disloyalty to American values and love of freedom and democracy. In the most practical terms, such an imaginative turn would mean getting teachers together into rooms in front of students, modeling intellectual community, making arguments, articulating diverse perspectives, challenging claims, responding to challenges in a respectful but compelling way, and inviting students to join in the conversation. Open forums, panel discussions and Q&As, conferences, and team-taught seminars, as well as online versions of these kinds of encounters, should be at the core of intellectual life in American schools and colleges. Not too long ago, it seemed to be the case that students were only able to witness public discussion of controversial issues in crude, shallow, and contentious forms provided by cable news channels. Today, many students do not even get that because their encounters with controversial issues are filtered through the increasingly narrow ideological channels made possible through digital media.

S. BENTON

In a democratic society, schools should be able to offer a robust alternative, but too many have bought the widely-supported notion in American popular fiction and film that schools are morally suspicious and ill-equipped to introduce students to complex ideological and intellectual issues. "The Legend of Sleepy Hollow" supports the view that the iconic American village might be better off without teachers whose loyalty to the nation is suspect. The *Little Women* novels support the view that the best educators are those who turn their backs on the wider intellectual community and retreat to a more narrowly circumscribed ideological enclave where message control is assured. Educator-hero films like *Freedom Writers* support the view that the best teachers are those who protect their students from the arrogant, cold-hearted policies of experienced experts and administrators. We can't blame popular culture for the ways these attitudes affect our collective pedagogical imagination, but we can pay attention to it, imagine something better, and take practical steps to bring an alternative narrative to life.

REFERENCES

Alcott, Louisa May. (1986). *Little men. 1871*. New York, NY: Signet Classic.
Alcott, Louisa May. (1995). *Jo's boys. 1886*. New York, NY: Bantam.
Alcott, Louisa May. (2000). *Little women. 1868/1871* (S. Cheever, Intro.). New York, NY: Modern Library.
Fiedler, Leslie. (1966). *Love and death in the American novel* (1960, rev. ed.) New York, NY: Stein.
Flint, Timothy. (1967*). Biographical Memoir of Daniel Boone, 1833* (J. K. Folsom, Ed.). New Haven, CT: College and University.
Irving, Washington. (2001). The legend of sleepy hollow. 1820. In *The legend of sleepy hollow and other stories, or, the sketch book of Geoffrey Crayon, Gent* (pp. 293–320). New York, NY: Modern Library.
Paulding, James Kirke. (1954). *The Lion of the West: retitled The Kentuckian, or a trip to New York. A Farce in two acts* (1830 rev., 1833 rev.) (J. A. Stone, W. B. Bernard, & J. N. Tidwell, Eds.). Stanford, CA: Stanford University Press.
Rowson, Susanna. (1986). *Charlotte Temple. 1794* (C. N. Davidson, Ed.). New York, NY: Oxford University Press.
Weems, Mason L. (1962). *The life of Washington* (1800, rev. ed. 1809) (M. Cunliffe, Ed.). Cambridge, MA: Belknap Press of Harvard University Press.

STEPHANIE SCHROEDER

2. SCHOOLING THE STATE

Teachers and Democratic Dispositions on The West Wing

ABSTRACT

The West Wing highlights the democratic dispositions of teachers and extends the larger historical narratives surrounding both the moral superiority of teachers and, as moral agents, teachers' central role in the cultivation of a democratic citizenry. Beyond the extension of these historical narratives, the depictions of White House Chief of Staff Leo McGarry's daughter, Mallory, a fourth grade teacher, or Mr. Willis, an eighth grade social studies teacher from Ohio filling his deceased wife's congressional seat, offer a counter narrative desperately needed both at the time the show aired and in the present day, as teachers are demonized as the problem, not the solution, to a national educational crisis. *The West Wing*, then, both builds on and challenges dominant depictions of teachers, all the while reminding us of the crucial role of teachers in a democratic society.

Keywords: democratic dispositions, teachers, counter-narrative, *The West Wing*

***

In the early days of the republic, just months after the ratification of the United States Constitution, Thomas Jefferson expressed his pleasant surprise at the willingness of the states to adopt a document that would greatly limit their individual sovereignty for the good of the fledgling nation. The widespread acknowledgement that a constitution of this sort was necessary to maintain the fragile nation signaled to Jefferson the undeniable significance of a well-informed citizenry. Jefferson explained to correspondent Richard Price, "a sense of necessity, and a submission to it, is to me a new and consolatory proof that, whenever the people are well-informed, they can be trusted with their own government; that, whenever things get so far wrong as to attract their notice, they may be relied on to set them to rights." This example, one of many, illustrates Jefferson's belief that education could motivate otherwise self-interested individuals to concern themselves with the common good. Having seen and experienced the inadequacies of the Articles of Confederation, well-informed representatives from the 13 states engaged in a collaborative and deliberative process to ensure that the fragile democracy they envisioned would survive. This required compromise, sacrifice, and an uneasy dialogue.

© KONINKLIJKE BRILL NV, LEIDEN, 2019 | DOI:10.1163/9789004398092_002

S. SCHROEDER

Illustrations of present-day politicians engaging in deliberation and other democratic dispositions are scarce, as "[p]rocedural wrangling and partisan gridlock have tied the Congress in knots" (Thurber, 2011, p. 4). Most Americans will recall the heightened partisanship in 2017 over the confirmation (or lack thereof) of former President Barack Obama's Supreme Court nominee Merrick Garland ("Confirm," 2016), a particularly ugly 2016 campaign season (Phillips, 2016), and President Donald Trump's blatant disrespect for constitutional democracy (Cooke, 2015). Citizens also lack democratic traits. Interest in voting, for example, arguably the most basic expression of citizenship, is low. In 2014, the *New York Times* reported that voter turnout was the lowest it had been in over 70 years, perhaps because of the sense of powerlessness that pervades the public consciousness ("Worst," 2014), resulting in both anger and apathy. "Most people have become passive listeners and viewers," David T. Sehr argues, "not active discussants and participants" (1997, p. 60). These trends in American politics have led some to posit that the United States, long considered a liberal democracy characterized by the rule of law and maintenance of individual liberty, is moving toward illiberalism. Freedom of speech and the press, the right to assemble, and the protection of other individual rights seem to be under attack (Van Buren, 2014), suggesting that the "norms and practices" of democratic behavior (Zakaria, 2016) are declining. Americans are once again embracing authoritarian tendencies, just as they did after the terrorist attacks on September 11, 2001 (Westheimer, 2009, p. 316).

Deliberation is one of these norms and practices of democratic behavior so central to democracy, and it is a skill that is desperately needed in the present day. Dating back to the early republic, many of the founders envisioned a democracy built on the pillars of deliberation and compromise. Noah Webster, for example, "sought to realize his republican ideal by fostering careful public deliberations that avoid inflammatory, divisive, or misleading speech. He valued compromise as a means to forge a common good and sustain the union" (Gustafson, 1992, p. 7). Similarly, James Madison, as historian Jack N. Rakove explains, favored "calm, patient, increasingly informed discussion" as the key to effective governing. As Walter Parker has noted, a commitment to facts and "evidence rather than prejudice" (104) should guide such deliberation, allowing individuals to weigh alternatives with informed and reasonable others. To James Madison, "having both knowledge and sympathy were the defining characteristics of being an effective representative" (Rakove, 2006). American democracy was thus built upon a commitment to dialogue, understanding, and knowledge, even as that foundation has cracked in recent decades.

Despite the lack of democratic practices in the United States, deliberation and other necessary democratic skills and dispositions are available to watch in abundance on the still-popular drama *The West Wing* (NBC 1999–2006) even if not evident among actual elected politicians. Democratic dispositions—such as the willingness to deliberate and change one's mind and the knowledge of history and civics—are portrayed in detail on *The West Wing* by teachers featured on the series instead of politicians or White House senior staff. These depictions are most notable in the first and second seasons of the series when teachers are cast prominently against the presidential backdrop. Though never shown in their classrooms, teachers on *The West Wing* are noble, intelligent, and revered. These juxtapositions are neither accidental nor without consequence.

The democratic dispositions of teachers on *The West Wing* extend the larger historical narratives surrounding both the moral superiority of teachers and, as moral agents, their central role in the cultivation of a democratic citizenry. The depictions of White House Chief of Staff Leo McGarry's daughter, Mallory O'Brien (Allison Smith), a fourth-grade teacher, or Mr. Willis (Al Frann), an eighth-grade social studies teacher from Ohio filling his deceased wife's congressional seat, offer a counter-narrative desperately needed both at the time the show aired and in the present day, as teachers are demonized as the problem—not the solution—to a national educational crisis (Kumashiro "Bad Teacher"). Other mentions of teachers and schools on the series provide support for this argument, such as when President Bartlet (Martin Sheen) is preoccupied with a seemingly inconsequential school board race in New Hampshire or a heated exchange later in the series between a staff member and a visiting school teacher regarding school choice vouchers. These examples suggest that *The West Wing* both builds on and challenges dominant depictions of teachers and schools while reminding viewers of the crucial role of teachers in a democratic society.

The first appearance of a teacher on *The West Wing* takes place in the pilot episode. White House Deputy Communications Director Sam Seaborne (Rob Lowe) is running late to a presentation he has been asked to give to a class of fourth-graders. Under the mistaken impression that one of the students is the daughter of his boss, Leo McGarry (John Spencer), Sam is concerned about making a decent impression but fails to do so when he arrives both late and unprepared. Sam begins with a brief introduction then the room falls silent. When asked by the teacher Ms. O'Brien to speak a little about history—meaning the history of the White House—he instead offers a history of himself. When Ms. O'Brien clarifies, he improvises, stammering, "The Roosevelt Room is very famous. It is named after our 18th president, Franklin Delano Roosevelt. The chairs that you are sitting on today are fashioned from the lumber of a pirate ship captured during the Spanish American War." At this point, Ms. O'Brien abruptly ends the conversation, saying, "All right kids, I need to speak with Mr. Seaborne." Outside of the room, she scolds Sam, "I'm sorry to be rude, but are you a moron? The 18th president was Ulysses S. Grant, and the Roosevelt Room was named for Theodore." Sam replies, "I'm not good at talking about the White House." Apologetic and pleading, Sam then requests that Ms. O'Brien tell him who his boss's daughter is so he can at least ensure she has a nice time at the White House. As part of his apology, he notes his extremely bad day, including having (accidentally) slept with a professional call girl. Sam is then surprised and clearly mortified to discover that Ms. O'Brien is, in fact, Leo McGarry's daughter, further complicating his already disastrous day. The scene ends with Ms. O'Brien, in typical schoolmarm fashion—prim, brisk, no-nonsense—turning back into the Roosevelt Room, leaving Sam dumbstruck and concerned.

In this scene, a flustered, self-centered White House staffer stands in stark contrast to the proper, knowledgeable, quick-witted teacher. O'Brien's depiction likely brings to mind for viewers the traditional narrative surrounding teachers as moral agents who are dedicated to cultivating in children industriousness and virtue. This historical view of teachers as moral agents extends as far back as the 1840s when a shift began in American public consciousness and Americans began to view the common school as the primary site of moral development in American life. Triggered in part by the rise of immigrants to the United States and the strains of nation building and Westward Expansion, education reformers believed schools should provide a common sense of morality that would be necessary to maintain the social order in a diverse and expanding country (Kaestle, 1983). As a result, "future citizens—and the women who as mothers and teachers would train them—not only needed to know some United States geography, history, and law but also needed to be impressed with the moral responsibility of protecting American institutions" (Kaestle, 1983, p. 97). Teachers, then, would have to teach and model such morality.

Figure 2.1. Sam Seaborn (Rob Lowe) and Mallory O'Brien (Allison Smith) on The West Wing *(NBC 1999–2006)*

Mallory O'Brien's character on *The West Wing* demonstrates both her knowledge of the United States and her moral commitments to students and the nation. She tells Sam, "These children worked hard. All of them." Having worked hard, they deserve a decent and factual introduction to the White House, the most American of institutions. When compared to Sam, O'Brien's morality and historical knowledge stands in stark relief, thus perpetuating the historical narrative of teacher as moral agent and highlighting her democratic sensibilities.

SCHOOLING THE STATE

Five episodes later, in "Mr. Willis of Ohio," a teacher's democratic sensibilities yet again become the focal point of the political drama. Mr. Willis, an eighth grade, social studies teacher who has assumed the role as U.S. Congressman after the death of his wife, is part of the swing vote in a House committee to approve an amendment banning the use of census sampling from the House appropriations bill. The White House wants the amendment removed and without removal will veto the bill. Communications Director for the President Toby Ziegler (Richard Schiff) must convince the men to drop the amendment or face a lengthy floor fight on a coveted holiday weekend. The other two congressmen have weekend airline tickets and are anxious to leave, explaining to Toby that their committee chairman would be extremely displeased if they changed their votes. To everyone's surprise, Mr. Willis is happy to remain at the White House to hear the arguments Toby wants to set forth. After a few tense hours and a reading of Article 1, Section 2 of the U.S. Constitution, Toby ultimately convinces Mr. Willis to change his vote, causing Toby to claim later that he has met "an unusual man" who "didn't walk into the room with a political agenda" or "with his mind made up."

During the hours of deliberation over the amendment, it becomes clear that Mr. Willis, as compared to his peers in Congress, possesses greater knowledge of the Constitution than other Congressional representatives as well as the ability to weigh reasonable alternatives in a manner unmarred by partisan influence. To influence his vote, Toby has a colleague read only partial lines from the Constitution. The other representatives in the room are unaware that she has left out essential information—namely, the three/fifths clause that counted all enslaved persons as three/fifths of an individual. One man claims in defense, "None of us is a constitutional scholar!" Mr. Willis, a dedicated, eighth-grade history teacher does know which lines have been removed, however. After this reading of the Constitution—and connecting its relevance to the proposed amendment focused on sampling portions of the population rather than door-to-door headcounts—Mr. Willis decides the committee should drop the amendment. The other congressmen leave frustrated and noticeably flustered. Moments later, as Toby and Mr. Willis prepare to leave the room, Toby asks, "What changed your mind?" "You did," Mr. Willis replied. "I thought you made a very strong argument." Toby, bemused, says, "I'm smiling because around here the merits of a particular argument generally take a backseat to political tactics." Both Mr. Willis and Ms. O'Brien are teachers who are able to deliberate, reason, and use knowledge about the American democratic system, and these characters are juxtaposed to great effect against stubborn, seemingly ignorant, and unreasonable politicians.

Although depictions of Ms. O'Brien and Mr. Willis carry forward traditional narratives of the moral teacher on a crusade to cultivate citizenship in their students, this very same narrative was under attack in the United States at the same time the series was broadcast. These depictions of teachers as intelligent, informed, deliberative, and—most of all—democratic are important because they offer a counter-narrative desperately needed both at the time the show aired and

17

Figure 2.2. Rep. Joe Willis (Al Frann) on The West Wing *(NBC 1999–2006)*

in the present day because teachers are regularly demonized as the cause of—not the solution to—a perceived national educational crisis (Kumashiro, 2012). Kevin Kumashiro explains that three "overlapping movements—namely, neoliberalism, Christian fundamentalism, and neoconservativism" coalesced in the 1990s to form the New Right, a group whose attacks on public education have come to be seen as "common sense" (2010, p. 57). At the time *The West Wing* aired, the New Right had been gaining momentum for some time, having developed "think tanks, advocacy organizations, and political action committees with aligned missions and coordinated strategies" (Kumashiro, 2010, p. 58). The rise of the New Right altered "the basic categories we use to evaluate our institutions and our public and private lives," most notably by inscribing the beliefs in the power of the free market, increased competition, and individualism on our collective ideologies (Apple, 2009, p. 239). In an environment governed by New Right ideology, "all of education rests on the shoulders of teachers," which causes teachers to be vilified as "all that is wrong with … public schools" (Kumashiro, 2012, p. 10). In contemporary politics, this is manifested as the derogatory usage of the term "educational establishment" or the blaming of radical and selfish teachers unions for student failure. *The West Wing* refuses to engage in such characterization, depicting only overwhelmingly qualified teachers against the backdrop of an increasingly polarized and ineffective political establishment. Additionally, Mr. Willis's depiction as an African-American man also complicates the notion that the public school should be "embodied in the White woman teacher" and that it should play "a central role in maintaining racial and cultural hegemony throughout the history of U.S. national growth" (Kaestle, 1983, p. 62). Instead, Mr. Willis directly challenges racial and cultural hegemony by voting against the amendment in question, as Toby explains that it would likely be detrimental to the African-American community. In this way, both the presence and the actions of Mr. Willis challenge the ideology of the New Right, which works to maintain Whiteness as the cultural norm. Likewise, the knowledge and commitment of both teachers to their students is clear, directly refuting many of the New Right talking points about teachers as lazy or selfish.

The assumption that producers and writers of *The West Wing* depicted teachers in such a way unwittingly is unlikely. An episode early in the second season, "The Midterms," suggests that the show's writers understood the political stakes around education and sought to make viewers aware, too. In this episode, the show's many characters are concerned about the impending midterm elections. To the surprise and confusion of many on his staff, the President is more preoccupied with a school board race in his home state of New Hampshire, in the district where his children attended school, than he is concerned about any congressional race. Early in the episode, President Bartlet asks his Chief of Staff Leo McGarry, "Leo, did you know Elliot Roush is running for the school board in Manchester? I beat him in my first congressional campaign. I want some polling numbers on that race." Leo is displeased and annoyed and attempts to shut down the conversation. Dismissing the President, he says, "I don't want you focusing your attention on a school board race in New Hampshire." The President is undeterred and works on his own to have the polling completed. In between making campaign donation phone calls, Bartlet discovers that Roush is polling at 46% and launches into a tirade against the man, calling him a "man who makes the Spanish Inquisition look like a Barbara Walters special." It comes out later in the episode that Elliot Roush is a Christian fundamentalist, hell-bent on using the position to impose his Christian beliefs in the public realm. Despite the President's concerns, no one at the White House seems to understand his obsession. Frustrated, he explains to White House Press Secretary C.J. Cregg (Allison Janney), "You don't take these people seriously cause they don't get anywhere nationally, but they don't have to. All they have to do is bit by little bit get themselves on the boards of education and city councils because that's where all the governing that really matters to people really happens." C.J. nods and changes the subject. Even Bartlet's daughter finds his obsession over Roush annoying, rolling her eyes at her father. By the end of the episode, Roush wins the election, reflecting the growing power of the New Right in public institutions at the time.

President Bartlet's concerns about Elliot Roush are well founded, and the way his staff and family treat his concerns is perhaps more meaningful than it appears at first glance. Bartlet knows that this is much more than just one school board race; it is symbolic of a larger trend that most progressive Americans were willfully ignoring or even ridiculing. Indeed, comedian and former senator Al Franken and commentators such as Stephen Colbert and Jon Stewart, among others, often lampooned the Christian Right, making it appear to be a marginal group with no real power (Fry, 2014). Such characterizations, however, were misleading, as groups such as the Philanthropy Roundtable and Business Roundtable, made up of wealthy—often religious—families and businesses, were making headway into local politics. As Kumashiro explains, "the business sector ... has a long history of influencing public education." In fact, "the business elite influenced school governance not only by constituting its governing bodies but also by structuring its model of management"

(2010, p. 63). While they may have been laughable, they were not powerless. As Kumashiro notes, religious conservatives "called for the entire school system to be privatized, made into a free enterprise" (2010, p. 67). Their method to get there would be through the use of school vouchers—funding programs meant to defund public schools in favor of private institutions. Bartlet's near obsession with this school board race and his staff's apparent lack of interest offers a window into the American psyche, mirroring how many Americans had lost interest in politics at the local level. The writers of *The West Wing* may have intended to suggest that the rest of America start paying attention to the small, seemingly inconsequential, political races to avoid a slow infiltration of religious zealots into local boards and councils.

An exchange between Sam and Mallory O'Brien later in the series tackles the issue of school vouchers head on, as Mallory misunderstands Sam's position on the issue. Bringing her grievance to her father's office, she says, "He's in favor of school vouchers, Dad." Leo replies, "No, Mallory, he's really not. It's opposition prep." Sam has been given the task of writing the opposing perspective on school vouchers and, to her disbelief, proceeds to explain to her his real position. He says,

> Mallory, education is the silver bullet, education is everything. We don't need little changes—we need gigantic, monumental changes. Schools should be palaces. The competition for the best teachers should be fierce. Schools should be incredibly expensive for government and absolutely free of charge for its citizens, just like national defense. That's my position. I just haven't figured out how to do it yet.

Sam's opposition research on vouchers and Elliot Roush's campaign for a seat on a local school board offer glimpses into the very real challenges to public education at the time. The perspectives—combined with the moral, knowledgeable, and democratic teachers depicted on the show—position public education as worthwhile. The scenes may be brief, but they demonstrate that education is essential to the growth and protection of democracy seemingly under threat from the New Right then and now.

While teachers play a decidedly marginal role in the rest of the series, the few representations examined here matter. As Soyini D. Madison reminds us: "How people are represented is how they are treated" (2012, p. 5). Dalton and Linder concur. They write, "How we characterize teachers directly reflects the collective opinion about the larger enterprise of formal education" (2019, p. 6). Of course, the only view of teachers at this time did not come solely from *The West Wing*, but these depictions are instructive nonetheless because they provide a look into historical and contemporary narratives that have guided the way we think about teachers and the role of education in a democracy. They also push back upon newer narratives, urging us to question their accuracy. As Kumashiro explains, "What counts as 'common sense' is not something that just is. … It is something that is developed and learned and perpetuated over time, and some groups are better at remaking common sense than others" (2010, p. 63). Depictions of teachers on *The West Wing* have the potential, when taken together with other similar depictions, to reframe the common sense debate over our public schools. Indeed, it is "up to us to think about the possibilities of new policies and practices that will create schools where social justice is more important than perpetuating the class system in America, and leading children to self-actualization and civic engagement is more important than preparing them to meet the wants and needs of business interests" (Dalton & Linder, 2019, p. 220), which means we must take the depictions of teachers on *The West Wing* seriously and demand that our educational policy and practices live up both to our expectations and media depictions.

REFERENCES

Apple, Michael. (2009). Can critical education interrupt the right? *Discourse: Studies in the Cultural Politics of Education, 30*(3), 239–251.

Confirm Merrick Garland and end the partisan pettiness over the supreme court. (2016, November 15). *Los Angeles Times*.

Cooke, Charles C. (2015, December 8). Trump, the anti-constitutional authoritarian—liberty lovers, beware. *National Review*.

Dalton, Mary M., & Laura R. Linder. (2019). *Teacher TV: Seventy years of teachers on television*. New York, NY: Peter Lang.

Fry, Karin. (2014). *Beyond religious right and secular left rhetoric: The road to compromise*. London: Palgrave Macmillan.

Gustafson, Thomas. (1992). *Representative words: Politics, literature, and the American language, 1776–1865*. Cambridge: Cambridge University Press.

Jefferson, T. (1789, January 8). *Letter to Richard Price*. Paris.

Kaestle, Carl. (1983). *Pillars of the republic: Common schools and American society, 1780–1860*. New York, NY: Hill and Wang.

Kumashiro, Kevin. (2010). Seeing the bigger picture: Troubling movements to end teacher education. *Journal of Teacher Education, 61*(1–2), 56–65.

Kumashiro, Kevin. (2012). *Bad Teacher!: How blaming teachers distorts the bigger picture*. New York, NY: Teachers College Press.

Madison, Soyini D. (2012). *Critical ethnography: Method, performance, and ethics*. Thousand Oaks, CA: Sage Publications.

Phillips, Amber. (2016, November 28). How the ugly 2016 presidential election could change the way we vote in future ones. *The Washington Post*.

Rakove, Jack N. (2006). James Madison and the creation of the American republic. London: Pearson.

Sehr, David T. (1997). *Education for public democracy*. Albany, NY: SUNY Press.

Thurber, J. (2011). What's wrong with congress and what should be done about it? In I. Morgan & P. Davies (Eds.), *Can Government be repaired? Lessons from America*. London: Institute for the Study of the Americas Press.

Van Buren, Peter. (2014, June 17). Whistleblower crackdowns, self-censorship, stonewalled FOIAs: The 1st amendment under attack. *Mother Jones*.

Westheimer, Joel. (2009). Should social studies be patriotic? *Social Education, 73*(7), 316–320.

Worst voter turnout in 72 years. (2014, November 11). Editorial. *New York Times*.

Zakaria, Fareed. (1997, November.–December. 1997). The rise of illiberal democracy. *Foreign Affairs*.

Zakaria, Fareed. (2016, December 29). America's democracy has become illiberal. *The Washington Post*.

ANDREW WIRTH

3. RETHINKING STUDENT-TEACHER RELATIONSHIP INTIMACY AS ATTACHMENT

ABSTRACT

Without a doubt, The Hollywood Model has provided media theorists academic tools to analyze the meaning of educators within the broader apparatus of popular culture. Most notably, The Hollywood Model has utilized queer theory to analyze the gender roles and sexuality of educators. However, this piece argues that previous definitions of queer theory have been too restricting to limit its use to only gay and lesbian educators. This chapter seeks to examine queer theory through Michael Warner and Lauren Berlant's approach to queer theory as queer criticism. Thus, expanding queer theory as the study of sexuality toward the study of attachment and belonging. To illustrate this point, this chapter examines the film *Detachment* (2011) to illustrate the role of intimacy and belonging between teachers and students. Reading *Detachment* through intimacy and belonging illustrates the potential for the expanded use of queer theory beyond films pertaining to gay and lesbian educators. In turn, illustrating that the belonging between teacher and student goes beyond the physical relationship to include emotional narratives and belonging to moments that do not exist within the present moment.

Keywords: The Hollywood Model, educators, queer theory, gender, sexuality, gay, lesbian, sexuality, intimacy, *Detachment*

***

Since Dalton's introduction of The Hollywood Model, film and cultural theorists have had the potential to trace the relationship between popular representations of teachers and the public consciousness. The model establishes a leaky rubric that categorizes traits common to the various representations of "good" teachers in Hollywood films by identifying them as: outsiders not typically liked by other teachers; forming personal connections with students; learning from their students; engaging in conflict with administrators; personalizing the curriculum to meet their students' needs; and, sometimes, possessing a ready sense of humor (2017, pp. 21–41). The Hollywood Model functions as a theoretical departure from theorist William Ayers, who posited the "good" teachers in movies as disciplinarians dividing their students into two broad categories: the salvageable and the lost causes (2017, p. 147). Dalton contests

© KONINKLIJKE BRILL NV, LEIDEN, 2019 | DOI:10.1163/9789004398092_003

A. WIRTH

Ayers's assessment by arguing that Hollywood portrays the Good Teacher as not necessarily saving students, but rather the Good Teacher is the educator who can reach students considered the hardest cases (p. 23). Through The Hollywood Model, Dalton's focus on the representation of the Good Teacher includes a discussion of educators establishing emotionally intimate connections with students in different contexts (2017, pp. 28–32). I expand upon Dalton's commentary about intimacy.

In *The Hollywood Curriculum: Teachers in the Movies*, Dalton also establishes queer theory as a lens to read the representations of gay, lesbian, bisexual, and transgender teachers, educators, and students (2017, pp. 99, 111–130). Berlant and Warner maintain that queer theory does not seek to establish a systematic explanation of "how oppression and sublimations around sex and sexuality" cause "other kinds of violence and oppression—with exploitation, racial formation, the production of the feminine subjectivity or of national culture" (1995, p. 347). Instead, queer theory directs critics and viewers toward reading the ways texts allow/foreclose the possibility of distinct acts of sex and intimacy and how normative understanding of sexuality and intimacy intersect with other forms of violence (Berlant & Warner, 1995, p. 347). I will expand upon the lens of queer theory by gesturing critics toward an intimate lens that focuses on the different genres of connection narratives within The Hollywood Model.

I theorize the lens of intimacy as useful for disclosing the ways Hollywood portrays the Good Teacher as forming attachments toward their students' educational and social futures in ways that are usually defined by the teacher's chosen curriculum. Understanding intimacy as attachment pushes critics and viewers to trace the process of how attachment occurs from small gestures of affection accumulated in mere moments. Hollywood teaching films feature different forms of attachment, and the concept of attachment expands beyond the typical teacher-student connection to include a teacher's attachment to their student's personal, social, and educational success. I maintain that a focus on intimacy discloses three types of Hollywood teaching films: establishment, sustainment, and the missed connection. The establishment narrative focuses on a Good Teacher attempting to establish an attachment toward their students. In these films, the teacher is not able to catalyze an attachment with students until after the rising action, climax, or falling action of the narrative. The sustainment narrative frequently portrays the teacher attempting to maintain an attachment throughout the film and often shows teachers with great pre-existing relationships with students or shows teachers establishing a connection early within the movie. The drama in these films threatens the durability of the attachment. Both establishment and sustainment narratives end with the relationship between teacher and student intact. The missed-connection film features "good" teachers who are unable to establish and sustain an attachment with their students, but this lost connection functions as a life lesson for both parties. Hollywood often presents good teachers also learning valuable life lessons from students. I would like to note that the boundaries delineating these three categories are "leaky" at best.

In this chapter, I explore teaching as forming attachments through a close reading of the film *Detachment* (2011). As a revisionist Good Teacher film, the story focuses on

24

Henry Barthes (Adrien Brody), a professional substitute teacher who does not desire to become a full-time teacher. Barthes is considered one the best substitute teachers since he can understand the emotional turmoil his students face, but the nature of his job allows him to leave before becoming attached to his students. The classroom storyline centers around Barthes's relationship with his student Meredith (Betty Kaye), who—in what has become a bit of a stock character in school films—is the troubled, suicide-prone loner. Reading *Detachment* through the lens of intimacy and attachment illustrates the compelling narratives of the student-teacher relationship. In the following sections, I will reflect on the concept of intimacy as a connection between individuals and how those formations establish collective attachments toward particular futures before examining Meredith's suicide in greater detail.

RETHINKING TEACHING AS INTIMACY AND ATTACHMENT

In the introduction to *Intimacy: A Special Issue*, Berlant maintains that "to intimate is to communicate with the sparest of signs and gestures, and at its root intimacy has the quality of eloquence and brevity. But intimacy also involves an aspiration for a narrative about something shared, a story about oneself and others that will turn out in a particular way" (1998, p. 281). Put more simply, intimacy solidifies collectives with a particular orientation that strives toward something that does not entirely exist within the present moment. In *Detachment*, one brief scene features Barthes as he peers into Sarah Madison's (Christina Hendricks) classroom during lunch. He witnesses her helping one student complete a math project. She exclaims, "Wow. I don't care what they say, you're doing great," and "I had a hard time with math too. It takes time." Barthes witnesses one moment of teacher-student intimacy that carries particular intensity. The brevity of the teacher-student intimacy is punctuated by two individuals basking in silence with minimal discourse about the student's success. Barthes did not witness a simple, heartfelt moment between Madison and her student, but rather, he sees the manifestation of the teacher-student attachment that leads toward the solidification of the teacher-student attachment. Barthes's longing for detachment is juxtaposed with Madison's longing for teacher-student connection.

As The Hollywood Model is played out in mainstream movies, the word intimacy can often be a loaded term. Within queer theory (as with other areas), sex and intimacy should not be understood as synonymous and interchangeable concepts. One-night stands do not promise intimacy, and the student-teaching relationship does not guarantee sex. Berlant argues that the distinction between sex and intimacy reminds us that these attachments occur outside of the "purview of institutions, the state, and an ideal of publicness" (1998, p. 285). In other words, attachments that exist outside intimate relationships will inevitably inhabit common spaces, yet an approach to intimacy as attachment reveals the process where social formation adheres to particular, "concrete" areas. These "connections" emerge in particular places such as the classroom (1998, p. 285). A lens that focuses on attachments urges the cultural critic toward processing the fixation of Hollywood and the larger

A. WIRTH

dominant culture on the potential impact of a Good Teacher on a challenging student. The film presents a critical medium for viewers to initiate a cultural studies critique of the contrast between media's representations of teaching attachments and Hollywood's obsession to remain attached to its narratives of attachments. These forms of intimate cultural criticism allow critics to trace repetitive attachments through teacher films and to connect those attachments to larger ideological structures and affective forces. Berlant maintains, "These spaces are produced relationally; people and/in institutions can repeatedly return to them and produce something, though frequently not history in its ordinary, memorable, or valorized sense, and not always 'something' of positive value" (1998, p. 285). The lens of intimacy discloses the public's attachment to the Good Teacher as providing emotional comfort, and the perspective describes the values that shape the public's obsession with Hollywood narratives of teachers and students.

The Hollywood Model's use of intimacy between students and teachers hinges upon the contours of public and private spheres. Berlant traces the dichotomy as a relic of the "Victorian fantasy that the world can be divided into a controllable space (the private-affective) and an uncontrollable one (the public-instrumental). Berlant finds the word fantasy may not fully disclose the individual's attachments to a dualism that has historically "organized and justified other legally and conventionally based forms of social division" (1998, p. 283). Teacher films reify these forms of social delineation through the construction of the school as public space for work while more intimate relationships occur within the private sphere. Hollywood portrayals suggest that most of the problems of "hard to reach students" begin within their private lives. Berlant maintains that intimacy functions as a means of creating a world and spaces within the public sphere (1998, p. 282). Hollywood portrays the intimate process of establishment and maintenance of areas surrounding the teacher and student as crevasses that allow their students to escape the violence of the private. The teacher-student conglomeration also functions as a space for existence for students who feel no place of belonging within the school or the rest of the public sphere. In *Freedom Writers* (2007), Erin Gruwell (Hilary Swank) accepts a teaching job at an "at-risk" school in Los Angeles shortly after the 1994 LA riots. The film features Gruwell attempting to establish a connection with her students. In doing so, Gruwell becomes attached not only to her students but also to their futures. Gruwell gives the students composition books and asks them to use the pages for diary entries that only she will read. The journals provide the teacher a channel to connect with students and see into their private lives. Once Gruwell has established an intimate connection with her students, she soon begins staying later into the evening at school so her students may remain in her classroom instead of dealing with the torment of their private lives.

Hollywood often creates films in which teachers are only seen within the school (public), and any personal information that is not appropriate for students is featured at home or away from students (private). In *Detachment*, Barthes witnesses a teenage sex-worker named Erica (Sami Gayle) performing oral sex on a man on a bus as he rides home from a nursing home where he visits his grandfather. Barthes witnesses

26

the man refuse to pay Erica for her service, which results in the two getting into a physical and verbal altercation. Erica follows Barthes as he gets off the bus and tries to solicit him, which results in yet another fight on the street. A few days after, Barthes notices Erica on his way home and invites her back to his apartment, which she interprets as Barthes soliciting her services. Barthes's surprise gesture implies he wants to see her crotch because he wishes to have sex with her, but actually he has noticed she is bleeding. He asks if she has been sexually assaulted or has had an HIV test while he cleans away the blood. He offers to let Erica stay with him until she can get back on her feet, and she voluntarily performs domestic chores while he is away. Later on, Barthes goes out on a date with his co-worker Madison, and he arrives home late to see that Erica has cooked dinner and elaborately set the table with candles and other decorations she could find around the house. The moment marks her disappointment, and—in the process—Hollywood portrays different iterations of intimacy based on the sphere in which a scene occurs.

The home of bad teachers is typically portrayed as a space devoid of sustainable intimacy. *Detachment* features scenes of teachers teaching as well as scenes revealing their private lives. One scene features Principal Carol Dearden's (Marcia Gay Harden) husband rubbing her feet and attempting to console her after a long day's work. Immediately, Dearden accuses her husband (Bryan Cranston) of being disingenuous, which eventually leads to inter-relational conflict and ends with Mr. Dearden destroying a sentimental vase the pair bought on a romantic trip to Europe. In another example, a bad teacher goes home to a emotionally distant family. Sarge Kepler (William Peterson) is the film's token bad teacher. Throughout the movie, there are images of Kepler failing to discipline his class. Kelper comes home to his wife to find her eyes glued to the TV. When he attempts to start small talk, she ignores his inquiries and continues to remain focused on the television.

The Hollywood Model uses the public and private distinction as a means for delineating between "good" and "bad" forms of "intimate." In the *The Hollywood Curriculum: Teachers in the Movies*, Dalton tackles the taboo subject of teacher-student sexual relationships, and observes, "If the law and school policies are clear in forbidding sexual relationships between teachers and minor-age students … that does not mean the problem has gone away, and it also doesn't mean that 'blurring the line' and 'crossing the line' have uniform meanings in each case" (2017, p. 132). I believe the line that Dalton is referring to is established in large part by the public and private distinction. In *The History of Sexuality*, Michel Foucault presents the repression hypothesis—the concept that the Victorian era was pure—yet disproves it by maintaining that the discourse of sex and sexuality was not absent, just relegated to the private sphere (1990, pp. 3–5). As Berlant has stated, sex has been associated with the institution of marriage and kinship, which situates it in the private sphere. In the films featuring teacher-student sexual relationships, the narratives document and disclose the events that cause teachers to blur the line between "public" and "private" life with their students. It is important to note, however, that not all sexual relationships between students and teachers are "intimate." Intimacy requires sex to be more than

A. WIRTH

just passion. Intimacy requires sustained belonging and the building of something more. In this context, truly intimate sexual relationships require that teachers and students long to build a private life together. The lens of intimacy does not assume all connections or attachments are inherently good or wanted by both sides.

SLOW DEATH, DETACHMENT, AND THE SUICIDE OF MEREDITH

In an interview with Robert Levin, director Tony Kayne remarks that *Detachment* is a film about this collection of people and their humanity rather than an issue film about teachers and schools, although the experiences of screenwriter Carl Lund, a former public school teacher, inform the script. As a substitute teacher, Henry Barthes is alienated from his full-time teaching cohort, but if viewers expect a political commentary about education reform, they will be disappointed according to the director. Kayne describes it is "a movie about those kinds of things ... a microcosm of our lives. ... It's not deep enough [and] it's not rounded enough, to be those other things. It's like [how] Star Wars isn't a movie about robots fighting each other. It's about something else" (Levin, 2017). I disagree with Kayne's assertion that Barthes's job as a substitute teacher is not insignificant because I believe that his characterization represents well how Good Teachers strive to help students accomplish something and build a future that is better than the present. John Fisk argues that critics must have a "double focus"—where one must focus upon structures of texts in tandem with a relationship between how an individual's praxis for "coping" with the system shapes the ways they read texts—in order to analyze the multiple meanings within a particular text (1989, p. 105). The lack of sustained intimacy between Barthes and Meredith can be used as a means to examine the small, ordinary things Kayne describes.

Detachment introduces Barthes as a Good Teacher who can connect with the emotional pain felt by his students. The substitute initiates intimacy with his students, especially those who are victims of harassment, but the temporary nature of his position allows him to leave before becoming attached to his students. Throughout the film, a series of flashback sequences comprised of home movie clips imply that Barthes's orientation toward detachment from individuals and institutions is due to his Grampa's (Louis Zorich) sexual abuse of Henry's mother throughout her life, a trauma that leads to her suicide. Barthes's fear of loss hinders his ability to establish and sustain intimate connections with other individuals.

On the first day of class, Barthes kicks a student out for calling Meredith (Betty Kaye) a dyke, and she interprets Barthes's simple gesture as a communication of the possibility that they might establish intimacy. The film features shots of teachers and students inside and outside the school, and the depictions of Meredith's life in public and private spheres reveals that both seem inescapably horrible. Dalton argues that The Hollywood Model establishes the representation of the Good Teacher as an outlaw, one often disliked by the administration and seen as a radical threat to the status quo (2017, p. 27). According to Dalton, these outsider characters are central to

Figure 3.1. Henry Barthes (Adrien Brody) in Detachment *(2011)*

narratives that have "traditionally championed individualism so long as that rugged individual presented as the focal point of countless film narratives remains a loner without the power of a collective force" (2017, p. 25). Within the genre of teachers establishing intimate attachments with their students, the individualism of the Good Teacher outsider appeals to students who also feel excluded.

The rising action of the film features Meredith in Barthes's classroom thanking him for making her feel valued. When she attempts to hug him, he immediately brushes her off, signifying his rejection of her desire to form an attachment. Barthes's rejection causes Meredith to leave the classroom crying, which prompts Madison to investigate the situation. Madison witnesses Meredith's attempt to establish a warm embrace with Barthes and soon begins questioning him about having inappropriate contact with a student. Madison incorrectly interprets the situation in part because Barthes has not asked her out on a second date. The climax of the narrative begins when Meredith prepares cupcakes with white frosting decorated with a smiling face, and she also makes one cupcake—laced with poison—anointed with a frowning face. The climax of the film is achieved when she eats the poisoned cupcake after Barthes apologizes for rejecting her hug. The scene ends with Meredith coughing up blood and slowly dying while faculty members attempt to resuscitate her.

The sustained intimacy subgenre often portrays the Good Teacher as outsiders who can connect with the students who feel foreign in comparison to their classmates. Dalton argues that these outsiders are often represented as not being well liked by administrators because they are viewed as a radical threat to the status quo (2017, p. 24). Hollywood frames the outsider as a unique conductor for establishing attachments with students who also identify as social outsiders. Dalton reminds us that the radical teachers often are not revolutionary because they do not present a praxis for shaking these institutions, let alone escaping or dismantling them (2017, p. 191). I would add that radical teachers fail to call into question our attachment toward education structures and the promised futures they provide students.

A. WIRTH

As a revisionist film, *Detachment* reminds us that not only does The Hollywood Model valorize the intimate connection between student and teacher, but the rubric suggests that a Good Teacher is one who sustains attachment with students as spaces for them to dwell within while inspiring them to strive for a better future. Meredith's suicide demonstrates Berlant's concept of slow death and articulates death not as a process but as an event (2007, p. 754). Jasbir K. Puar argues that the suicide of Tyler Clementi (the gay teenager whose death inspired the It Gets Better Project) is an exemplar of slow death because Clementi did not die the moment he hit the ground after jumping off a bridge. Clementi's death began the moment he did not fit within the heteronormative kinship narrative, which slowly exhausted him until he could no longer bear feeling the pain (2012, pp. 150–151). Meredith's process of dying begins before she makes the deadly dessert. *Detachment* illustrates how Meredith's slow death occurs within her dysfunctional family and extends into her social isolation within the school. One of Meredith's domestic scenes features a paternal authority figure exhibiting frustration over her obsession with art. He maintains that art has no potential of being a sustainable future occupation and asserts that he spends the entire day working to provide a good life for his family.

Hollywood often portrays teachers becoming intimately invested in their students and in the ability of these students to achieve a shot at living the "good life" and escaping the "bad life." Berlant says individuals seek to escape the bad life for "the good life's normative/utopian zone," but the individual is "stuck in what we might call survival time, the time of struggling, drowning, holding on to the ledge, treading water, not-stopping." According to Berlant, attempts of individuals to transgress the bad life for the good life solidify the zones as a binary where subjects either have the good life or they struggle to obtain its promises in a process made manifest through the ordinariness of the everyday (1998, p. 284). Stewart defines ordinariness and the everyday as "a shifting assemblage of practices and practical knowledge, a scene of both liveness and exhaustion, a dream of escape or the simple life" (1998, p. 1). Meredith's suicide could be read as nothing extraordinary because exigency for the event is not brought upon by a singular crisis; her exhaustion is the result of social exclusion from the folds of the happiness implicitly promised in the everyday. Barthes's coping mechanism of detachment is not a sustainable praxis for his students because it neither changes the material conditions that make ordinary life unbearable nor helps establish alternative fantasies beyond the good life.

An intimate reading of Meredith's suicide illustrates that the film fits within the connection subgenre as a missed-connection narrative. The ending of the movie presents Meredith's death as a life lesson for Barthes on the importance of attachment, intimacy, and utopian zones. Meredith's suicide reminds Barthes how his praxis of detachment is not sustainable, especially in the case of his Grampa from whom he could not entirely detach—he relives scenes through flashbacks whenever visiting his grandfather. While I do not classify this film within the sustained-intimacy subgenre due to Meredith's suicide, I do believe the sustained-intimacy narrative illuminates how Barthes functions as Good Teacher who is an outsider as described by The Hollywood Model. Meredith's suicide is framed as a pivotal moment for Barthes, which pushes the teacher to reflect upon his "detached" life. In the end, Barthes realizes the price of detachment: an unbearable and cruel existence.

CONCLUSION

In this chapter, I propose the Berlant frame for a rethinking of intimacy as attachment as a mechanism for finding deeper meaning within texts about teachers:

> Rethinking intimacy calls out not only for redescription but for transformative analyses of the rhetorical and material conditions that enable hegemonic fantasies to thrive in the minds and on the bodies of subjects while, at the same time, attachments are developing that might redirect the different routes taken by history and biography. To rethink intimacy is to appraise how we have been and how we live and how we might imagine lives that make more sense than the ones so many are living. (1998, p. 286)

The purpose of this chapter is not to invalidate already-existing readings of student-teacher intimacy. Instead, this perspective is meant to move critics to examine the value of particular attachments—ranging from teacher-student intimacy to our own affective attachments—while analyzing depictions of Good Teachers and assessing how such values and representations influence the structure of institutions of education. Rethinking intimacy pushes us to a reconsideration of the teacher-student relationship as the process in which the Good Teacher strives both to establish and maintain connections with their students. Intimacy as a lens follows Fiske's recommendations of a structural critique by asking what forms of attachments keep us invested within current representations of education. This perspective is meant to supplement other existing frameworks by connecting ideological critiques with questions of attachments. I believe examining intimacy as attachments allows us to ask new questions, such as what purpose is served by becoming attached to Good Teacher movies as radical narratives if the structure of education does not move and what ideological motives shape students' attachments to fantasies of good lives after education?

In the grand scheme, the purpose of my analysis is to illustrate that gays and lesbians do not a have a monopoly on intimacy. Put differently, queer theory is a theoretical lens that can be applied to a milieu of films. Queer theory has gone beyond the study of sexuality; it examines how our intimacy for another goes beyond the current temporal moment. The transition from sex to intimacy suggests the possibility for queer theory analysis in the other areas of The Hollywood Model. Thus, future analyses of teachers teaching in media may find queer theory as a fruitful theoretical lens even when examining texts of heterosexual educators of students.

A. WIRTH

REFERENCES

Ayers, William. (1993). A teacher ain't nothin' but a hero. In Pamela Bolotin Joseph & Gail E. Burnaford (Eds.), *Images of schoolteachers in twentieth-century America: Paragons, polarities, complexities* (pp. 147–156). New York, NY: St. Martin's Press.

Berlant, Lauren. (1998). Intimacy: A special issue. *Critical Inquiry, 24*(2), 281–288.

Berlant, Lauren. (2007). Nearly utopian, nearly normal: Post-Fordist affect in La Promesse and Rosetta. *Public Culture, 19*(2), 273.

Berlant, Lauren. (2007). Slow death (sovereignty, obesity, lateral agency). *Critical Inquiry, 33*(4), 754–780.

Berlant, Lauren, & Michael Warner. (1995). Guest column: What does queer theory teach us about X? *Publications of the Modern Language Association of America, 110*(3), 343–349.

Dalton, Mary M. (2017). *The Hollywood curriculum: Teachers in the movies rev* (3rd ed.). New York, NY: Peter Lang.

Fiske, John. (1989). *Understanding popular culture*. Boston, MA: Unwin Hyman.

Foucault, Michel. (1990). *The history of sexuality: The use of pleasure* (Vol. 2). New York, NY: Vintage.

Levin, Robert. (2012, March 16). 'Detachment': A movie about teachers, not education reform. *The Atlantic*.

Puar, Jasbir K. (2012). Coda: The cost of getting better suicide, sensation, switchpoints. *GLQ: A Journal of Lesbian and Gay Studies, 18*(1), 149–158.

Stewart, Kathleen. (2007). *Ordinary affects*. Durham, NC: Duke University Press.

JEFF SPANKE

4. MR. MILLER GOES TO WAR

Saving Private Ryan *and the Children Left Behind*

I wasn't going to add my film to a long list of pictures that make World War II "the glamorous war," "the romantic war" ... If you cheapen it, if you make it more palatable, if you somehow diminish what went on there, I think you end up doing a great disservice to what the movie as a whole is trying to communicate.

—Steven Spielberg, Director, *Saving Private Ryan*

ABSTRACT

Since the passing of No Child Left Behind and the subsequent creation and adoption of the Common Core State Standards (CCSS), the rhetoric of American education has grown increasingly militaristic in tone. Amid a barrage of external pressures, social distrust, achievement gaps, and accountability models, the discourse (Gee, 1989) of teaching has become entrenched in a seemingly endless series of "fights," "battles," "strikes," "missions," and "fronts." Within this bleak backdrop of institutional warfare and professional casualties, this chapter argues that the present depiction of teachers should abandon the reductively saccharine images of past teacher narratives, and instead reflect the very real conflicts teachers currently face. As a metaphor for today's beleaguered educators, Steven Spielberg's 1998 film, *Saving Private Ryan,* offers teachers and teacher educators a refreshing—albeit disturbing—glimpse into the trials and tribulations of contemporary education. While not traditionally framed as a teaching narrative in itself, the film illustrates the risks and rewards shrouded in one teacher's mission to literally leave no child behind.

Keywords: experiential learning, teacher, war films, WWII, public pedagogy professional development, attrition, pragmatism, narrative, *Saving Private Ryan*

***

He never took his eyes off the screen. Instead, with a slight tilt of his head, my father whispered in my ear, "That means Fucked Up Beyond All Recognition." I lied and whispered simply, "I know." It was the first time I ever heard him cuss, but I didn't really think anything of it. In a way, the vulgar simplicity of his words matched the brutal reality of the grisly images unfolding before us. Bullet-riddled bodies were

© KONINKLIJKE BRILL NV, LEIDEN, 2019 | DOI:10.1163/9789004398092_004

J. SPANKE

washing lifelessly to the shore. Screaming hordes careened to cliffs, some searching for their own limbs in the wake of crimson tides. The opening scene alone was more bloody, haunting, beautiful, and horrible than anything I'd seen in my brief fourteen years on suburban Earth. Yet, we watched. Our eyes affixed to the cine-madness of *Saving Private Ryan* (1998): a father and son alone in a theater packed with strangers, all united under the banner of watching actors share Our Story on film. When it was over, no one said a word, as if we were collectively bound by the unspoken consensus that our experience somehow defied discussion. I heard some people crying, but it sounded more like the muffled grief of funerals than the tearful joy at the end of *Sleepless in Seattle* (1993). These were tears accompanying a real sense of loss. We left in silence when the credits ended and the lights came up.

PART I: ONCE MORE INTO THE BREACH

For nearly 20 years, critics and audiences have lauded *Saving Private Ryan* as arguably the most poignant, authentic, and vivid depiction of war ever put on screen ("Saving Private Ryan," 1998). The film garnered 11 Academy Award nominations (winning five), and his portrayal of Captain John Miller earned Tom Hanks his fourth nomination for Best Actor. Yet, despite the accolades and profound international response the film achieved, few have examined the story of Captain Miller's perilous search for Private Ryan as anything other than an unprecedented war epic. When viewed through a less conventional lens, however, I argue that *Saving Private Ryan*—and particularly the role of Captain Miller—offers perhaps the most poignant, authentic, and vivid depiction of *teachers* ever put on screen.

I can certainly appreciate that framing a war film like *Saving Private Ryan* as a teacher movie may seem farfetched. On the surface, the genres of war films and teacher movies occupy entirely different cinematic continents. One brings to light the violent struggle of a ragtag band of youth, trapped behind enemy lines, enlisted on a mission whose completion seems perpetually out of reach all the while engaged in a raging fight against oppression and tyranny with only their cunning (and each other) to survive. The other is about war.

Still, at the time of its release, *Saving Private Ryan* was considered anything but a teacher film. And, nearly two decades later, little has changed. It premiered less than ten years after such iconic teacher sagas as *Lean on Me* (1998), *Stand and Deliver* (1988), and perhaps the paragon of pedagogical prowess, *Dead Poets Society* (1989). When pairing the latter teacher film with *Saving Private Ryan*, we juxtapose a barely post-pubescent Todd Anderson (Ethan Hawke) waxing poetic atop his private school desk with another captain—Oh, Captain!—teaching his boys to build sticky bombs and blow up Nazi panzers. These young men didn't have time to read Keats; they were too busy seizing D-Day (Spanke, 2016, pp. 216–26). In the end, Anderson's teacher gets fired, and some of the students cry. Private Ryan's savior just gets fired at.

Saving Private Ryan is also flanked on both sides by other contemporary teacher films, such as *Dangerous Minds* (1995), *Mr. Holland's Opus* (1995), *Music of the*

34

Heart (1999), *Finding Forrester* (2000), *School of Rock* (2003)*, and *Freedom Writers* (2007)*. There are, of course, many others, but the almost dogmatic exclusion of *Saving Private Ryan* from the canon of teacher movies is consistent with America's insistence that teachers be confined to classrooms and that learning can only occur in schools (Dewey, 1916, pp. 25–32; Pinar, 2012, pp. 15–42). This reductive prescription of the educative process consequently renders cinematic portrayals of teachers and teaching as woefully severed from the experiences of the professionals in the actual profession (Shoffner, 2016, pp. 1–10). A critical consideration of these teachers' experiences, however, reveals a unique discursive system that I argue aligns much more closely with the unforgiving, combative world of Captain Miller than the dangerously simplistic tableau of well-intentioned teacher-saviors civilizing a bunch of rowdy Black kids or inspiring rich, prep schoolers to read Whitman in caves after curfew.

While traditionally operating within two distinct paradigms, the respective language structures deployed by curriculum and combat seem to mirror each other in compelling and provocative ways. In fact, a simple Google search for "battle, schools" yields over a million results containing those two words. Granted, thousands of these likely have little, if anything, to do with appropriating war as a viable metaphor for education, but the first several results pages alone illustrate the extent to which scholars, civilians, and other stakeholders have often couched schools in militaristic terms. Whether writing about "the battle against soft drinks in schools" in the face of rising health consciousness, "the battle for public schools" amid a spark of religious fundamentalism, the "battle for books" in an age of censorship, or—simply—"the battle for better schools" or "the battle for America's future," these results suggest that people familiar with schools have little difficulty thinking of education as a metaphorically violent enterprise. Furthermore, this metaphor often extends beyond the institutional level. "Students compete against one another," argues Anthropology Professor Susan Blum:

> We identify winners and losers. Schools compete against each other, with military-style bands and the uniforms that identify the opposing teams. Students struggle against teachers, who are seen as authorities to evade. Cleverness and tactics, on both sides, are seen as necessary. Schools fight the public, unions fight administrations, and many urban schools are best described as "war zones."

Given the rhetorical bonds between SLOs and POWs (Student Learning Objectives and Prisoners of War, respectively), it stands to reason that what might be the cinematic archetype of authentic war films, *Saving Private Ryan*, might also epitomize the trials not only of today's gallant teachers but also of the students who exhaust their youths following orders in hopes they can one day enjoy the lives for which they fight so feverishly. Granted, SLOs typically are written objectives, whereas POWs are actual people. But, when we consider that for the majority of the film, Private Ryan functions as both an actual person *and,* quite literally, the

J. SPANKE

soldiers' objective, then we can begin to see the congruency between the objects and the subjects of our educational pursuits. Despite our best inclinations, sometimes students devolve into *what,* as opposed to *whom* we teach.

If we view Captain Miller's mission to save Private Ryan as analogous to the tribulations of today's teachers, we may find that many of the tenets of teacherdom that often wash ashore in more conventional teacher narratives also have their place on the beaches of Normandy and the fields, towns, and rubble of Nazi-occupied France. In reality, thousands of soldiers never made it off those beaches, and every year, thousands of students never make it onto the bus. A teacher's story—like Captain's Miller's special assignment—begins with the kids who make it to school. The rest are either bodies in the sand or blank squares in a yearbook.

PART II: OF BUSES AND BEACHES, SCHOOLMARMS AND SOLDIERS

Of all the moments in *Saving Private Ryan* that resonated with me as a kid—and there were certainly many—none had a greater impact on my youthful sense of narrative complexity than a scene in which Captain Miller reveals his former profession. After months of concealing his "job back home" from his unit, Captain Miller and company find themselves traversing the French countryside in the days following the Normandy Landings. When Miller orders the release of a German prisoner, who, in a previous ambush, had killed one of Miller's men, his troops begin threatening desertion. As a means of quelling the impending mutiny, Miller calmly addresses a bet that his soldiers have long-since wagered on what their Captain "did back home" and discloses an identity he'd previously shrouded in secrecy. "I'm a schoolteacher," the Captain confesses. "I teach English Composition in this little town called Addley, Pennsylvania. The last eleven years, I've been at Thomas Alva Edison High School. I was coach of the baseball team in the springtime. Back home, I tell people what I do for a living and they think, well, now that figures. But over here, it's a big, a big mystery." Miller's revelation alleviates the dissention in the ranks, ultimately granting new perspective to the men's seemingly futile objective. Rather than allowing them to succumb to the absurdities of war, his testimony revives in his soldiers their latent awareness of life *beyond* war: of their homes, families, and futures. By distinguishing person from purpose, Miller invites his men to do the same: to recognize that their humanity is greater than their present function as soldiers and that they were all people once.

This scene has the additional effect of personifying War as a character in its own right, not too unlike the role of School in other teacher films: an evolving, imposing, corporeal force whose sole purpose is to coerce submission through the use of oppressive and dehumanizing tactics. While, on the surface, both war and school usually operate as common processes, experiences, or mere *things* in their respective narratives, they may also often function as proper nouns, endowed with all the grammatical and rhetorical privileges of being a *particular* type of process, experience, or thing. In other words, their shift from the common to the proper

36

highlights the degree to which the particulars of their presence inform the narrative arcs of the characters. Cinematic soldiers, in this sense, not only have conflicts with other soldiers but also with War itself. Likewise, students on screen may struggle with common elements of school—tests, bullies, teachers, etc.—but also with the paradigm of School writ large. In the case of *Saving Private Ryan*, the fact that Miller's men begin to conceive of themselves in terms independent of their rank, despite the suffocating confines of War-as-character, suggests the enlightening impact that Miller's words have on their previously dormant senses of self.

The deconstruction of personhood in *Saving Private Ryan* is significant because, unlike the prominent depiction of adolescents in paradigmatic teacher movies, these men exist as soldiers *and* people. The transparency of their function creates a certain temporality in which their humanity takes precedence over and exceeds their role as soldiers. These men are people before, during, and after their temporary fight in and with War. As audience members, we find pleasure in seeing past their uniforms to discover who these men actually are when they're not playing soldiers overseas.

Figure 4.1. Private Jackson (Barry Pepper), Corporal Upham (Jeremy Davies), Private Mellish (Adam Goldberg), Sergeant Horvath (Tom Sizemore), Medic Wade (Giovanni Ribisi), and Private Reiben (Ed Burns) in Saving Private Ryan *(1998)*

On the contrary, the cinematic portrayal of adolescence often conflates identity and function into one all-purpose Student-as-Person. Students in teacher movies rarely exist outside the parameters of their actual school; their extracurricular lives, if featured at all, remain inextricably tethered to their academic function. Thus, their roles as students—roles that have been imposed upon them by external, colonizing forces—eclipse their identities as anything other than people called Students in a world called School. Thus, in addition to serving thematic and narrative ends,

J. SPANKE

Miller's mountaintop sermon-of-sorts also unearths an intriguing yet rarely showcased element of American culture: that despite our tendency to conceal, deny, hide or otherwise dismiss the inconvenient reality, teachers and students have always engaged in a battle of sorts.

At its core, *Saving Private Ryan* shares many of the same essential values, messages, and themes with its more traditional teacher-movie counterparts. Amid treacherous waters of doubt, fear, confusion, and chaos (in the case of *Saving Private Ryan*, a literal sea), emerge heroic depictions of courage, friendship, victory, and loss. Whether the threat of War manifests as a domineering headmaster or a swastika-clad German bomber, the scenes remain consistent among war films and teacher movies: soldiers and students fighting to preserve their hopes for lives better than the ones through which they're currently slogging. Granted, the stakes are always greater in *Saving Private Ryan* than failing a calculus test—and dropping out of school is never the same as actually dying for your country—but the dramatic stakes in the films are not that different. The ways both sets of teacher narratives depict issues of performance, attrition, objectives, and success demonstrate that, at least on screen, failing that calculus test *is* often a matter of life and death, if only in academic terms. That kid who dropped out of school may still be alive somewhere, but his peers who stayed behind have no choice but to view him as just another casualty of a War already in progress.

This struggle to negotiate identity and function extends beyond students and soldiers. From the beginning of the film, a beleaguered Miller conceals certain aspects of his personhood, ostensibly because any divulgence of personal details would compromise the integrity of his position and, by extension, their mission. Miller's choice to limit his identity to his present functionality has an inherent othering effect on the people around him. Prior to his confession, he is only a captain: *not* a private, corporal, general, or Nazi. He chooses to create a relationship with his troops predicated on difference and isolation. Teacher movies tend to follow suit. Because of the way they're portrayed, prototypical movie teachers, while seeking an earnest connection with their students, can never fully achieve such a relationship because they, like Captain Miller, are *necessarily* different from their students. The relationship between teacher and student (and, prior to his speech, between Miller and his men) is based upon an inherent power disparity that prohibits authentic liberation (Freire, 2000, pp. 43–69) and insists upon continued adherence to the rules of School/War, however destructive they may be.

Teachers on film don't often have the luxury of being depicted as anything other than what they do. Since these teacher characters are seldom portrayed as whole people, the relationships they form with students are just as rarely anything beyond performative and, at least to some extent, artificial. When Captain Miller-Soldier transforms into Mr. Miller-Teacher, however, he welds the boundary between himself and his students, thus ushering in a multiplicity of personhoods, purposes, and future possibilities. To say that *Saving Private Ryan* is a teacher movie simply because the protagonist is, in fact, a professional educator does a tremendous disservice to both *Saving Private Ryan* and professional educators. Mr. Miller's employment as a teacher doesn't necessarily make him one, especially one worthy of headlining a teacher movie. In fact, the significance of his profession prior to the war pales when compared to the innate pedagogical disposition he commands during the war. He could have just as easily been an auto-mechanic, an amateur golfer, a circus clown, a burgeoning hand model, or an ice-cream vendor. The job itself isn't nearly as important as his speech's reminder that both teachers and soldiers have complete lives somewhere far away in their own little towns with their own pleasant spring seasons.

No, what makes *Saving Private Ryan* a teacher movie is that the main character, quite simply, teaches. His actions determine his function, not the other way around. Contrary to other portrayals of teachers, Captain Miller is neither bound to nor limited by his profession. That he is, in fact, an actual teacher—a convenient occupation, granted, given the scope and trajectory of this piece—distracts us from accepting that teaching manifests in wildly different fashions and that you don't need a license to change students' lives. Beneath the immediate, surfaced themes in the film, *Saving Private Ryan* tells the story of one educator's inner-battles reconciling his various roles in the midst of surrounding chaos. Like so many real-life teachers, Captain Miller strives to reconcile the intricate and often competing versions of himself (Alsup, 2005, pp. 125–146) in the face of daunting external pressures, mounting institutional commands, and the persistent threat of insubordination. His mission to save Private Ryan is administered under circumstances to which most teachers can relate.

After the successful capture of the beach (arrival at school), his commanding officer (principal) calls him to headquarters (the front office) where Miller reports the casualties (absences) and is given his next order (lesson plan). As a metaphor for a year in the life of one teacher's classroom—a temporal convention typical of teacher movies—*Saving Private Ryan* extends fairly evenly. Every town Miller and his men encounter—every burned bridge, eviscerated village, or charred chateaux—serves as yet another curricular milestone on their journey toward that elusive construct of success. Near the beginning of the film, Miller's group is even joined by a New Kid—an awkward, bookish translator named Corporal Upham (Jeremy Davies)—who must adjust to the unique classroom culture created by Miller and his students. As a character, Corporal Upham offers an alternative lens through which viewers can inspect the intricacies of Miller's classroom; Upham's outsider vantage point further humanizes the curricular space, allowing us to see ourselves in Miller's students, their conflicts, defeats, and desires. We recognize their dispositions and empathize with their struggles, even though few of us have ever lost a friend to a Nazi sniper cowering in a French bell tower.

Indeed, as is customary in the teacher movie canon, Miller's class does experience its share of student attrition. On their journey to find Private Ryan— the personification of a capstone educational objective—Captain Miller loses two soldiers to enemy fire. Again, this loss of life is not unique to war films. Whether it's institutional or actual, teacher movies often feature student attrition as a means of accentuating the dire stakes of public education, coupled with the tragic likelihood

J. SPANKE

that not all kids will survive the harsh and unceasing perils of life in school (Cameron, 2012, pp. 83–118).

As Mr. Miller and his class navigate the harsh and monstrous borderlands of preservation and annihilation, his students look to him for guidance. As a teacher abroad, Miller negotiates the pedagogical nuance of granting autonomy while demanding obedience. He fosters collaborations, differentiates instruction, clarifies learning objectives, offers constructive feedback, and incorporates a variety of formative and summative assessments, all to ensure that he and his men make it home at the end of the day. He is masterful in content and technologically resourceful, loyal to his administration while also cognizant of its flaws. He instills in his men a lifelong love of learning and living as he strives to reach them at their own levels to ensure their individual development and the successful (and sustained) completion of their task. Captain Miller excels at classroom management and epitomizes student-centered learning, encouraging his pupils to pursue the professional avenue at which they individually thrive. In Miller's case, these avenues range from translator, sniper, medic, and munitions expert. Real-life teachers can see these analogs in their own students. Just like an orchestra conductor must differentiate instruction for each individual musician, so too must Miller cater to the respective learning needs of each individual soldier. Miller's sniper, for example, becomes a choir director's soprano, and his translator, an art teacher's illustrator: each soldier skilled to achieve a particular objective. Snipers can hit a target from long range; a soprano can hit high notes and may have a wide range.

In perhaps the most literal sense, Captain Miller anchors his pedagogy in immersive, experiential, problem-based learning. Echoing John Dewey's call for "experience gained in more direct associations" (1916, p. 11), Miller cultivates lessons not in some detached, inauthentic, contrived institutional setting but, rather, in organic, indirect, real-world environments. By initiating his transformative experiences under broad and often chaotic circumstances, Captain Miller perpetuates Dewey's lauding of education as a social function predicated on "mutual accommodation and adaptation" (1916, p. 60). Along these lines, as one inherently rooted in a series of trials and tensions, Miller's pedagogy embodies Paulo Freire's notion of "problem-posing education" in that it serves dually as a "humanist and liberating praxis" (2000, p. 86). Freire argues that this approach to education:

> enables teachers and students to become Subjects of the educational process by overcoming authoritarianism and an alienating intellectualism; it also enables people to overcome their false perception of reality. The world—no longer something to be described with deceptive words—becomes the object of that transforming action by men and women which results in their humanization. (2000, p. 86)

Through their literal mission to defeat Nazi authoritarianism and the alienating, fascist intellectualism that accompanies it—and, perhaps more importantly, in their battle against War itself—Miller and his men subsequently transcend their false perception that they have no greater world than War. If we extend this metaphor to more traditional academic settings, Freire argues that when students become the Subjects of their own learning, they too may overcome the authoritative, alienating oppression of School. But this subjectification—this liberation and transcendence of false realities—must derive solely from the students/soldiers themselves, lest these lessons, as Dewey warns, become "remote and dead—abstract and bookish, to use the ordinary words of depreciation" (1916, p. 9).

Freire's plea for humanization underscores Captain Miller's final spoken words of the film. As he lies fatally wounded in battle, the dying Captain pulls Private Ryan close and whispers in his ear, "Earn this. Earn it." Whether it's Ryan's future death that Miller is imploring he earn, or the life he'll lead prior to it, Miller's final orders complement Freire's advocacy of liberating education. "Only power that springs from the weakness of the oppressed will be sufficiently strong to free both" (2000, p. 44). With his final breath, Miller realizes that Ryan's life was never his to save. Removing Ryan from War wouldn't have saved him. Not dying is never the same as truly living. Indeed, Miller's last words serve to underscore that the only person who can save Private Ryan is Ryan himself.

Figure 4.2. Captain Miller (Tom Hanks) and Private Ryan (Matt Damon) in Saving Private Ryan *(1998)*

Indeed, the character of John Miller—in his intertwining functions as teacher, coach, and captain—offers a refreshing reimagining of the popularized conception of teachers and teaching. Rather than function independently from his life outside of war, Miller's proclamation of his past occupation simultaneously synthesizes and troubles what he did and who he was. As a teacher, Mr. Miller sought to prepare his students for life after school. As a soldier, Captain Miller just wants to get his boys home. His is not some vague aspiration for college and career readiness or blasé adherence to arbitrary state standards. As Captain, Miller has no time for abstraction and little room for contemplation. He yells "Down," and his men duck or die. He doesn't care where his soldiers have come from, how poor they are, what color they are, whom they love, or even why they're there. As long as his men have fired a weapon in basic training, he welcomes them to his company with open, loaded arms.

Ironically, it's Miller's pragmatic, obedient maneuvering that ranks him among the most liberating, agentic, and empowering teachers ever to storm the screen. Captain Miller's calculated disruption of the pedagogical exchange typifies that not all learning occurs in school, and curricular spaces can exist even in the fields of Nazi-occupied France (Burdick & Sandlin, 2013, pp. 1–12; Pinar, 2012, pp. 226–238). Rather than approach his classroom with the same cavalier recklessness with which so many of his fellow movie teachers seem to combat School, Teacher Miller instructs his students never to question their superiors: to follow orders, yes, but only in the name of protecting what they already have. As opposed to other, more renegade movie teachers, Captain Miller is governed by orders and decorum and procedure and tact. He positions his pedagogy in direct opposition to fascist oppression while simultaneously grounding it in a system of rules, regulations, and power inequity. His classroom stands in stark contrast to the otherwise transcendental and celebratory spaces immortalized in movies like *Dead Poets Society.* While John Keating (in an iconic performance by Robin Williams) incites rebellion while insisting that his American Scholars *carpe diem* by ripping pages from archaic texts, Miller's men keep their heads down, their guards up, and their mouths shut. They strive to save bridges, not burn them, and to live for tomorrow instead of seizing the day. While the professional lives of too many movie teachers end before the credits—their careers dying in a blaze of fubar glory—Captain Miller fights for life, that of his men and his own.

Miller's deliberation and restraint distinguish him as the antithesis of traditional movie teachers. He's not flashy, sexy, or edgy. He honors the System and its Code and refuses to question either. In the same vein in which he refers to Private Ryan early in the film, John Miller humbly lives each day as "a needle in a stack of needles." He cares nothing for self-promotion or popularity and is impervious to sudden, emotional songs of himself. He commands his soldiers to fall in line rather than think outside the box. As one, they march to the beat of a drummer greater than themselves. Yet, in this unquestioned submission, we find Miller's greatest strength, and in the fragility of his function, his greatest value. Through his principled dedication to his mission, Captain Miller emblematizes what other movie teachers often don't: in the most literal and all-encompassing sense, John Miller is an ally.

It would cheapen his character to suggest that Miller's ultimate goal as a soldier is to kill Germans. "Just know that for every man I kill, the farther away from home I feel," Miller tells his men after a particularly harrowing incident. As opposed to his troops, many of whom went to war precisely to kill Germans, Miller's goal seems to resist the continuous loss of life. In Miller's case, the enemy never had to be Nazis. Miller's fascist enemy was always just an obstacle masking his primary objective. It could have been the Japanese, or disease, or PTSD, or a spelling test, STI, or crosstown baseball rival. Sometimes the people of the other village win, sometimes they lose (Lux, 2011, p. 428); but in themselves, the faces of opposition never matter as much as opposition itself. Instead, Miller's conviction rests not in War, nor in defeating the enemy. Because Miller realizes that his true enemy is War itself, he fights to defeat War altogether: to escape, transcend, rinse, and repeat. Therein lies his heroism. Miller believes that by surviving War, soldiers will have overcome War; likewise, by outlasting School, students conquer School. Of course, rarely is sheer survival included on a list of state standards, even though simply getting through the system remains the solitary purpose for thousands of students for which they storm, year after year, once more, into the beach.

Inasmuch as he casts teachers in a new light, Captain Miller also models what all embattled teachers humbly try to do: train their students to resist oppressive mental occupation while equipping them with the skills necessary to beat their Wars. Still, despite the profound impact he has on his soldiers—and on Private Ryan in particular—Miller's name will likely never top a list of all-time great movie teachers. In the final scene of the film, an elderly James Ryan returns to Arlington National Cemetery to visit the grave of his Captain and beg his wife for assurance that he's led a good life in accordance with his savior's dying orders. Perhaps this powerful reckoning makes the case that Miller's name should be placed prominently on that list.

PART III: CAPTAIN MILLER'S PUBLIC RELATIONS MISSION

"I don't know anything about Ryan. I don't care," Captain Miller admits days before meeting the fated soldier. "The man means nothing to me. He's just a name, but if finding him so he can go home, if that earns me the right to get back to my wife, well then, that's my mission." When Captain Miller first receives the command to find Private Ryan—an assignment he learns came "straight from the top"—he calls it a "public relation's mission." And, so it goes. James Francis Ryan of Iowa was a Private in the 101st Airborne during the invasion and was one of those Captain Miller dubs "airborne miss-drops" somewhere over France. Thus, from his narrative introduction, Private Ryan personifies a mistake, a snafu, something to be remedied, corrected, fixed, made right. Furthermore, Captain Miller soon discovers that not only was Private Ryan's mission botched, but his ticket home comes with a steep price. His only three brothers have already died in combat. Private Ryan is the proverbial child left behind. The mission's public relations agenda, therefore, essentially serves to remind outsiders that fighting a War does not preclude compassion and that some mistakes are swiftly addressed.

What does it mean to *save* Private Ryan? Who *is* Ryan, and why is it worth risking the lives of eight men to ensure that he gets home safely? If we view War as analogous to School, how does saving Private Ryan challenge education's prevailing imperative to leave no child behind? What can teachers glean from the fact that when Miller finally does meet Ryan in the final act of the film, he chooses *not* to bring him home but instead resolves to help him defend his position, aware that by doing so,

J. SPANKE

he's defying the very system to which he has previously pledged allegiance? What does it mean that he dies in the process?

As a comment on our current political climate, *Saving Private Ryan* problematizes the notion of what it means to leave a child behind. Contemporary education insists that to "leave no child behind"—to save them, so to speak—means making sure that students stay *in* school instead of flunking out or quitting. In other words, failure-a la-removal is not an option. Yet, in the case of Private Ryan, removal serves as the primary mechanism for saving him. Saving Private Ryan doesn't mean leaving a good soldier behind; it just means taking him someplace else. Rather than fighting an alternative war or somehow accommodating his present one, saving Private Ryan means severing his dependency on War altogether. Especially since he's already lost three brothers to War—an interesting parallel when considering the number of American families who have "lost" several members to the public school system (Birioukov, 2016)—it means getting him, as one officer says in the movie, "the hell out of there." Since war-as-process and War-as-character are each unapologetically destructive and dehumanizing, it stands to reason that the only way to guarantee a soldier's life would be to detach them from the source of destruction.

To a certain degree, the potential for destruction has always warranted expulsion. We rely on the presence of various toxins to determine what to engage and what to avoid. When canaries died in coal mines, the miners didn't keep sending in more canaries in hopes that things would just get better (Cameron, 2012, pp. 83–104). They wouldn't ignore the dead birds, and they wouldn't pretend that the birds somehow brought death upon themselves. They would just find a new mine. The birds weren't deficient; the mines were toxic. Nobody questioned the strength or motivation or effort of the canaries; nobody sought better, more well-trained miners; and, nobody ever looked at the mines as somehow independent of the toxicities lurking within. Toxins kill, birds die, and people accepted that. Sometimes mines kill people. Period. In their own right, school-as-process and School-as-character are each arguably just as destructive, dehumanizing, and poisonous as coal mines and War (Burdick, 2013; Giroux, 2002). While thousands of students every year suffer at the hands of systemized, standardized, sterilized education (Giroux, 2002), we insist that these students stay in the mine. Even though they may anguish at the prospect of another test, torment, or trigger, they must all stay in the name of not leaving them behind.

As an innovative reframing of the teacher movie, *Saving Private Ryan* inverts the relationship between toxicity and salvation. Saving Ryan, in this case, means leaving War not demanding that Ryan simply fight harder or that Miller captain better or that War not kill as much. The film offers a disturbingly gruesome testimony to the carnage of War, leaving no doubt that War really is *that bad.* Teacher movies, on the other hand, don't often authentically reflect the brutality of School or the absurdity of keeping kids in a system in which they're constantly under fire. As *Saving Private Ryan* suggests, however, maybe it's time for teacher movies to reevaluate why being left behind is so inherently bad and why being brought along

MR. MILLER GOES TO WAR

is so unquestionably good. Or, maybe it's just time we do away with the linear model of education altogether and start using wind farms instead of coal mines. "He wants to stay here, fine. Let's leave him and go home," suggests Captain Miller's close friend and Sergeant, Mike Horvath (Tom Sizemore) upon hearing Ryan's refusal to abandon his post. "But another part of me thinks, what if we stay, and by some miracle we actually make it out of here alive? Someday we might look back on this and decide that saving Private Ryan was the one decent thing we were able to pull out of this whole godawful, shitty mess."

Ultimately, what makes Captain John Miller an exemplary movie teacher is his willingness to meet (in his case, literally) his students where they are. He listens to their concerns, gives them space to voice their goals, does not judge them for their prior conduct, treats them as humans, and, perhaps most importantly, grants them autonomy to exercise their own agency, even if doing so means they are ignoring orders that have come straight from the top. After spending the entirety of the film meandering through various obstacles in the increasingly desperate search for an elusive objective, when Miller meets Ryan, he first begins to appreciate the subjectivity of Success. Captain Miller realizes that his mission might not necessarily align with Ryan's or the rest of his student soldiers. Miller accepts that he may want something from War that maybe Ryan doesn't and that his personal agenda might not be in the best interest of his men or his mission. What sets Miller apart from other movie teachers is that he allows himself to be influenced by Ryan in such a way as to consciously reexamine not only War in general but his respective role in sustaining War. Maybe there are other ways to beat War, he begins to think. Maybe we should occasionally listen to our soldiers and take our commands from them. Maybe the best way to beat War is to address the immediate needs of each individual soldier instead of unquestioningly compromising those needs for the good of the collective. Maybe that's what it means to leave no child behind.

In *Dead Poets Society,* the first thing John Keating does is give his students orders. Yes, they're new and neat and fun and exciting, but they're orders nonetheless. Keating never asks his students what *they* want from School; he just spends the movie telling them how to live. Interestingly, the film doesn't even end until Mr. Keating has the final word ("Thank you, boys"). Captain Miller, on the other hand, risks his career (and his life) helping his soldiers achieve *their* objectives, earn *their* successes, and defeat *their* Wars. Miller knows that beating War means little if Success doesn't derive from true student agency. The kids standing on their desks at the end of *Dead Poets Society* may have stuck it to the man, but they're all still getting expelled. School won in the end.

Miller's decision to dismiss his assignment and stay with Ryan's fledgling unit signifies authentic, student-centered learning, putting the students' needs ahead of his own teaching agenda. Of course, the decision not to bring Ryan home ultimately costs Captain Miller his life. War, like School, can't accommodate a leader who disobeys orders. The miner who ignores the dead canary always dies. Yet, as opposed to other movie teachers whose careers also perish at the end of their stories, Captain

Miller doesn't die until after he defeats War. With his last breath, he fires his pistol at an incoming Nazi tank. Moments later, an allied aircraft destroys the tank and screams over the town in victory. Miller's life is over, but as that plane flies above him, he knows that War is over, too. With a smile on his face, Mr. Miller finally gets to go home. In the end, Captain Miller meets the same fate as so many of his cinematic teacher counterparts. By rejecting direct orders and allowing his soldiers to exercise their own free will, he loses everything; his life as a teacher, coach, and captain literally ends on the bridge between fascism and freedom. Rather than expel a student from School, Captain Miller helps a soldier fight the good fight. He could have saved Private Ryan, removed him from War, and may have even gotten to see his wife again. Instead, he chooses to let Ryan save himself. Because of that supreme sacrifice, in his death, lives his greatest triumph.

REFERENCES

Alsup, Janet. (2005). *Teacher identity discourses: Negotiating personal and professional spaces.* London: Routledge.

Birioukov, Anton. (2016). Beyond the excused/unexcused absence binary: Classifying absenteeism through a voluntary/involuntary absence framework. *Educational Review, 68*(3), 340–357.

Blum, Susan D. (2012). Education is war, according to a term-paper mill: A metaphor to justify by. *Huffington Post.*

Burdick, Jake, & Jenny Sandlin. (2013). Learning, becoming, and the unknowable: conceptualizations, mechanisms, and process in public pedagogy literature. *Curriculum Inquiry, 43*(1), 142–177.

Cameron, Jeanne. (2012) Canaries reflect on the mine: Dropouts' stories of schooling. Charlotte, NC: Information Age Publishing.

Dewey, John. (1916.). *Experience and education* (Reprint Edition, 1 July 1997). Free Press.

Freire, Paulo. (2000). *Pedagogy of the oppressed* (30th Anniversary ed.). Bloomsbury Academic.

Gee, James P. (1989). Literacy, discourse, and linguistics: An introduction. *Journal of Education, 171*(4), 5–14.

Giroux, Henry A. (2002). Neoliberalism, corporate culture, and the promise of higher education: The University as a democratic public sphere. *Harvard Education Review, 72*(4), 425–463.

Lux, Thomas. (2011). The people of the other village. In *The penguin anthology of 20th century American poetry.* New York, NY: Penguin.

Pinar, William F. (2012). *What is curriculum theory* (2nd ed.). London: Routledge.

Saving Private Ryan. (1998). *Rotten Tomatoes.*

Shoffner, Melanie. (Ed.). (2016). *Saviors, scapegoats & schoolmarms: Examining the teacher in fiction and film for teacher education.* London: Routledge.

Spanke, Jeff. (2016). No human left behind: falling skies and the role of the pedagogue in the post-apocalypse. In Melanie Shoffner. (Ed.), *Exploring teachers in fiction and film: Saviors, scapegoats & schoolmarms: Examining the teacher in fiction and film for teacher education* (pp. 216–224). London: Routledge.

Spielberg, Steven. (1998, June 23). Spielberg aims to tell truth about war in saving private Ryan. *CNN. com.*

ELIZABETH CURRIN

5. IN LOCO PARENTIS REDUX

Bob and Linda Belcher at Wagstaff School

ABSTRACT

Grounded in a critical historical understanding of the feminization of teaching, this chapter explores representations of teaching in the Fox animated series *Bob's Burgers*, featuring Wagstaff School's well-intentioned but inept guidance counselor, Mr. Frond, an oft-villainous counterpart to Tina, Louise, and Gene Belcher's own parents, Linda and the eponymous Bob. Because both Bob and Linda each take a turn as substitute teachers, in addition to the usual parent-teacher conference or chaperone fare, *Bob's Burgers*, aside from being an underrated commentary on the American working class, also stands to make a significant contribution to scholarly conversations about education in pop culture.

Keywords: parents, guidance counselors, gender, *in loco parentis*

***

Though I entered the teaching profession intending to work *with* young people rather than birthing any of my own, I was loath to become another old maid schoolteacher. The punishing gender stereotype loomed a little too close for my anxiously single, twenty-something comfort, reinforced by the near-daily refrain of my good-natured department chair. On his way out the door, he inevitably dispensed unsolicited advice to my fellow novice and me. I understand that "Y'all need to get some kids" was a gentle jest, spurring us toward a little work-life balance, yet my workaholic colleague and I invariably replied, "We already have more than a hundred, thank you" and returned to our labors of love.

Historians of education have ably traced the shift from American schoolmarms and masters—your Ichabod Cranes—to the prevailing mores that comfortably conflate parenthood and the education profession. Carl F. Kaestle's account of the antebellum quest for common schools notes how "the two arguments in favor of female teachers—their cheapness and natural superiority as instructors of young children—appear together so often that it is difficult to determine which was the more important as a motive" (1983, p. 124). Kaestle further argues, "the feminization of teaching and the professionalization of teaching"—marked by the appearance of a decidedly patriarchal administrative class—"were compatible

© KONINKLIJKE BRILL NV, LEIDEN, 2019 | DOI:10.1163/9789004398092_005

and reinforcing," serving "to bridge the widening gap between family culture and school culture" (1983, p. 125). In part, this was because "feminization" was a far cry from "feminism" (Sugg, 1978, p. 18), owing to the enduring ideals of republican motherhood. Founding Father Benjamin Rush had advocated for women's education because "instruction of children naturally devolves upon women [… as the] most important duty of mothers" (2014, p. 25). Turning teaching into a pink profession, at least in theory, restored the perceived breach between cradle and classroom (Grumet, 1988, p. 56). Entrusted to maternal pedagogues and paternal principals, students thus became acquainted with the *in loco parentis* functions of increasingly systematic schooling.

As women broke fertile ground in a new profession, however, they tended to be of the barren variety themselves, whether by choice or by circumstance. At the dawn of the 20th century, women comprised approximately seventy percent of the nation's teaching force, nearly all of them unmarried; this societal shift was only possible, Jackie Blount reasons, because "recognizable sub-cultures of single women teachers emerged that sometimes served as surrogate families," providing requisite social, emotional, and practical support to sustain single ladies apart from their parents' protection (2005, p. 45). In rural areas where such affordances were rare, women were known to live in their schools, entirely dismissing the question of work-life balance posed by my well-meaning department chair (Blount, 2005, p. 48). Even in urban areas, women educators were constrained in their attempts to delineate separate public and private spheres (Carter, 2016, p. 60), all the more so when they sought to disrupt the spinster status quo. In 1913, a New York City teacher who dared to grant herself maternity leave prompted the board of education to declare, "married women who are teachers are inefficient and undesirable" ("Reports against Married Teachers," 1913, p. 2).

The unwed teacher trend, though financially appealing and in some cases legally mandated, ultimately proved untenable. Amid rising concern about the perceived threat of lesbianism, the National Education Association insisted, "'marriage and parenthood are likely to enrich a teacher's understanding of childhood and family life and thus will help her be a better teacher'" (qtd. in Blount, 2005, pp. 75–76). Today, the image of the prim, old maid teacher perhaps lingers only in neophyte minds like my own, but the feminization of teaching persists, and the twice-told joke in Jason Reitman's *Juno*—"Pregnant? Like our moms and teachers?"—attests to the concomitant staying power of the conflation of teaching and motherhood. As Lillian Mongeau (2016) posits, "Caring for young children can't be separated from teaching them," a warning doubly true for teacher-parents.

Attending this sociohistorical linkage of teaching and parenting is a corresponding uneasiness with or distrust of the childless, a population evidently perplexing otherwise incessant advertisers (Strauss, 2016) and gaining some attention amid the Brexit brouhaha across the pond. When Andrea Leadsom suggested her rival was less qualified to be Prime Minister simply by eschewing the option of progeny (Adam, 2017), the late Benjamin Rush no doubt would have been pleased. Theresa May ultimately proved victorious, albeit seen as "a stern headmistress walking into a room of rowdy children just as things were getting out of hand" (Reidy, 2016). Though women have, indeed, infiltrated the administrative echelons of school and society, teaching demographics continue to skew noticeably female, to the great consternation of those who advocate for parity of student and teacher populations in terms of gender, race, and ethnicity (McClain, 2016; Rich, 2014). Extant disparities have the potential to provoke and exacerbate fraught relationships between families and schools.

Such rifts are not without precedent. Adam Laats has explored the "long history of questioning the proper relationship between school, child, and parent" (2015, p. 131), and as historian John Rury has noted, "Ideas about education are inevitably influenced by social norms and expectations regarding children" (2016, p. 50). Likewise, those norms and expectations can be both governed by and reflected in visual media, giving rise to a branch of cultural criticism devoted to teachers on TV. Existing scholarship has noted the significance of cartoons like *The Simpsons* (Fox 1989–), *King of the Hill* (Fox 1997–2010), *South Park* (Comedy Central (1997–), and *Daria* (MTV 1997–2002) for their literally animated portrayals of educators that both exhibit and problematize traditional teacher behavior (Dalton & Linder, 2019, pp. 113–114), but Fox's animated comedy *Bob's Burgers* (Fox 2011–) has yet to join the scholarly conversation, despite being rife with the sociocultural themes outlined above.

Initially panned as another would-be *Simpsons* (Hale, 2011; Lowry, 2011; Stuever, 2011), *Bob's Burgers* has since garnered a cult following and critical acclaim. The eponymous lead, Bob Belcher (voiced by H. Jon Benjamin), runs a burger joint with his dutiful wife, Linda (voiced by John Roberts), and the help of their three quirky but loveable children: Tina (voiced by Dan Mintz), Louise (voiced by Kristen Schaal), and Gene (voiced by Eugene Mirman). An observably working-class family, the Belchers take pride in their establishment, and the ups and downs of owning a small business inherently offer rich plot possibilities—not to mention sharp social commentary on our populist present. In fact, because the family lives above the restaurant, the kids are trapped in what amounts to a perpetual work-study situation, a progressive educator's dream (Perlstein, 2016, p. 128). Because the Belchers are equal opportunity stars, viewers also spend a considerable amount of time at Wagstaff School, which all three children—of young but indeterminate ages—attend and where Bob and Linda each take a turn as substitute teachers in addition to attending the usual parent-teacher conference or chaperoning school events. Admittedly, this requires the viewer's willing suspension of disbelief: how does the restaurant survive such irregular hours? Verisimilitude notwithstanding, the Belchers's support of Wagstaff yields frequent encounters with the childless Mr. Frond (voiced by David Herman), a well-intentioned guidance counselor who proves to be almost villainously inept, consistently disproving the claim, "Parents are amateurs, but *teachers* are professionals" (qtd. in Huneven, 2015, p. 140). The expert blending of home, school, and workplace evokes the deeply integrated lives of colonial-era schoolchildren (Kaestle, 1983, p. 4), and the fluidity with which the characters move throughout these spheres has the makings of the "radical openness"

E. CURRIN

envisioned by third-space theorists (Hulme, Cracknell, & Owens, 2009, p. 540). The social dynamics yoking parents, children, and counselor—traversing all seven seasons and counting—are undoubtedly worthy of critical attention.

Focusing on key episodes featuring the fictional Bob, Linda, and Mr. Frond not only exposes authentic tensions between families and schools, but by giving so much airtime to a guidance counselor rather than the archetypal teacher or administrator, *Bob's Burgers* also invites much-needed critical analysis of that role. Honoring the altruistic intentions of such characters as Ms. Friedenberg (Florence Stanley) in *Up the Down Staircase* (1967) and Mr. Rosso (Dave Allen) in *Freaks and Geeks* (NBC 1999–2000), Mr. Frond joins a long line of caricatures of those overreaching specialists that infiltrated American schools during the 20th century. Intended to enable "the pupil to understand himself and others," guidance counselors swelled in number after the passage of the National Defense Education Act in 1958, turning their attention to home-school relations in the midst of the turbulent 1960s (Royster, 1964, pp. 6, 8). Practitioner journals of the era devoted whole issues to the problem of "aimless, maladjusted youth" (Brison 41) and counselors' potential to serve "as an institutional balance wheel" (Popper, 1970, p. 232). Proclamations like "the specialist is born" (Schlegel 30) and "the guidance counselor, contrary to public opinion, is quite human" (Calia, 1955, p. 431) praised their Herculean efforts, but *Bob's Burgers* tells a decidedly different story.

Wagstaff School—yet to be explicitly identified for viewers—makes a brief but significant appearance in the show's very first episode. The plot of "Human Flesh" pivots on a pernicious rumor that Bob's titular burgers are made with a little help from the adjacent crematorium. When confronted by the health inspector, Bob immediately suspects young Louise as the source, picturing her deeply engaged in a morbid round of "Show and Tell" at school. From the beginning of the series, then, the Belchers's school, work, and home environments are interconnected, a relationship that increases in richness and in risk with each passing season.

Following on the heels of "Human Flesh," the second episode, "Crawl Space," contributes to the children's character development, inevitably relying on school to achieve that aim. As with the first episode, the title indicates the crux of the action: Bob, having attempted to fix a leak in the attic in anticipation of a visit from his in-laws, finds himself happily stuck in the crawl space and thus unable to entertain his wife's family. Like the rest of the Belchers, however, he cannot escape the off-putting sounds of their geriatric lovemaking, which Gene impishly captures on his keyboard to accompany his report in class the next day. He is transferred forthwith to Mr. Frond's office, bedecked with posters urging students to wear "Re-spect-acles" and "Hop on the Self-E-Steam Boat." Louise lands in Frond's office, as well, having convinced her peers that the ghost of her father is haunting the restaurant. Though the prior episode showed viewers Louise's devious personality, Mr. Frond has yet to catch on, playing right into her trap by seizing the opportunity to counsel a "grieving" student. His motivation increases when Tina also earns involuntary guidance for having followed in her dad's crawl-space footsteps all the way to the boys locker room to satisfy her vivid adolescent imagination.

This culmination of incidents, aside from fleshing out the cartoon's young characters, fills Mr. Frond with purpose. Over a dramatic soundtrack, he shrieks, "You are kids. In. Crisis! We need to conduct a home visit TODAY." Gathering grief puppets and crisis crayons, he soon learns that Bob is not, in fact, dead. Linda explains that Louise "just likes messing with people she thinks are stupid," and thus we have an explicit sense of how she views Mr. Frond—a portrayal Linda does not refute. George M. Schlegel assured *School and Society* readers that guidance counselors are, indeed, necessary because "everybody cannot guide and counsel" (1961, p. 31). No doubt Louise would disagree, yet Mr. Frond's actions in this episode indicate the persistence of the specialist ideal.

Contrary to expectations, Linda's mother proves to be the hero of the episode. As Frond frantically dials social services to save the "troubled" youth, Gloria (voiced by Renée Taylor) blocks him with a motherly monologue: "Are you married? 'Ya have kids? My daughter is the best mother in the world. And this one? (She gestures to Bob.) He's nuts. But guess what? Having a family makes you go nuts. So, if you don't have kids, I don't think you know enough to be calling anyone." Despite Gloria's final exhortation to "Leave this family alone!" Mr. Frond is a regular fixture on the show and a significant foil to Bob and Linda as he tries to figure out how to serve *in loco parentis*. Surveying their key interactions provides an opportunity to reflect on the question Gloria implicitly raises here: whether or not schools know what is best for the students they serve.

That question takes an interesting turn when parents become the pedagogues. In Season 2, "Synchronized Swimming" opens with the Belcher matriarch bestowing unconditional love upon her progeny in the form of homework help, that perennial motherly pastime. Bob feels she is a little too generous, which can only lead to trouble. Then again, sitcoms traffic in trouble. Over lunch, the kids discuss their mutual hatred of physical education. Gene loathes the shirts vs. skins routine, and Tina cringes at the recollection of a pummeling montage. Louise's grievance is arguably more serious. She dreads being told by a hat-wearing teacher that hats are not allowed in P.E. Though viewers have no idea why, Louise has never appeared without her pink bunny ears, yet her parents permit the unique self-expression without judgment. The gym teacher's rule, then, amounts to a serious threat to Louise's identity, prompting her to act. "Let's stop by Mr. Frond's office. He's highly suggestible," she suggests to her likewise impressionable siblings.

Once again attesting to her keen ability to read Mr. Frond, Louise converses with the others outside his office door, falsely lamenting, "When I'm in P.E. class, I feel like I'm not living up to society's warped image of fitness." Tina follows suit, claiming, "I feel like I'm not being valued as a woman." Gene humorously adds, "Me neither. I need guidance. And counseling," inspiring the hopelessly heroic Frond to try out some slang and empathize with their "feeling P.O.-ed about P.E."

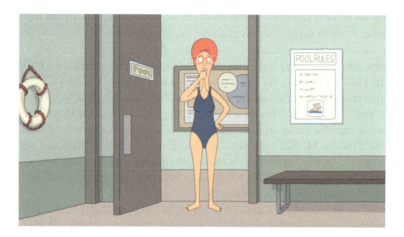

Figure 5.1. Linda Belcher (voiced by John Roberts) on Bob's Burgers *(Fox 2011–)*

while ultimately acknowledging the need to uphold state curricular requirements. Ever resourceful, Louise talks him into letting her take an independent study in synchronized swimming—as the episode title indicates, though she wisely manipulates him into thinking it is his idea.

Forging Linda's signature of agreement to teach the swimming class buys the young Belchers some respite from P.E. until Linda encounters Mr. Frond at a craft store and the proverbial jig is up. Bob reminds an irate Linda of the danger of her habitual coddling of the children, and she vows to "get tough," which in this case means actually coaching the fabled swimmers. With a parent for a pedagogue, the kids continue to play games, expertly relying on educational jargon by claiming that as "visual learners" they will succeed best by watching Linda do all the work. This class clown's dream attracts more students, and when Linda struggles to teach "other people's children" (Grumet, 1988, p. 164), she quits, harshly conceding, "You were right, Bob. I need to let my baby birds fly. My bratty little baby birds fly with their crappy wings." Ms. Belcher ultimately reclaims her class and proves to be an effective educator, though perhaps not so adept as Bob, as a later episode reveals. Regardless, this episode includes a rare apology from Louise: "Sorry we were such jerks," she tells her mom, and Linda replies, "That's why I quit being your coach, but I'll never quit being your mommy." Teaching, indeed, is a transient act, whereas parenthood has an air of permanence.

Over the course of the show's run, the airtime devoted to Wagstaff School has ebbed and flowed. The third season offers the delightful "Carpe Museum" in which Bob takes Linda's place as the parent volunteer for the annual field trip, a gig that requires one to wear an obnoxiously orange safety vest. Further underscoring the Belchers's consistent support of the school, Bob queries, "How did you survive eight years with Mr. Frond?" It appears that among his many responsibilities—providing guidance the least of them—Mr. Frond is also the field trip coordinator, and he is not exactly thrilled to have a green chaperone on the activity bus because "With great vest comes great responsibility." Despite dire warnings about "Missing Marvins" and "Walk-away Wendys," Bob manages to lose two of his charges, including Louise. This causes him to have to play "bad cop," which prompts Louise's designated buddy to issue the ultimate insult, "You remind me of my mom! She hates fun, too!" Bob's intense need for the children to like him leads to typical *Bob's Burgers* hijinks, neatly resolved in episodic fashion but not before Bob learns a thing or two about being a chaperone.

That knowledge serves him well the following season in "Bob and Deliver," the titular homage reinforced by the "Edward James Olive-Most Burger" advertised on the "Burger of the Day" board that regular viewers have learned to spot. Perhaps intentionally paralleling Linda's run-in with Mr. Frond in "Synchronized Swimming," the episode opens with Bob and the kids in a kitchen supply store where they, too, encounter Mr. Frond, who informs Tina that since her home economics teacher is out on disability, the class is to be combined with metal shop. Bob pipes up: "It's a shame to have to cancel Home Ec. I mean, everybody needs to learn how to cook, right? A lot of kids aren't lucky enough to grow up in a restaurant." Mr. Frond immediately suggests that Bob would make a great substitute, and the Belcher patriarch lights up, truly inspired by the prospect: "It is an honor to pass on what you know to the next generation, right? I mean … I might even change some lives." This exchange conveys Bob's perception of educators, which, judging by their reactions, Gene and Louise find to be a little inflated. Tina, however, is open to having a parent for a pedagogue, losing herself in a fantasy about being the teacher's pet.

Viewers continue to get a sense of Bob's notion of what a teacher is and does when he dons a business casual outfit for his first day on the job, complete with makeshift briefcase. This is a far cry from Bob's usual attire: grimy t-shirt, sweats, and comfortable clogs. He cautions the kids over breakfast to refer to him as "Mr. Belcher" and treat him like any other substitute. Louise retorts: "That means you get a mean nickname, and we assume you lead a horribly depressing life." Though Nicholson Baker has argued the substitute is "the lowest-ranking participant in American education" (2016, p. 1), Bob approaches the task with incredible solemnity and is subsequently horrified to learn the students' usual *modus operandi* is to watch films rather than engage in any hands-on learning. His threatened disruption of this status quo begins to incite mutiny until Mr. Frond enters, pacifies the children, and guides Bob into the hallway. "Kids are horrible! Why do we keep making them?" the novice teacher asks. Mr. Frond bluntly explains, "Home Ec isn't for honors students. It's where dumb-dumbs learn to make ice." Brushing aside Mr. Frond's having blatantly insulted his daughter, Bob asks, "Shouldn't we be challenging them?" Whereas Mr. Frond associates challenge with confrontation, Bob views it as central to teaching.

Processing his (stereotypically) rough first day in the comfort of his restaurant, Bob vows not to quit, hoping instead "to reach [his students]." Intuitively meeting them where they are, he slyly "tricks" the students into making kettle corn to accompany their daily feature, prompting Tina to admit, "I think Dad might be a great teacher." This is not so much a proud seal of approval as it is an expression of worry over the competition for teacher's pet. Bob's mixed reception at Wagstaff School also includes the cafeteria ladies, who rebuff his requests for supplies and attempt to chasten what they perceive to be his arrogance.

Figure 5.2. Bob Belcher (voiced by H. Jon Benjamin) on Bob's Burgers *(Fox 2011–)*

In truth, however, Bob is a pretty humble pedagogue, gently coaxing the defiant Zeke to try his hand at seasoning some soup. The music builds as Bob discovers Zeke's "perfect palate," and teacher and student share an emotional moment of recognition. The following musical montage shows signs of pedagogical progress, culminating in the idea to start a "Home Ec-staurant," ably utilizing each student's assets. Unfortunately, this turn of events alienates Tina and infuriates the cafeteria staff. Having run afoul of school bureaucracy, Bob must close the Home Ec-staurant and turn over the teaching reins to Mr. Frond. This leads to a *Dead Poets Society* (1989) send-up in which the students, led by the reformed Zeke, stand on their desks and radically rip their popcorn bags, just as Bob had once done. Very much in contrast to Linda's stint as swim coach, Bob's brief tenure as a teacher elicits genuine promise from the pupils. True to his word, he *challenges* them, thereby empowering them.

Mr. Frond, of course, sees children in a different light, a motif recurring in "Frond Files," when once again, the restaurant is inexplicably closed so the Belchers can attend a school event. Dismayed to find their children's "Why I Love Wagstaff" projects are not on display, they learn Mr. Frond found them "too creative" and thus unsuitable for the superintendent's eyes. Viewers are then treated to an imagining of Louise's *Terminator*-inspired (1984) theme, Gene's flatulent spoof of *Rock 'n' Roll High School* (1979), and Tina's trademark hormone-rich and zombie-filled fantasy.

All three vignettes feature a villainous Frond, who fails to take students' needs or interests into account, which explains the counselor's censorship and sharply contrasts with the schoolhouse style of Mr. Belcher. Demonstrably proud of their young writers, Bob and Linda attempt to assuage Mr. Frond's hurt feelings. "Maybe relax a little," Linda advises; "Try to talk to the kids about kid stuff, y'know. Relate to them. On their level." She, too, knows a thing or two about children, living up to her mother's praise all those seasons before and offering some pointed commentary on the childless Frond. Catching a glimpse of the high-strung and overworked guidance counselor, I have no doubt my former department chair would chide, "You need to get some kids," and yet, Linda's advice is not unlike suggestions made to counselors in the throes of desegregation: "they must be sensitive to the feelings of resentment and hostility in their clients without becoming upset and useless; they must be interested and committed to accepting the student for what he is" (Smith, 1971, p. 351). *Bob's Burgers* may make jokes at Mr. Frond's expense, but like any good satire, it acts as a corrective device: exposing in order to improve, a trend that continues through the show's eighth season, current as this chapter is written.

Dalton and Linder have posited, "How we characterize teachers directly reflects the collective opinion about the larger enterprise of formal education" (2019, p. 5). *Bob's Burgers* provides an additional layer by implicitly indicating how Bob and Linda characterize teachers when they step into that role, too. Though their involvement with Wagstaff School could contribute to "the popular belief that teaching is a job that anyone can do" (Tye, 2000, p. 127), viewers stand to gain from witnessing the Belchers's trials and tribulations in all three spheres of work, home, and school, as well as contemplating the productive overlap thereof. *Bob's Burgers* is by no means intended solely for an audience of educators, but the show's nuanced portrayal of complex interpersonal interactions has the potential to inform our understanding of the relationship between schools and society. Bob and Linda, by showing greater participation at Wagstaff than television viewers typically witness, illustrate what scholars have labeled as parental "*engagement*, rather than *involvement*, precisely to emphasize a more active and powerful role for parents in schools" (Warren, Hong, Rubin, & Uy, 2009, p. 2211). Along with the show's charming details and delightful hijinks that have attracted a cult following and overdue critical acclaim, *Bob's Burgers* thus invites willing viewers to contemplate the *in loco parentis* model—a worthwhile and significant pursuit.

REFERENCES

Adam, Karla. (2016, July 9). Finalist for British prime minister suggests motherhood makes her a better pick than childless opponent. *The Washington Post*.

Baker, Nicholson. (2016). *Substitute: Going to school with a thousand kids*. New York, NY: Blue Rider Press.

Blount, Jackie M. (2005). *Fit to teach: Same-sex desire, gender, and school work in the twentieth century*. Albany, NY: State University of New York Press.

E. CURRIN

Brison, David W. (1964). The role of the elementary guidance counselor. *The National Elementary Principal, 63*(5), 41–44.

Calia, Vincent F. (1955). The guidance counselor: the miracle man in education. *The School Review, 63*(8), 429–431.

Carter, Patricia A. (2016). From single to married: feminist teachers' response to family/work conflict in early Twentieth-Century New York City. *History of Education Quarterly, 56*(1), 36–60.

Dalton, Mary M., & Laura R. Linder. (2019). *Teacher TV: Seventy years of teachers on television.* New York, NY: Peter Lang.

Grumet, Madeleine R. (1988). *Bitter milk: Women and teaching.* Amherst: The University of Massachusetts Press.

Hale, Mike. (2011, January 8). Deadpan boundary-pushing in Bob's Burgers: Low-key approach taken in mildly funny new series. *The Houston Chronicle.*

Hulme, Rob, David Cracknell, & Allan Owens. (2009). Learning in third spaces: Developing trans-professional understanding through practitioner enquiry. *Educational Action Research, 17*(4), 537–550.

Huneven, Michelle. (2015). Amateurs. In Meghan Daum (Ed.), *Selfish, shallow, and self-absorbed: Sixteen writers on the decision not to have kids* (pp. 131–146). New York, NY: Picador.

Kaestle, Carl F. (1983). *Pillars of the Republic: Common schools and American society, 1780–1860.* New York, NY: Hill and Wang.

Laats, Adam. (2015). *The other school reformers: Conservative activism in American education.* Cambridge, MA: Harvard University Press.

Lowry, Brian. (2011, January 7). TV review: Bob's burgers. *Daily Variety*, p. 35.

McClain, Dani. (2016, June 9). America needs more black men leading classrooms. *Slate.*

Mongeau, Lillian. (2016, August 16). The underestimation of America's preschool teachers. *The Atlantic.*

Perlstein, Daniel. (2016). Class. In A. J. Angulo (Ed.), *Miseducation: A history of ignorance-making in America and abroad* (pp. 123–139). Baltimore, MD: Johns Hopkins University Press.

Popper, Samuel H. (1970). The guidance counselor as an institutional balance wheel in early adolescent education: A probe into latent role capacity. *Contemporary Education, 61*(5), 232–239.

Reidy, Padraig. (2016, July 29). Theresa may: The Hillary Clinton of Britain? *Salon.*

Reports against married teachers. (1913, June 24). *Los Angeles Herald.*

Rich, Motoko. (2014, September 6). Why don't more men go into teaching? *The New York Times.*

Royster, William B. (1964). Guidance in the elementary school. *The National Elementary Principal, 63*(5), 6–10.

Rury, John. (2016). *Education and social change: Contours in the history of American schooling.* New York, NY: Routledge.

Rush, Benjamin. (2014). Thoughts upon female education, 1787. In James W. Fraser (Ed.), *The school in the United States: A documentary history* (pp. 24–26). New York, NY: Routledge.

Schlegel, George M. (1961). Is the guidance counselor necessary? *School and Society,* 30–31.

Smith, Paul M. (1971). The role of the guidance counselor in the desegregation process. *The Journal of Negro Education, 40*(4), 347–351.

Strauss, Elissa. (2016, July 11). Why don't advertisers pay attention to childless women? *Slate.*

Stuever, Hank. (2011, January 9). In 'Bob's Burgers,' plenty to beef about. *The Washington Post.*

Sugg, Redding S. (1978). *Motherteacher: The feminization of American education.* Charlottesville, VA: University Press of Virginia.

Tye, Barbara Benham. (2000). *Hard truths: Uncovering the deep structure of schooling.* New York, NY: Teachers College Press.

Warren, Mark R., Soo Hong, Carolyn Leung Rubin, & Phitsamay Sychitkokhong Uy. (2009). Beyond the bake sale: A community-based relational approach to parent engagement in schools. *Teachers College Record, 111*(9), 2209–2254.

JILL EWING FLYNN

6. WHAT'S A NICE WHITE LADY TO DO?

*A Critical Literacy Lens on Teaching and Learning in
Pop Culture Portrayals*

ABSTRACT

This chapter explores the use of media literacy projects to foster critical understandings of texts, schools, teachers, and students. The framework of critical literacy facilitates understanding of how texts position readers, viewers, or listeners; how readers position texts; and how texts are positioned within social, cultural, historical, and political contexts. I describe how my undergraduate students, future English teachers, use a critical literacy approach in a course assignment, the Media Representations of Teachers Project. Excerpts from their projects show how studying media representations of groups can foster critical literacy in methods courses as well as secondary classrooms and other settings. In a world saturated by media, it is teachers' responsibility to equip students with such tools: to question and criticize, analyze and decide, talk back and make change.

Keywords: critical literacy, popular culture, teaching, media portrayals, White savior, teacher candidates, critical pedagogy

***

Each fall, the undergraduate students in my course Literacy and Technology—all future secondary English teachers—complete a project examining media representations of teaching. As I have written about elsewhere, the project provides students with several choices: they can work alone or with peers; they can choose any film or television show that portrays teaching and learning, whether inside or outside of school; and, they can present their findings via traditional paper or a multimedia presentation (Prezi, PowerPoint, blog, podcast, wiki, or iMovie). Their projects must consider how teaching and learning are portrayed in the film or series and how the roles of the teacher(s), students, administration, and/or the school system are depicted. I also ask the students to consider their own beliefs about teaching in the context of the readings completed in their coursework and to compare/contrast them with this media representation.

For the last five years or so, I have shown *MADtv*'s (Fox 1995–2006, CT 2016) "Nice White Lady" to prepare students for this project. I use this over-the-top parody of the White savior teacher movies to foster a critical literacy stance toward

© KONINKLIJKE BRILL NV, LEIDEN, 2019 | DOI:10.1163/9789004398092_006

J. E. FLYNN

films about urban teaching. In the video, the students are uniformly resistant and dangerous (one sharpens his knife using his gun—*during class*); the administration is unsupportive (a principal-type figure tells the teacher, "These students can't learn. They're minorities!" after taking a swig from his flask); and the teacher miraculously breaks through to her students by handing them pencils and composition books ("Write that down," she tells one, dramatically). When I show this clip, my preservice teachers can easily identify the elements it spoofs in many of the films they know. As the fictional tagline says, "When it comes to teaching inner city minorities, you don't need books, and you don't need rules. All you need is a nice White lady." The satire helps them discover why these features need to be examined with a critical lens and helps prepare them to complete their project on media representations of teachers.

One semester, our discussion of "Nice White Lady" became more nuanced than it ever had before. While the students still laughed at the clip and volunteers explained the satirical elements, I noticed frustration and distress on some faces. I called on a student, let's call her Mary,[1] to share what she was thinking, and she explained, "But *Freedom Writers* is one of my favorite movies!" Alexis volunteered, "I want to teach in an urban school. Is this supposed to mean I shouldn't just because I'm a White woman?" Jon agreed: "The fact is, I do want to be a teacher because I want to change lives, but this sketch makes fun of that." Diana ventured, "Yeah, and I actually think sometimes what we learn about students of color reinforces the stereotypes in this clip." Though class was ending soon, I was glad to continue the conversation. "Ok, let's unpack this a bit. Many of you in this room, including me, are White women. What does that mean for us as teachers?" Students began to discuss further. Some expressed a desire to move past race and see students as individuals. Others struggled with the issue of stereotyping—both of students and of themselves as White teachers. We weren't able to come to conclusions during that class, but Dan wrapped up our first day of discussion by emphasizing, "I understand we want to see past race, but the fact is that racism still exists. There are still many people who believe, consciously or unconsciously, that people of color just aren't as smart or as valuable in this world. We can't forget that."

I knew these issues needed further discussion. Luckily, I have the luxury of teaching these students in future semesters, including the fall of senior year in a project I have developed with colleagues to foster racial literacy where they closely examine their own racial identity and its impact on their teaching. I also remembered my own motivations for teaching and could relate to my students' feelings about their calling to make a difference. Still, we needed to continue to consider issues of race, identity, power, and representation and the way that "Nice White Lady" reveals important critiques. I decided to start the next class with the following post on the board:

From *Critical Pedagogy* by Kincheloe:

Freire argued that all teachers need to engage in a constant dialogue with students that questions existing knowledge and problematizes the traditional power relations that have served to marginalize specific groups and individuals. In these research dialogues with students, critical teachers listen carefully to what students have to say about their communities and the problems that confront them. Teachers help students frame these problems in a larger social, cultural, and political context in order to solve them. (p. 19)

[T]eachers must study how the world that is unjust by design shapes the classroom and the relations between teachers and students. By doing this, teachers can begin to discern concrete manifestations of the abstract concept of a world unjust by design. Here critical teachers make use of this knowledge not to "save" marginalized students but to provide a safe space for them and to learn with them about personal empowerment, the cultivation of the intellect, and the larger pursuit of social justice. (2008, p. 25)

I tagged the quotations with a note on the board for students to "Think about these quotations and their relationship to our discussion of the *MadTV* "Nice White Lady" clip last class."

Joe Kincheloe's explanation of some of the aims of critical pedagogy provoked a productive discussion. Students were able to identify possible problematic assumptions teachers might make when we say we want to "change students' lives" (2008). Kincheloe's explanation of critical goals for teachers helped us reframe that desire. We should not seek to rescue students, assuming that they need saving from dire circumstances. Instead, we can want to be positive forces in students' school experiences and to learn from and with students in order to affect positive social change. We also need to continue to use the tools of critical literacy to understand the texts—and the world—around us.

Critical literacy applies critical pedagogy to the study of English Language Arts. This framework facilitates understanding of: how texts position readers, viewers, or listeners; how readers position texts; and, how texts are positioned within social, cultural, historical, and political contexts. This approach gives students important resources not only for the English classroom but also for daily living in a world saturated by media. It is the responsibility of teachers to equip students with tools to question, analyze, talk back, and make changes.

Studying media representations of teaching and learning using a critical literacy orientation serves an important purpose for my students as they prepare to become educators. The assignment helps them examine the role media has played in their "apprenticeship of observation," the many hours of time we have all spent as students, hours that can lead us to believe (mistakenly) we have a full understanding of what teaching is (Lortie, 1975). Most prospective teachers have had a positive experience in school themselves and possess a limited view of what teaching entails. Films, television shows, and news reports influence their understanding of the profession, in addition to their own experiences. Yet, future teachers often do not realize how these media portrayals shape their beliefs unless prompted to do so. Teacher candidates need a more nuanced, well-informed, fully developed conception of the work of

J. E. FLYNN

teaching. They also need to see how their own experiences and those depicted in media can replicate dominant narratives about power, gender, urban students, and more. Studying media using a critical literacy approach has the potential to benefit both teacher candidates and the students they will serve in the future, giving them the means to incorporate the critical study of film, television, and other media into their future classrooms.

What are some examples, then, of students applying a critical literacy lens to pop culture portrayals of teaching and learning? The same group of students I wrote about above provided several models. To begin, students noticed that the "behind the scenes" work of teaching goes undocumented in films and television shows, except for the occasional short montage in which a teacher works alone and undisturbed. In their project on 1989 *Dead Poets Society* (one of this course's most popular films for analysis), Fiona, Kate, and Tara showed that "the portrayal of John Keating (Robin Williams) is strong and inspirational, but it is not necessarily realistic." They noted, "Teaching is so much more than standing in front of a room inspiring students every day. This movie leaves out the planning, grading, assessments and all of the other 'less exciting' aspects of teaching that we know to be a part of our lives as future educators." Fiona, Kate, and Tara recognized that teaching is much harder than the movie would have us believe; they observe the same about learning and note that "the viewer never sees the boys reading the complex texts that are meant to inspire them; it is inferred by the viewer that these boys are diving into the complex works of Walt Whitman, William Shakespeare, Henry David Thoreau, and Robert Frost" mostly on their own. Fiona, Kate, and Tara demonstrated their understanding of perspectives that are not shown in these movies, missing parts of the story. Furthermore, these three students explained how film techniques cultivate this portrayal:

> The film creates the tone of inspiration with its sweeping shots of scenery and Keating's classroom. The director ... shoot[s] him from a lower angle, giving him more of an air of grandeur and significance. By viewing him like this, the audience sees a figure of great intelligence and compassion, something that is strengthened by his words and relationships with the students.

> In addition to showing how camera angles position the audience, these students also pointed out the effects of costume, lighting, and editing techniques: Keating is always dressed in light colors, emphasizing that he is a benefactor of the boys, that his intentions are always good and pure. Most of the shots with Keating are brightly lit and clean; all are shot smoothly and without choppy transitions like the viewer sees when the boys are holding their Dead Poets Society meetings.

This example of student work showed how popular culture portrayals of teaching are partial and incomplete; recognizing the missing pieces is one skill nurtured by a critical literacy approach.

WHAT'S A NICE WHITE LADY TO DO?

Other student projects revealed additional problems with pedagogy in film and TV depictions of teaching. Analyzing an episode of *Glee* (Fox 2009–15), Sierra showed how Mr. Schuester (Matthew Morrison) never actually teaches students to dance and sing except through his own performance As she explained, "teachers are supposed to lead by example, but they don't have to flaunt their skills and make students feel inferior. It would have been enough for him to simply teach them the steps and then allow them to use them in their own ways." While Mr. Schue fails to teach, other teachers in the media rely on traditional, teacher-centered approaches, approaches that we don't want preservice teachers to replicate.

Figure 6.1. Jason Sherwood (Michael Angarano) and Ms. Sinclair (Julianne Moore) in The English Teacher *(2013)*

Sydney recognized this problem and explained that the type of didactic teaching shown in *The English Teacher* (2013) is rarely as effective as it is portrayed in the film. She points out that while the classroom is shown to be a happy, productive environment, it is unrealistic because Ms. Sinclair (Julianne Moore) "uses the Initiate-Respond-Evaluate model consistently, gives right/wrong feedback about students' ideas and does not encourage discussion among students"—practices Sydney did not intend to follow in her own future teaching. Ms. Sinclair "looks down on her students as vessels that need to be filled with knowledge rather than seeing them as equal individuals in a classroom community." Ms. Sinclair does not "give students a chance to construct their own understanding, but instead tells them what is right or wrong, which does nothing but promote the idea that all the 'right' answers in English class are right for no good reason other than that the teacher says so." Sydney highlighted these shortcomings to contest a traditional narrative about pedagogy and contrasted the depiction with her own intentions as a future teacher.

Examining relationships between teachers and students, we often find positive models lacking in popular culture portrayals. Students used this project to explore an issue very much on their minds as future teachers: the balance that needs to be struck between maintaining a professional distance and showing care and compassion for, and interest in, students. Many of my students showed how professional/ethical lines are frequently crossed in movies. They noted that, even when results are

J. E. FLYNN

seemingly positive, it is important not to normalize such behavior. Sierra discussed how Mr. Schue in *Glee* does not adequately address a student's crush on him. She wrote, "because it is a melodrama where nothing bad ever really [happens] ... things like this are satirized and the teacher is cast in a humorous role. At no point ... did Mr. Schuester go to his principal to tell him that there might be an issue with this student." Sierra explained how such a situation could be dangerous, an important concern for her to consider as a future teacher.

Building on our discussion following the screening of "Nice White Lady," some students took the opportunity to relate how shortcomings in the media helped them consider what role they want to play in students' educational experiences. Anthony and Nadia analyzed Mr. Feeny (William Daniels) from *Boy Meets World* (ABC 1993–2000) and his apparent distance from his students. They appreciated his professionalism but also wanted a model for building connections with students in their own future classrooms: "While we do find it crucial to remain respected as an educator among your students, we also think that it is important to allow them to feel as if you (as an educator) are an approachable person that they can trust." Similarly, Sydney questioned the initial, simplified portrayal of the self-sacrificing Ms. Sinclair in *The English Teacher*, who "literally has nothing else in her life except her work." She noted that the film "operates under the idea that teachers must be a little less human to be successful, but I think teachers' humanity is what makes them great." Yet, in analyzing Miss Day (Zooey Deschanel) in *New Girl* (Fox 2011–18), Kris reminded us that we cannot valorize the teacher above all else. As she noted, "In a real classroom, a teacher should be a resource, not the center of a student's universe." These careful investigations of relationships between teachers and students show consideration of how these texts are positioning viewers as well as how they are placed within social, cultural, historical, and political contexts, all key facets of critical literacy.

Other students' analyses show that media representations of school are filled with stereotypes—stereotypes that often go unchallenged. A number of students highlighted how power and authority play out in these school settings. Also examining *Dead Poets Society*, Tricia explained that Mr. Keating inherently has authority and "is a force that should go unquestioned" by his students. In a more extreme portrayal, Mike noted how teachers in *Fast Times at Ridgemont High* (1982) are all "apparently domineering despots with unlimited power." Recognizing the interplay of power relations is yet another important aspect of critical literacy. As Kincheloe notes, it is vital to have an education that "questions existing knowledge and problematizes the traditional power relations that have served to marginalize specific groups and individuals" (2008, p. 19).

Related to issues of power and control, students perceived the oversimplification of teacher and student roles, analyzing how archetypes are closely followed. Emma demonstrated how both teachers and students in an episode of *Bob's Burgers* (Fox 2011–) are shown as extremes: "the perfect teacher/student and the nightmare teacher/student." She also discussed how the satirical episode shows the teacher following

62

the typical journey: starting out idealistic, becoming discouraged, then managing "to make the whole student body love and respect them after an unrealistically short amount of time." In another analysis, Nick pointed out how Principal Vernon (Paul Gleason) in *The Breakfast Club* (1985) fails to show any redeeming or sympathetic qualities, embodying the stereotype of domineering administrator. Nick contrasted this portrayal with those of hero teachers in the other extreme—teacher savior films—concluding his project by asking if there is room for more nuance.

In her analysis of *Dangerous Minds* (1995), one of the films most directly parodied in "Nice White Lady," Taylor showed how urban teaching is stereotyped. As she explained, in films about city schools, teachers "face increasingly violent school environments in which they must become violent and aggressive to succeed." Furthermore, it is always the teacher "against the world" in situations where she must "fix the entire educational program herself." It is not only the teacher who is stereotyped, however. Urban students are shown to be "unteachable" by "normal" means, which creates a sense of hopelessness that firmly places blame on the students themselves. Taylor also noted important issues related to race: "by casting all of the disadvantaged students as ones of color," the film "enforces a stereotype that kids of different ethnicities are unintelligent and need to be *saved* by the White individual." Taylor's analysis clearly showed an understanding of the voices that were going unheard in this film. She also connected the depiction to stereotypes of teachers discussed earlier: "this creates an unrealistic image of what teachers are supposed to be doing in the classroom. Sure, it is great to inspire each and every one of your students, but will teachers get discouraged if they *can't* be superheroes? Will they think they are failing?"

Similarly, Ben and Alexis took on the challenge of analyzing *Freedom Writers* (2007), the other movie directly satirized in "Nice White Lady." In an analysis of two clips, they highlighted the portrayal of student George, who says that he can learn in Mrs. Gruwell's class because his life problems are outside of the room. Taking up threads from our class discussion, Ben and Alexis made an important point that while school *can* be sometimes be an escape, a place of refuge for students, this concept can be problematic as well. As they observed, students can't escape "real life" fully. They all return home for the majority of hours in the day. Furthermore, most students' real lives are not all gloom and doom. They usually have joyful moments and can bring resources to bear on their learning, as Kincheloe has noted. All of these examples of student work show how a critical literacy lens helps students question stereotypes and oversimplifications (2008).

Another common finding in student analyses was the prevalence of sexism and sexualization. In her analysis of *Buffy the Vampire Slayer* (CBS 1996–2003), Sarah pointed out the stereotype of the sexualized female teacher and how the shots and camera movement contributed to the objectification of this substitute's body. She also noted that students were subject to gender stereotypes as well: not all boys would be uninterested in school and titillated by the "sexy substitute" (or by women in general). Similarly, Nicole pointed out that while female students were few and

J. E. FLYNN

far between in *A Beautiful Mind* (2001), those present were overly sexualized with, for example, a camera angle exemplifying the "male gaze" on one female character's backside. Sam wrote about a minor teacher character from *Arrested Development* (Fox 2003–06, Netflix 2013–), Rita (Charlize Theron), who is portrayed as a sex symbol and desperate for money (yet another stereotype). Taylor showed how LouAnne (Michelle Pfeiffer) in *Dangerous Minds* licks her lips "seductively" to motivate one of her students to do his work, observing "women are sexualized in movies and can only hold power when they are being erotic, which is a stereotype in many films." Writing about *South Park* (Fox 1997–), Josh analyzed an episode about a teacher who has a romantic relationship with elementary student Ike (Milan Agnone). This relationship is actually celebrated by the police in the episode, who "congratulate Ike and repeat the phrase 'Niceeee' when they hear the teacher is hot, blonde, and young." In these depictions, females wield power through their sexuality, power that is inappropriately used on students, colleagues, and parents.

The sexism inherent in the above portrayals is obvious. In her analysis of *The English Teacher*, Sydney showed how the film promotes a different type of gendered stereotype: self-sacrificing teachers who have no room in their lives for romantic relationships. She illustrated the gender bias of this type of portrayal: "It suggests that women cannot be successful in their careers as well as their personal lives." Few female teachers are portrayed in films or TV as having healthy, thriving home and family lives outside the classroom. They have inappropriate relationships with students or other school/community members, or they are devoted only to their work. Once more, critical literacy provides tools for students to examine the ways in which media portrayals replicate dominant power relations that marginalize groups and individuals.

We also need to look for the silences in texts, considering who benefits and who is left out, and examine the dominant power relations and narratives that are expressed in texts. These critical literacy skills are vital because we live in the world as producers and consumers of media. Despite their initial difficulty, my students analyzed popular culture portrayals of teachers in the media; they had to grapple with the tension between their idealistic intentions and the dominant savior narratives satirized in "Nice White Lady." Through additional discussion and reflection using a critical pedagogy framework, they were able to reconcile that conflict (at least to some degree), and their projects show how they were able to apply elements of critical literacy to draw important conclusions. Their work demonstrated how critical media literacy can be addressed in methods courses in order to help preservice teachers reflect on their observations, but it could easily be adapted to secondary classrooms and other settings. Students could pick any social group or category they are interested in to analyze (there are several related teaching suggestions in Richard Beach's chapter 5, including gender, family, sexuality, race/ethnicity, and social class [2007]). Furthermore, as many advocates of critical pedagogy and critical literacy observe, it is not enough merely to point out the faults and failings of dominant narratives. It is also important to help students see action that they can take, as Beach

64

discusses in his book, perhaps by creating their own more nuanced, more accurate portrayals (2007). A nice White lady *can* be an effective teacher of any group of students, but she has to commit to growing and learning alongside her students and continuing to employ critical literacy tools for questioning the world around her.

NOTE

[1] I did not record this class discussion, so the dialogue is an approximation, and have used pseudonyms for all students referenced in the chapter. I did write down a summary immediately following class, however, and performed a member check with students to confirm that my depiction here and in later portions of the chapter is as accurate as possible.

REFERENCES

Beach, Richard. (2007). *Teachingmedialiteracy.com: A web-linked guide to resources and activities.* New York, NY: Teachers College Press.

Flynn, Jill Ewing. (2014). Studying media representations to foster critical literacy. In Kevin Kumashiro & Bic Ngo (Eds.), *Six lenses for anti-oppressive education: Partial stories, improbable conversations* (pp. 119–134). New York, NY: Peter Lang.

Kincheloe, Joe. (2008). *Critical pedagogy.* New York, NY: Peter Lang.

Lortie, Dan C. (1975) *Schoolteacher: A sociological study.* Chicago, IL: University of Chicago Press.

GARY KENTON

7. THE DIS-EDUCATION OF ROCK 'N' ROLL

ABSTRACT

Many factors have contributed to the decline in support for public schools in America. Most often, blame is directed at politically conservative groups and individuals that have resisted integration, affirmative action, and other programs associated with the Civil Rights Movement. But this essay considers the impact of popular as well as political culture on the marginalization of public schools, looking specifically at the negative portrayal of schools and formal education in rock 'n' roll. Song lyrics and other cultural information conveyed by rock and rap artists have tended to romanticize individual creativity and freedom and to discourage a communitarian, civic orientation. As an indirect consequence, Baby Boomers and Millennials have been muted in their defense of all things public, including education.

Keywords: education, rock 'n' roll, popular culture, cultural studies, Baby Boomers, Millennials

***

Grandfather:	Would you look at him? Sittin' there with his hooter scrapin' away at that book!
Ringo:	Well, what's the matter with that?
Grandfather:	Have you no natural resources of your own? Have they even robbed you of that?
Ringo:	You can learn from books!
Grandfather:	You can, can you? Pahh! Sheeps' heads! You could learn more by gettin' out there and living!
Ringo:	Out where?
Grandfather:	Any old where! But not our little Richard. Oh, no. When you're not thumpin' them pagan skins you're tormenting your eyes with that rubbish.
Ringo:	Books are good.
Grandfather:	Parading's better.
Ringo:	Parading?
Grandfather:	Parading the streets! Trailing your coat! Bowling along! LIVING!
Ringo:	Well, I am living.

© KONINKLIJKE BRILL NV, LEIDEN, 2019 | DOI:10.1163/9789004398092_007

Grandfather: You? Living? When was the last time you gave a girl a pink-edged daisy? When did you last embarrass a sheila with your cool, appraising stare?
Ringo: You're a bit old for that sort of chat, aren't you?
Grandfather: Well, at least I've got a backlog of memories! All you've got is—THAT BOOK!

A Hard Day's Night (1964)

Figure 7.1. Grandfather (Wilfred Brambell) and Ringo (Ringo Starr) in A Hard Day's Night *(1964)*

Education has been viewed as one of the key underpinnings of democracy in the United States since Colonial times. Beginning in 1852 with Massachusetts and ending in 1918 with Mississippi, every state has made it mandatory for children to attend primary school. This consensus began to erode in the 1960s and '70s when significant numbers of families began to seek alternatives to public schools. It is no coincidence that this trend began in the wake of the historic successes of the Civil Rights Movement and the court-mandated desegregation of public schools.

Based partially on racial history, the decline in support for public schools is most often blamed on groups and individuals resisting integration, affirmative action, and other programs associated with the Civil Rights Movement. These same, right-leaning forces have adopted other positions that have had the effect of undermining public schools, including an emphasis on testing and "accountability" that shift the locus of control to federal and state agencies and away from local school districts. They have also promulgated policies that divert government funding away from (predominantly urban) public schools in favor of charter and for-profit schools.

The relative lack of community support for public schools is too widespread to be attributed solely to racial politics or to one side of the political spectrum. Schools

THE DIS-EDUCATION OF ROCK 'N' ROLL

in historically left-leaning communities have also suffered shrinking resources, lack of parental involvement, and a loss of students to charter schools and private institutions. Since these communities identify predominantly with groups and parties that adopt policies supportive of public schools, a political analysis alone is not adequate to explain the situation. There is a need to go beyond scoreboard watching—the recognition that anti-public-school forces are winning and pro-public-school forces are being routed—and consider the impact of popular as well as political culture on the marginalization of public schools. As Cameron McCarthy, Glenn Hudak, Shawn Miklaucic, Paula Saukko, and others have pointed out, popular culture is often overlooked by academics who do not recognize the critical role it plays in the lives of young people and in society (1999).

This chapter looks at the messages conveyed regarding schools and teachers in rock 'n' roll and rap music. Christopher Richards is among the scholars who have described the functions of popular music in "the formation of and cultural reproduction of identities [and] the development of a sense of place and social context ... " (McCarthy et al., 1999, p. 7). While rock and rap artists often defy easy left or right political categorization, their music is overwhelmingly concordant with anti-authoritarian and counter-cultural tendencies that are invariably associated with political progressivism. What the lyrics of their songs impart to listeners about schools and schooling, however, is unremittingly negative. This expression of disaffection has served to undermine support for public schools among a cohort of Baby Boomers and Millennials that is counted, on almost every other public policy issue, as solidly liberal.

Although many consider rock and rap music fandom to be part and parcel of normal teenage rebellion—a near-universal rite of passage—this widely held view is a rather recent historical development.[1] While the tension between independence and family cohesion is a long-established facet of developmental psychology, especially in the West, the notion that rejection of parental and institutional authority is an inherent aspect of adolescence did not become popular until the 1950s. The disaffected, anti-social teenager was epitomized by two iconic film stars: the rebel portrayed by James Dean in *Rebel Without a Cause* (1954) and the outlaw biker portrayed by Marlon Brando in *The Wild One* (1953).

When asked, "What do you rebel against?" Brando's character responds, "What have you got?" To older viewers, this exchange perfectly encapsulated the alarming combination of negativity and irrationality they associated with teenagers. Predictably, the more volatile and negative the reaction to these black-leather-clad hoodlums, the more young people identified with them. As Barbara Ehrenreich puts it, " ... despite all the developmental psychology and high school 'life adjustment' texts, maturity just wasn't sexy" (1983, p. 57). The defiant Brando and the wounded Dean, of course, *were*. Even more than the movies, rock 'n' roll became the soundtrack for adolescent nonconformity and the beginning of a broader cultural upheaval.

If rock 'n' roll became the sound of the 1950s, high school was the place. James S. Coleman documents the importance of the institution of high school as the

69

G. KENTON

most significant site for the transmission and development of youth culture in this time period. Rock 'n' roll and television were primary media influences, and high school was the geographic locale where teenagers processed the new information and formulated their individual and collective responses (1961). While high school became an important way station early in the 20th century, adolescence underwent a seismic change in the 1950s. High school populations increased significantly in that decade due to the baby boom and a reduction in truancy, the latter a reflection of both greater enforcement of compulsory education laws and a greater public appreciation for the economic advantages afforded by a diploma. Among minority groups, especially Blacks and immigrants, education was firmly established as the proximate means to the end of social mobility and financial independence that accompanies it.

Not only was there a greater number of high school students in the 1950s, but an almost wholly-new activity rapidly moved to the center of their social universe: dating. If compulsory education guaranteed nothing else, it created a large pool of potential romantic partners. In earlier days, most after-school activities had been designed for groups and were often chaperoned, but in the 1950s, dating became an entrenched ritual engaged in by young couples that contributed to a hothouse environment featuring constant romantic positioning and negotiation. Part of the appeal of rock 'n' roll in the 1950s was that it reflected this hyperactive social environment and helped students navigate it.[2] Rock music spoke with compelling immediacy to what Lawrence Grossberg called "the affective extremism of youth" (qtd. in Epstein, 1994, p. 33).

In addition to serving as a mirror of high school life for those living it, rock 'n' roll also had a dramatic influence upon it. A counter-cultural attitude came pre-baked into the rock 'n' roll ethos, and the music unleashed powerful transgressive energies. Rock was, after all, congenitally *miscegenistic,* the love-child of Black (blues, jazz, R&B) and White (country, folk, Western) genres. The very term "rock and roll" was an oft-used euphemism for sexual intercourse in rhythm & blues in the 1940s; even if the teenagers who cottoned to Chuck Berry and Elvis Presley were not aware of the semantic appropriation, the risqué connotations remained.

That the music was inherently emancipatory, conveying overt and implicit anti-social messages, was not lost on parents and cultural traditionalists. Almost as soon as rock 'n' roll manifested itself in the early-to-mid 1950s, a substantial backlash developed, framing this new force in popular culture as "the enemy—a surreptitious and corrosive force brought into schooling and the public sphere by the minority other and by white working class youth" (McCarthy, et al., 1999, p. 2). Many of the most vocal anti-rock voices came from religious leaders who decried the immorality and vulgarity in the music. One psychiatrist was quoted in *The New York Times* referring to rock 'n' roll as a "communicable disease" (Braceland, 1956, p. 33). According to Linda Martin and Kerry Segrave, "No other form of culture, and its artists, has met with such extensive hostility"[3] (1993). Predictably, however, the anti-rock backlash barely slowed the rock 'n' roll juggernaut, falling—one might say—on deaf ears.

70

In addition to reflecting the social maelstrom of high school, many popular rock songs held up school for ridicule, pitting the demands of schoolwork against the unfettered joy of the music. It was hardly a fair fight. Although ambivalence toward school had been expressed previously in blues, R&B, and country & western music, the gauntlet was thrown down in 1957 by Chuck Berry in "School Days," which starkly contrasted the mean teacher and "the burden" of history and math with the after-school dancing to "something that's really hot." With "the beat of the drums, loud and bold" emanating from the juke box, offering deliverance from "days of old," Berry's song comes across with the power of a prison break.

Figure 7.2. Chuck Berry performing "School Days" on The Dick Clark Saturday Night Beechnut Show, *August 23, 1958*

One of the first TV rock idols, Ricky Nelson, closely copied this narrative and musical formula later that same year for his hit "Waitin' in School." Sam Cooke's "Wonderful World" (1960) is delivered in a more muted manner but conveys a similar perspective with the singer placing education far below romance on his list of priorities. The singer readily (proudly?) admits that he "don't know much" about history, biology, science, or French, but is secure in the knowledge that his love will make it "a wonderful world."[4]

The Everly Brothers, Buddy Holly, and Eddie Cochran are just a few other early rock hit makers whose songs characterized school as, at the very least, an impediment to social interaction. Gary U.S. Bonds summed it up with his 1961 hit "School is Out" on which the listener can literally hear the party going on in the background as the singer exults that summer means trading in books and studies for fun with his buddies. In the coming years, rock 'n' roll music began to take on broader cultural meanings. Complaints about school were no longer focused narrowly on teachers, homework, and social distractions, but on the role of school in society.

As rock 'n' roll and the baby boomer generation came of age in the mid-1960s, concern over juvenile delinquency, epitomized by Dean and Brando, was replaced by something much broader and deeper: a true counter-cultural movement. While it was opposition to the Vietnam War that brought most young people onto the streets—not least because they were eligible to be drafted into the armed services—these were rebels with many causes: civil rights, women's rights, environmental degradation ... the list goes on. Although not on the front burner, the anti-establishment rhetoric found another target in education, which is hardly surprising considering that the only institution with which most young people had first-hand experience was their schools. As part of a repudiation of conformity of all kinds, protesters opposed the pragmatic, utilitarian approach to education. The so-called "factory model" in education had been introduced in the United States by Horace Mann in the mid-19th century, but it was in the post-World War II period that it became influential in the design of school buildings and curriculum. With an emphasis on efficiency and rote-learning of information delivered in lecture format by the teacher,[5] the factory model was anathema to young people who felt themselves to be harbingers of a new consciousness on the cusp of a political revolution.

In the headlong rush away from "the establishment," baby boomers were all too willing to paint education with a broad brush. The factory model fairly begged for disruption, but voices raised in defense of academics and the role of education in a democracy were dismissed as unhip. Referring to 1960s youth as the "New Romantics," Frances FitzGerald said that "because the New Romantics saw the technocracy[6]—intellectual and otherwise—as the main enemy, they tended to look upon all intellectual pursuits as narrow, 'academic,' and stunting to the psyche" (1979, p. 200). Most teachers discouraged students in their newfound civic interests, which, of course, only made the rallies and protests more attractive. Where the classroom imposed physical and psychological confinement, the streets were full of action.

Sex, drugs, and rock 'n' roll became the handy shorthand descriptor for the 1960s. Timothy Leary, the Harvard psychologist who promoted the use of LSD and other psychotropic drugs, famously urged the Baby Boomers to "Turn On, Tune In, and Drop Out" in 1966. School was seen as an obstacle to personal enlightenment. Four years later, John Lennon sang about the psychological damage inflicted at school in "Working Class Hero," describing the dysfunction that arises after "they've tortured and scared you for twenty-odd years." One can only be sympathetic to Lennon's searing description of the mind-numbing cruelty of the British public school, but the cumulative effect of more than a decade of school bashing was gradually evolving into a broader skepticism, not only toward school but toward literacy itself.

Nowhere was the romance of anti-literacy more hopefully and sincerely championed than in Charles A. Reich's best-selling *The Greening of America* where rock 'n' roll was hailed as the leading wedge in a "soft" revolution. For Reich, rock music was not just a particular genre "but the pleasure and happiness that results from immersion in music" (1970, p. 279). Reich characterized school as a funnel that corralled young people into the military, the corporation, and other fossilized institutions. "They are prisoners of the technological state," he wrote (266). In the

Figure 7.3. John Lennon (center) at Quarry Bank High School, Liverpool, England, May 1957

love-embrace of what Reich called "new knowledge," it was all too easy to reject whatever the schools had on offer, which was—by definition—"old knowledge." If, in the 1950s, schools were considered "a drag" by beatniks and delinquents, a much larger cohort in the 1960s came to see school as a straightjacket, a mechanism of mainstreaming.

In 1972, Alice Cooper raised the ante further with "School's Out," in which school is not just out for summer vacation, but forever. Flaunting a persona more reliant on shock value than authenticity, Cooper (née Vincent Furnier) took an incendiary approach to school ("my school's been blown to pieces"). But if "School's Out" could be dismissed as the faux revolutionary stance of teenage punk rebellion, Pink Floyd's full-frontal analysis several years later could not be so easily set aside. In "Another Brick in the Wall Part 2," from *The Wall*, their mega-hit album (1979) and film (1982), Pink Floyd composer Roger Waters explicitly equates education with thought control. In *The Wall*, Waters expresses concern with broader societal issues of isolation and alienation, but "Another Brick in the Wall Part 2" takes dead aim at school. Of all the songs on the double-album, it received (and still receives) by far the most attention and radio airplay. Phil Rose describes what takes place in the film as the song plays:

> The children are marched mechanically through a maze and onto a conveyor belt where they disappear behind a brick wall. They reappear on the other side of the wall sitting at their desks and are now wearing the pink masks that rob them of their identities. Along with the cogs and wheels that run this huge mechanical apparatus are hammers, which ultimately force the children into a mincer from which they emerge in a ground-down state. (p. 20)[7]

Meanwhile, a chorus of schoolchildren chants "we don't need no education," undoubtedly the most abject anti-school anthem in the rock canon. Here, a quantum

G. KENTON

leap has been taken. School is being portrayed not just as boring and retrograde but as an instrument of fascism.

Anti-school sentiment only became more widely assimilated in subsequent decades, as administrators force-fed No Child Left Behind policies focused on testing and accountability at the same time that Gen Xers and Millennials demanded individual expression and personal fulfillment. Some messages hardly changed from the 1950s. Student fantasies were overwhelmingly carnal, not pedagogical, as evidenced by "Hot for Teacher," a hit song and video for Van Halen in 1984. For Waldo, the nerdy young protagonist in the video (with millions of views on YouTube), boarding the morning bus is just the beginning of the school nightmare, which is relieved only by the discovery that his new teacher is a bikini-clad beauty pageant queen. The chorus sets up the choice: on one hand, there is homework; on the other, a striptease set to a jungle beat. The video ends by showing where the "students" (the members of Van Halen) ended up in life; lead singer David Lee Roth becomes a TV game show host.

In an essay about the Van Halen video, Christine Mallozzi describes how female teachers are on display and forced to be strategic about how they dress and behave lest they be accused of encouraging the sexualized male gaze, or worse (2017, pp. 101–107). Erica McWilliam describes this as the choice between "schoolmarm or seductress" (4). Yet, even as these scholars explore the important issues of gender and sexualization, there is no consideration of the underlying anti-school message. Mallozzi criticizes Val Halen for going "over the top," but the only thing that set Van Halen's contribution to the "sexy teacher trope" apart from hundreds of others is that it is accompanied by a titillating video (2017, p. 106).

Just as students in the 1960s found validation for their anti-school sentiments in the campaign that opposed the factory model, young people in the 1980s and 1990s found common cause with the marginal but influential deschooling movement. The radical idea that schools were no longer preparing students to live fulfilled, spiritually balanced lives was introduced by Ivan Illich in the 1970s but gained momentum in subsequent decades through the work of Gatto, Noddings, Llewellyn, and others. The deschoolers faulted educational institutions not just for falling short of their pedagogical goals but for doing damage to the students placed in their care. The emphasis was on replacement, not on reform. Although the movement was limited in impact, it added fuel to the fire of flight (predominantly White) from public schools in favor of a growing number of private, charter, and parochial schools, as well as increased interest in home schooling.

In some ways, the anti-school attitudes expressed in earlier decades by rock artists became so entrenched that it came to constitute a default position for many young people. It is certainly prevalent in the world of rap music and hip-hop. While schools often deliver on the promise of career preparation and competitive advantage to White students, it is accepted in African-American communities that the path to success for Black students is far more problematic. If racism is properly understood as a social construct, manifested not only through the bias of individuals but indirectly through

THE DIS-EDUCATION OF ROCK 'N' ROLL

institutions throughout American society, then schools can be seen historically as a primary (and secondary) system within which White students are advantaged and Black students are disadvantaged. The calamitous fact that there are more young, Black men in prison than in college speaks much more profoundly to a failure of the school system than to a lack of preparedness or academic orientation on the part of Black youth.[8]

Although rap music brings its own particular set of cultural attitudes, it is unsurprising that rap and hip-hop artists express similar sentiments as rock artists toward school. If there are fewer direct references to school in rap lyrics, this can be attributed largely to the fact that, while school remains a part of daily life for a significant portion of the rock audience, most rap music is made by and primarily for a cohort that is either not in school or does not perceive school to be as central to its experience.[9]

Even a rapper such as Common (née Lonnie Lynn), known as a pro-social commentator in comparison to many of his compatriots, dismisses the idea that school could be a place where he might find the information he needs. On his 1997 album *One Day It'll All Make Sense*, guest Cee Lo Green raps on the song "G.O.D. (Gaining One's Definition)" about the African-American history that is "purposely hidden" in school curriculum. Beginning in the Black church, the singer embarks on a journey of discovery because "Damn, somethin' in me wanna know who I am." A clear analysis emerges in which school is not a benign repository of a shared history but an institution in which large portions of historical content related to the Black experience are systematically omitted.

A recurring theme on Kanye West's 2004 album *College Dropout* is the frustration felt by many Black students as a result of not fitting in at White-dominated colleges and not finding the path to middle-class employment that is the basis on which the time and expense of college is most frequently justified. On "Graduation Day" West is ready to "break the rules" but there is an understanding that he may well be hurting his chances of getting "a good ass job." But, on "School Spirit Skit #2," he also expresses the hard reality that, even when a Black man stays in school and graduates, it is hardly a guarantee of success. He looks around and sees other guys "making money all these ways," while he is struggling, lamenting that his academic degrees are not "going to keep me warm." Empirically, Black youth have particular reason to be wary of the schooling process and skeptical about its benefits, but neither West nor his rock 'n' roll peers ever seem to credit their time in the classroom for helping them develop the tools of logic and critical analysis that allow them to make a reasoned judgment.

Perhaps it takes a non-American rapper, Suli Breaks (née Darryll Suliaman Omaoko), to bring greater objectivity. His popular 2012 rap and video "Why I Hate School but Love Education" (over eight million views on YouTube) is neither cheerleading nor naysaying, raising up famous figures who achieved greatness without the benefit of a college degree (i.e. Steve Jobs, Malcolm X) but not suggesting that education is unnecessary. His view is clear-eyed:

75

G. KENTON

If there was a family tree hard work and education would be related,
But school would probably be a distant cousin,
Because if education is the key,
School is the lock,
Because it rarely ever develops your mind to the point where it can perceive
as red and green
and continue to go when someone else said stop.
Now, I'm not saying that school is evil and there's nothing to gain,
All I'm saying is: understand your motives and re-assess your aims …
Redefine how you view education,
Understand it's true meaning,
Education is not just about regurgitating facts from a book,
Or someone else's opinion on a subject to pass an exam,
Look at it…
There's more than one way in this world to be
An educated man.

Breaks, himself a college graduate, makes the all-important distinction between school—a system—and education—a process, one that all individuals navigate with varying degrees of interaction with academic institutions.

Yes, a few popular songs have held school in a positive light. The Beach Boys "Be True to Your School" (1963) stresses loyalty, but the emphasis is on identification with the school students, not academics, and the "rah rah, sis boom bah" chorus flirts with parody.[10] Responding to growing alarm over high school dropout rates, James Brown scored a hit in 1966 with "Don't Be a Drop-Out" ("Mr. Man said, without an education you might as well be dead"), but the concern was socioeconomic, not academic. The fact is, regardless of genre, songs that hold up education as a fundamental, salutary enterprise are virtually nonexistent. It is difficult to imagine that such prolonged and consistent negativity reflected in music aimed primarily at young people has not had an impact on attitudes. Such messages may be easily ignored by students who excel in school, but for the majority of average students, anti-school sentiments expressed in rock 'n' roll have resonance. And, for those who don't find school to be a hospitable environment, whether the disaffection is socially or academically rooted, songs that point blame at the school would surely hit a responsive chord. It is perhaps the ultimate hidden curriculum.

The ramifications of this dis-education extend beyond the schoolhouse walls. It's not just a lack of enthusiasm for reading, writing, and arithmetic that has been fostered but also a loss of appreciation of the broader lessons learned in the pursuit of knowledge. In addition to curriculum content, guided reading (which is the foundation of academics) also imparts the value of logic, rational discourse, and the scientific methodology of research. In the process of fomenting antipathy toward schools, rock music has contributed to the mainstreaming of anti-intellectualism in America. Donald N. Wood is among the scholars who have recognized this trend.

THE DIS-EDUCATION OF ROCK 'N' ROLL

Following the work of sociologist P.A. Sorokin, Wood warns that the attitudes of the baby boom generation were not limited to being countercultural but contributed to "the collapse of print culture" (1996, pp. 67–70) and "the blossoming of post-intellectualism" (1996, p. 103).

In the late 1980s, Allan Bloom warned of the moral effects of rock, seeing it as a stepping stone toward sex, violence, and drugs.[11] But, his greatest worry was that the music was "hostile to reason ... I believe it ruins the imagination of young people," he said, "and makes it very difficult for them to have a passionate relationship to the art and thought that are the substance of liberal education" (1987, pp. 71, 79). While Wood and Bloom raised legitimate questions about the physiological effects of loud, fast music, they fail to provide evidence for widespread negative effects on brain function or critical thinking. More constructively, Robert Albrecht points out that "rock, rap, and other loud, aggressive forms didn't create the disharmony and disorientation of the modern world; they are an expression of it" (2004, p. 44). The argument being made in this chapter has nothing to say about direct influences of rock or rap music on intellectual capacity. Nor does this chapter dispute the Marxist analysis that schools in the United States generally perform the capitalist function of turning out graduates who are, by and large, compliant and accepting of the goals of progress, productivity, and efficiency. The focus here is on indirect, sociopolitical influences of anti-intellectual messages contained in the music and disseminated by popular musicians. It has been an inadvertent, stealth campaign, but it has helped to create a world in which the lack of education is often seen as a refuge from inconvenient facts and elitist authority.

For example, in an interview in *Playboy*, David Bowie expressed disdain for the very idea that rock 'n' roll might carry mental weight. "I have no message whatsoever," he said. "Show someone something where intellectual analysis or analytical thought has been applied and people will yawn. But something that's pretentious—that keeps you riveted" (Crowe, 2009, p. 330). Similarly, Kate Pierson of The B-52's told *Rolling Stone*, "As an American, I feel everyone has a right to be stupid" (Neely, 1990, p. 27). In the 1990s, the phrase "I'm With Stupid" entered the slang mainstream. The problem, as Wood suggests, is that although it may be a peculiarly American right to be "with stupid," it is a self-defeating one. "Citizens in a true democracy," he says, "do not have the right to remain uninformed and uninvolved. Liberty is not a license to remain ignorant" (1996, p. 252).

Recent national political developments have raised deep concerns about fake news and media manipulation and demand that we consider the historical roots of the post-literate world in which we find ourselves. Numerous signs point to the backlash against modernism, which for many Americans in the 1950s and 1960s was epitomized by rock 'n' roll. The boisterous, defiant music served as a surrogate for more generalized anxieties about technology, industrialization, and the acceleration of social changes. Even forward-thinking communication scholar Marshall McLuhan reflected the puritanical attitude of his generation toward rock 'n' roll, referring to it as "a central aural form of education which threatens the whole educational

77

G. KENTON

establishment," going as far as to say that "If Homer can be wiped out by literacy, literacy can be wiped out by rock" (McLuhan "Part 5").

There has always been a deep strain of anti-intellectualism in American life. Thomas Jefferson's Agrarian Ideal was based not only in an abiding faith in the common man but a deep skepticism toward the professional, credentialed class. The ascendance of the Tea Party and Donald Trump have made visible a situation that had been developing for decades, combining anti-elitism and anti-intellectualism in a way that is new to the United States. Over decades, the backlash against changes wrought by technology (industrial and digital), by the New Deal and the Great Society, by hippies and Millennials, energized a coalition of evangelicals, blue-collar workers, and libertarians. This bloc, deftly organized into common purpose by the Republican Party, blamed schools for leading young people away from religion, social custom, individualism, and "family values." The reactionary flames have been fanned by a burgeoning conservative media, led by Fox News, talk radio, and the information silos created by the Internet and social media. The result has been a widespread turn away from science, history, and the facts that those disciplines reveal.

Unlike some on the political right, rock and rap artists do not, as a rule, purposefully disseminate misinformation, but they convey a similar distrust of institutional authority. Most rock and rap stars espouse egalitarian viewpoints, and many take overtly progressive stands, but their more persistent, affective messages have tended to romanticize individual creativity and freedom and to discourage a communitarian, civic orientation. As an indirect consequence, the Baby Boomers have been muted in their defense of all things public, including education. Rock and rap artists may show a general preference for street smarts over scholarship, but— Ringo's grandfather notwithstanding—they say nothing to discourage the reading of books or the pursuit of knowledge. What these artists do is to undermine what should be a natural constituency for public education. One might say, they set a tone.

NOTES

[1] Although the magazine *Popular Science* used "teen-ager" in 1941, the word did not enter common usage until the early 1950s.
[2] Gunilla Holm, Paul Farber, and B. Lee Cooper are among the scholars who have explored the connections between rock 'n' roll and the school experience.
[3] Rap artists who emerged in the 1970s and 1980s might disagree.
[4] According to Cooke biographer Peter Guralnick, Cooke had to convince his co-writers on this song, the estimable Herb Albert and Lou Adler, to emphasize the school-related theme. In the song, the protagonist eventually buckles down to his studies but only because he thinks that "being an A student" will improve his odds romantically.
[5] The factory model was sometimes referred to as the "sage on the stage" method where all knowledge and wisdom is seen to reside with teacher and only selectively doled out in pre-measured dollops.
[6] Neil Postman defined technocracy in *Technopoly: The Surrender of Culture to Technology* as a culture in which technological tools are no longer integrated but dominant (1992).
[7] As Rose notes, the metaphor of the school as a meat grinder was first employed by Marshall McLuhan in 1951: "Our educational process is necessarily geared to eliminate all bone. The supple, well-

THE DIS-EDUCATION OF ROCK 'N' ROLL

adjusted man is the one who has learned to hop into the meat grinder while humming a hit-parade tune …" (2015).

[8] Michelle Alexander's *The New Jim Crow* establishes the historical link from the segregationist Jim Crow era to the development of the school-to-prison pipeline in subsequent decades (2010).

[9] While rock and rap have become readily accepted as subject areas for scholarly research and promoted as topics for college courses, and rap music is increasingly being used as a teaching tool in public schools, little attention is paid to what rock and rap *say* about the experience of schooling. The music is being celebrated and utilized by the very institutions that songs generally hold in low regard.

[10] The MC5 use the same "rah rah sis boom bah" chorus on their 1970 song "High School." Yet, where The Beach Boys might have considered dating a cheerleader, such unalloyed school spirit would only be a target of ridicule for The MC5.

[11] Bloom leveled similar attacks against feminism. His track record as a prognosticator is spotty. Referring to the lead singer of The Rolling Stones, he said, "Jagger has begun to fade." Three decades later, Mick Jagger is still performing; Bloom passed away in 1992.

REFERENCES

Print

Albrecht, Robert. (2004). *Mediating the muse: A communications approach to music, media, and cultural change.* Cresskill, NJ: Hampton Press.

Alexander, Michelle. (2010). *The new Jim Crow.* New York, NY: The New Press.

Bloom, Allan. (1987). *The closing of the American mind.* New York, NY: Touchstone/Simon & Schuster.

Braceland, Francis J. (1956, March 28). Rock 'n' roll called communicable disease. *New York Times.*

Coleman, James S. (1961). *The adolescent society.* New York, NY: The Free Press.

Crowe, Cameron. (2009). Interview. In D. Brackett (Ed.), *The pop, rock, and soul reader* (pp. 328–33). New York, NY: Oxford University Press.

Ehrenreich, Barbara. (1983). *The hearts of men.* Garden City, NY: Anchor Press.

Epstein, Jonathon S. (Ed.). (1994). *Adolescents and their music.* New York, NY: Garland Publishing.

FitzGerald, Frances. (1979). *America revised.* New York, NY: Vantage Books.

Guralnick, Peter. (2005). *Dream Boogie: The triumph of Sam Cooke.* New York, NY: Little, Brown.

Illich, Ivan. (1971). *Deschooling society.* New York, NY: Harrow Books.

Mallozzi, Christine. (2017). When worlds collide: Van Halen's "hot for teacher" and gender in the classroom. In Mary M. Dalton & Laura R. Linderedited by aryandaura (Eds.), *Screen lessons: What we have learned from teachers on television and in the movies* (pp. 101–107). New York, NY: Peter Lang.

Martin, Linda, & Kerry Segrave. (1993). *Anti-rock: The opposition to rock 'n' roll.* Boston, MA: Da Capo Press.

McCarthy, Cameron, Glenn Hudak, Shawn Miklaucic, & Paula Saukko. (Eds.). (1999). *Sound identities: popular music and the cultural politics of education.* New York, NY: Peter Lang.

McLuhan, Marshall. (1951). *The mechanical bride.* Boston, MA: Beacon Press.

McWilliam, Erica. (1996). Seductress or schoolmarm: On the improbability of the great female teacher. *Interchange, 7*(1), 1–11.

Neely, Kim. (1990, August 9). Rockers sound off. *Rolling Stone.*

Postman, Neil. (1992). *Technopoly: The surrender of culture to technology.* New York, NY: Vintage Books.

Reich, Charles A. (1970). *The greening of America.* New York, NY: Random House.

Rose, Phil. (2015). *Roger waters and pink floyd: The concept albums.* Madison, NJ: Fairleigh Dickinson University Press.

Wood, Donald N. (1996). *Post-intellectualism and the decline of democracy.* Westport, CT: Praeger.

G. KENTON

Music

Alice Cooper. (1972). School's out. *School's Out*. Warner Bros.
Beach Boys, The. (1963). Be true to your school. *Little Deuce Coupe*. Capitol Records.
Berry, Chuck. (1957). School days. *After School Session*. Chess Records.
Bonds, Gary U.S. (1961). School is out. *Dance 'til quarter to three with U.S. Bonds*. EMI Music Publishing, Sony/ATV Music Publishing LLC.
Brown, James. (1966). Don't be a drop-out. *James Brown Sings Raw Soul*. King Records.
Common (aka Lonnie Lynn). (1997). G.O.D. (Gaining One's Definition). *One Day It'll All Make Sense*. Relativity Records.
Cooke, Sam. (1960). Wonderful world. *The wonderful world of Sam Cooke*. Keen Records.
Lennon, John. (1970). Working class hero. *John Lennon/Plastic Ono Band*. Abbey Road.
MC5. (1970). High school. *Back in the USA*. Atlantic Records.
Nelson, Ricky. (1957). Waitin' in school. *Ricky*. Imperial Records.
Pink Floyd. (1979). Another brick in the wall, Part 2. *The Wall*. Pink Floyd Music Publishers.
Suli Breaks (née Darryll Suliaman Omaoko). (2012). Why I hate school but love education. *Suli Breaks*. Retrieved from https://www.youtube.com/watch?v=y_ZmM7zPLyI&t=168s
Van Halen. (1984) Hot for teacher. *1984*. 5150 Studios.
West, Kanye. (2004). Graduation day. *College Dropout*. Springtime Music, Inc.
West, Kanye. (2004). School spirit skit #2. *College Dropout*. Springtime Music, Inc.
West, Kanye. (2004). *College dropout*. Springtime Music Inc.

Films

A Hard Day's Night. United Artists, Lester, Richard, dir. 1964.
Hot for Teacher. Angelus, Pete, and David Lee Roth, dirs. Van Halen, 1984.
"Part 5: University of South Florida Lecture." *Living in an Acoustic World*. McLuhan, Marshall. 1974. Retrieved from http://www.mcluhan-salon.de/en/selected-contents
Rebel without a Cause. Ray, Nicholas, dir. Warner Bros, 1955.
The Wall. Parker, Alan, dir. Pink Floyd. Metro-Goldwyn-Mayer, 1982.
The Wild One. Benedek, László, dir. Columbia Pictures, 1953.

CHAD E. HARRIS

8. PROMOTED TO CONTROL?

School Office Culture in HBO's Vice Principals

ABSTRACT

HBO's *Vice Principals* (2016–17) does not execute the magic of entertaining while also providing meaningful, well-thought-out critiques of toxic masculinity and crude educational philosophies. Instead, the show depicts male school administrators who pull every trick, action, and word to undermine the woman who gets the job they desire. I argue that the series does not do its work in good faith but rather irresponsibly plays out, for laughs, damaging representations of the education system that leave its audience primed to believe that the real system is, too, a big, damaged joke. Yet, I could not write about this show without highlighting the aspect that almost redeems it. This is Dr. Belinda Brown, the principal. Dr. Brown is rare onscreen and in real life—she is an African-American woman principal, and she does not fit into any of the three main categories we see in onscreen principals, all reductive to draw on easily packaged conflict: the buffoon, the autocrat, or the bureaucrat. Dr. Brown falls into what Mary M. Dalton terms "principal as caring pragmatist," a principal who is written as a fully realized character in her approach to her work. Caring pragmatics are rare onscreen, so it is important to bring this character into view, even if she is a part of a show that leaves so much else to be desired.

Keywords: caring pragmatist, principals, administrators, episodic television, school administrators on television

INTRODUCTION

In a promotional interview for the HBO comedy *Vice Principals* (HBO 2016–18), Walton Goggins (who plays Vice Principal Lee Russell) says, "These guys are trying to be the principal of a *high school*. It's not a high school that's a feeder to Harvard. It's like *really*?" (*Vice Principals: Behind-the-Scenes*, 2016). Dalton, in *The Hollywood Curriculum: Teachers in the Movies*, defines "principal as buffoon" as a character who "is played for laughs and cannot be taken seriously by students or teachers" (2017, p. 180). Goggins correctly implies that the characters Lee Russell and Neal Gamby (Danny McBride) are buffoons—after all, the series is a farce—and he also

© KONINKLIJKE BRILL NV, LEIDEN, 2019 | DOI:10.1163/9789004398092_008

notes how many Americans view school administrators. Though I could not disagree more with this position ideologically, the series reinforces Goggins's attitude: if you are going to stoop to unimaginable lows, you should do so over something more "important" than a job at a high school. These "culturally shared cognitive models" (qtd. in Glanz "Images of Principals,"1997, p. 295) have far-reaching effects, which is why a silly series merits serious consideration. In buffoonish ways that cross the line into sinister, Neal and Lee unleash unprovoked havoc on the new principal, Dr. Belinda Brown (Kimberly Hébert Gregory), an African-American woman to whom, in their minds, they lose out on a promotion. To viewers, it is obvious that she eclipses both of the men in terms of experience, competence, and intelligence.

It is important to note, however, that male buffoonery is inextricably linked to hypermasculinity. Because the series portrays masculinity as sexism resulting in toxic indignation rooted in entitlement as a member of the privileged sex (compounded by the privilege accorded their race), *Vice Principals* is a dangerous cultural representation. In striking contrast is its non-stereotypical and honest portrayal of Dr. Belinda Brown, who, despite the show's otherwise damaging and reductive depiction of school leaders, belongs in Dalton's only positive category of administrators, "principal as caring pragmatist," a character type rarely seen on television or in the movies (*Hollywood Curriculum*, 2017, p. 186). Setting the portrayal of administrative competence represented by Principal Brown in opposition to the toxic, White masculinity of Vice Principals Russell and Gamby *almost* redeems the series, and the competing messages dominating the narrative as well as its prominence in the cultural landscape as a heavily promoted show on a premium channel make it worth consideration. Unfortunately, professionalism is no match for the privilege of two White men.

*Figure 8.1. Lee Russell (Walton Goggins) and Neal Gamby
(Danny McBride) on* Vice Principals *(HBO 2016–18)*

What is it about our culture that makes *Vice Principals* popular? As Caroline Heldman puts it in the documentary *The Mask You Live In* (2015), Neal Gamby and Lee Russell represent "the man-child, or the mook, a male who is in perpetual adolescence. His body doesn't typically have a lot of muscle, but he tends to project masculinity in other ways, through the degradation of women [and] engaging in high-risk activities." Heldman reminds us that this is a prevalent representation and harmful if viewed uncritically. The man-child archetype represents masculinity packaged as sexism, a distinction that also accrues to other archetypes according to Heldman, such as "the thug," "the superhero character," and "the strong, silent guy." Why do I take a farce so seriously? It seems dangerous not to do so because no text resides in isolation but reinforces the dominant ideology of a culture; in this case, the exaggerated antics of these vice principals overshadow—and thus downplay—the ways in which their behaviors are steeped in sexism and racism.

MASCULINITY AS SEXISM

While audiences laugh at Neal and Lee, viewers should not ignore shared behaviors more likely to be associated with characters who embody other archetypes of hypermasculinity (e.g., Donald Draper, a "strong, silent type" in *Mad Men* [AMC 2007–15]). Neal and Lee, living within narrow confines of what it means to "be a man," are trapped in eternal adolescence, unable to express themselves authentically, and use words to diminish what they fear. The word "bitch" is uttered about 50 times during the first season's nine episodes. Neal and Lee use the word to refer to Belinda 21 times, and they also use it to refer to one another as a way of demeaning what is considered "feminine." When this language is directed toward a man, the implication is that he is homosexual because he displays a characteristic associated with "femininity." Imposing binaries—such as between "gay" and "straight" or "man" and "woman"—is reductive, and Heldman says that bifurcations are employed "to try to organize and simplify the world." In practice, the word strips men of their masculinity, the hegemonic variety (Smith, et al., 2015, p. 161) to which American culture—and thus *Vice Principals*—clings tightly.

In "The Principal," the two men unite under the word "bitch" to bring down the new, female principal, who is hired from another state, while they have been administrators at North Jackson High School for years. In "Circles," Neal mouths, "Bitch" when Belinda tells him he needs to "adjust" his attitude. In "The Foundation of Learning," the men refer to English Department Chair Ms. LeBlanc (Robin Bartlett) as "LeBitch" because she is a good teacher who stands up for herself. In "Gin," Mi-Cha (June Kyoto Lu), Lee's live-in mother-in-law and enemy, repeatedly calls him "bitch boy" as he picks up Belinda's dry cleaning. This language reflects the cultural practice of using words to keep marginalized groups on the margins. One problem with *Vice Principals* is that the word bitch is deployed for cheap laughs in sexist contexts without critical reflections, not to mention space and context to invite competing or even complex readings of the text. Instead, the series endorses hegemonic masculinity, "the normative ideology that to be a man is to be dominant in society and that the subordination of women is required to maintain such power" (Smith et al., 2015, p. 161). To me, there is nothing humorous in performances that reinforce rather than challenge the basest examples of masculinity as sexism, a tradition existing in popular film and television for decades.

*Figure 8.2. Dr. Belinda Brown (Kimberly Hébert Gregory)
on* Vice Principals *(HBO 2016–18)*

TOXIC INDIGNATION

Defenses against threats to hegemonic masculinity can lead men to feelings of indignation that result in "toxic practices ... that stabilize gender dominance in a particular setting" (Connell & Messerschmidt, 2005, p. 840). Toxic masculinity arises from "the aspects of hegemonic masculinity that ... are, thus, socially destructive" (Kupers, 2005, p. 717). As Rachel M. Smith et al. note, men like Neal and Lee who act within the confines of hegemonic masculinity "are more likely to experience stress in situations where masculinity is threatened" (2015, p. 161). This "masculine gender-role stress" (Eisler, Skidmore, & Ward, 1988, pp. 134–135) takes the form of indignation, which then becomes toxic, as does their masculinity. Three situations in which the two characters demonstrate this crossover into toxicity follow three of Terry A. Kupers's five characteristics distinguishing toxic masculinity from hegemonic masculinity: "stigmatization and subjugation of women, gays, and men who exhibit feminine characteristics," "a readiness to resort to violence," and "extreme competition and greed" (2005, p. 717).

Stigmatization and Subjugation of the Other

In "The Principal," Neal assigns Matthew Potter (Ryan Boz) to in-school suspension against the advice of English teacher Amanda Snodgrass (Georgia King), who attests that he is being bullied and not involved in the conduct violation. One morning, Neal picks up Matthew from the bus stop with the plan to take advantage of Matthew's nonassertive personality by coercing him into staging a walkout against Belinda: "You know what happens to smart kids like you in I.S.S.? You get turned the fuck out. You know what "turned out" means? It's when a straight dude rolls in to prison and gets his ass fucked, then becomes a girl." After providing more graphic detail, he offers Matthew an early pass out of I.S.S. to lead the walkout. Like the boys who bully Matthew, Neal labels Matthew as "feminine" because he does not conform to toxic masculinity. Taking it further, Neal uses the language of violence, shaming victims of prison rape by labeling them "girls." The implication is that they are "weak" and "gay" because they are overpowered by seasoned prisoners, who display violence as the way of claiming their place at the top of the "hierarchy of intermale dominance" (Kupers, 2005, p. 716). What goes on in prisons finds its way into popular culture, and it is used to espouse gender norms and to scare men into staying on the right side of the law to avoid prison and the possibility of losing their "manhood" there. The effects of John Fiske's "leaky boundaries" (2010, p. 101) are clear here, as *Vice Principals* perpetuates this damaging narrative, reinforcing it for those familiar with it and introducing it to those who are not.

A Readiness to Resort to Violence

Of everything Neal and Lee do to showcase their toxic indignation toward a woman for taking what they believe to be their rightful place, most shocking is that they burn down Belinda's home. After going through Belinda's trash, they break a window in a door and proceed to break eight objects and ransack two rooms before Lee decides to set the house ablaze. Belinda embodies the basis of what they fear: a feminine presence far beyond their capacity for understanding women. Because they reject any identification with femininity, subordination to a woman is unacceptable to them (Smith et al., 2015, p. 161). Regardless of whether a man or a woman were named to the post of principal instead of one of them, the vice principal(s) stuck in the support position would experience "masculine gender-role stress." Neal sees an enemy in nearly every person he encounters, including the man married to his ex-wife, Gale (Busy Phillips). Ray Liptrapp (Shea Whigham) is a loving and positive influence on Neal and Gale's daughter, Janelle (Maya G. Love). While Ray is a constructive male presence, the character is not enough to counteract stronger, bolder, messages of toxic masculinity wrapped in slapstick situations and throwaway lines delivered as jokes. Both Ray and Belinda are characters that could be used more critically and effectively to mount challenges to toxic, White masculinity and to the sexism and racism that is its stock-in-trade.

C. E. HARRIS

Extreme Competition and Greed

In "The Foundation of Learning," Neal's unilateral feud with Ray is an impetus for his high-risk behavior, a feature Heldman tells us to look for in the "mook" archetype (2015). When Janelle decides to give up horseback riding for motocross, Neal is both furious and jealous because he believes Janelle's interest in the latter comes from Ray's involvement in the sport, part of a deceptive plan for him to replace Neal as Janelle's "real" father. Neal vows to learn motocross in an appallingly short period of time so he can show up at Janelle's race and prove his dominance over Ray. Despite moderate success during the practice, overconfidence leads to a spectacular wreck as the bike smashes into a building located next to spectators. An irate official expels Neal from the premises, and Janelle is not impressed. In "Gin," Belinda offers Neal a promotion (and it is implied that she plans to fire Lee), but he acts out of jealously when he hears about the past relationship between Amanda Snodgrass and history teacher Bill Hayden (Mike O'Gorman). Neal enters Bill's classroom while he is teaching and turns over a cabinet then later has a conversation with Amanda during which he regresses into adolescent behavior, leading Amanda to say, "This is not how you communicate with people, Neal. What are you, 12?" It is true that neither Neal nor Amanda is blameless in the scenario, but Neal's extreme defensiveness and his ineptness in emotional ("feminine") situations reflect "masculine gender-role stress." This type of reaction is a standard practice in media texts and often goes unchallenged because it reflects lived experience. Characters ranging from *Mad Men's* Don Draper (a dapper, attractive executive) to Neal and Lee (crude, unsophisticated buffoons) rely on patriarchal structures to justify their combativeness and greed to preserve their male privilege. Even in comedies—maybe particularly in comedies because laughter comes from emotional connection—representations of men should be taken seriously because the consequences are never trivial.

THE PRIVILEGE OF MALE ENTITLEMENT

In *Hollywood Goes to High School: Cinema, Schools, and American Culture*, Robert C. Bulman provides a structure for understanding how Neal and Lee's toxic indignation is a byproduct of the entitlement they feel as members of the privileged sex (2015). Because of similarities in subject matter and research findings, as well as HBO's production style, Bulman's study of films can be applied to television. As White, suburban men, Neal and Lee have privilege, not only in American culture and media but more specifically in the context of what Bulman calls "suburban school films" (2015, p. 10). These films focus on "expressive individualism"—a type of American individualism "that values not material achievements but the discovery of one's unique identity and the freedom of individual self-expression" (2015, p. 10). Students are the heroes of these suburban school films (86). The opposite is true in "urban school films" (2015, p. 10). In films such as *Blackboard Jungle* (1955), *Stand*

and Deliver (1988), *Dangerous Minds* (1995), and *Freedom Writers* (2007), students are taught "utilitarian individualism," "that strain of American individualism that celebrates hard work, materialism, and individual self-sufficiency" (2015, p. 10). The heroes of urban school films are the middle-class teachers who swoop in to "save" poor, urban students (2015, p. 31). This difference between how suburban and urban students are educated coheres to Jean Anyon's findings in "Social Class and the Hidden Curriculum of Work." In her sample of New Jersey schools, Anyon observed that, depending on the socioeconomic status of the school, "curricular, pedagogical, and pupil evaluation practices emphasize different cognitive and behavioral skills" with the purpose of preparing children to occupy the same jobs held by their parents, thereby creating a "reproduction of unequal social relations" (1980, p. 90). High school films also reflect these inequities, and they no doubt reinforce prejudices that viewers already hold about social class, sex roles, sexuality, race, and other markers of identity.

Bodies of Entitlement

An HBO interview with Danny McBride and Walton Goggins reveals that *Vice Principals* is essentially a suburban high school film—with adult instead of teenage stars. In the *Vice Principals: Extra Credit* supplement to the episode "The Good Book," McBride describes episodes of the series as "almost love letters" to the 1980s teen movies he and Goggins watched while they were growing up. *Vice Principals* is not about academics. Teaching and learning may not be a focus of this series, but merit is considered because that is how Belinda gets the top job at the high school. Nevertheless, Neal and Lee feel entitled to the job because they are White men, and they respond to not getting it by spitting in her coffee, burning down her house, and otherwise sabotaging her life, which puts them on equal footing with the teenage heroes of suburban school films. In "Run for the Money," Lee tries to drug football players so the team will lose the game, making Belinda appear weak as a leader. In "The Good Book," Belinda's young sons get high on marijuana, and Lee smokes it with them to garner their cooperation. Lee shows pornographic videos to Belinda's sons as a bribe to get them to reveal secrets about their mother. Bulman cites *American Pie* (1999) as an example of how the pursuit of sex is a common narrative convention of suburban school films. Like Jim (Jason Biggs) and his friends in *American Pie*, Neal spends a significant amount of time trying to have sex with Amanda. He also has a sexual relationship on school grounds with Spanish teacher Ms. Abbott (Edi Patterson), a woman he repeatedly disrespects and humiliates. This "salute," as McBride calls it, to 1980s teen movies may seem like an amusing, nostalgic experience, but it is a shallow approach. Just when it seems there might be an opportunity for more depth in *Vice Principals*, the series simply reinforces simplistic tropes and formulaic scenarios that are comfortable for mainstream Hollywood but not good for social progress.

C. E. HARRIS

A Note on Complexity

There is a more complex aspect of male entitlement in this show that should be considered. In the episode "Gin," Lee says to his wife, Christine (Susan Park), "This is about me, being a man, getting the goddamn respect I deserve." The scene takes place in their kitchen, and Lee wears an apron with a floral pattern, a visual joke to undermine his masculinity. He tells Christine that she and his mother-in-law would not care if he committed suicide, to which Christine replies, "Why are you saying that?" This exchange recalls the earlier conversation in the same episode between Neal and Amanda ("What are you, 12?"). In both cases, entitlement causes masculine gender-role stress, but in Lee's case, there is a dimension that shows how "antifemininity" (Smith, et al., 2015, p. 162) can come in any form in the "plurality of masculinities" (Connell & Messerschmidt, 2005, p. 846). The flowery apron is but one metaphor. Lee's style of dress (colorful, patterned bow ties, blazers, and sweaters), the way he walks, his disinterest in sports and fighting, and his physical appearance (thin and prissy) are also neither stereotypically nor traditionally associated with hegemonic masculinity in American culture. Lee illustrates that even a man who embodies "nonhegemonic masculinities" (p. 846) can come to embody hegemonic masculinity or assert his maleness to claim power over women. Lee copes with his fears through actions that do not involve face-to-face confrontation or physical activity. He spits in cups, burns down houses, and drugs water coolers, but his motives are both sexist and rooted in misogyny. Lee demonstrates that masculinity does not fit into one mold but still fails to offer a compelling critique of any representation of male entitlement, hegemonic masculinity, toxic masculinity, or sexism.

TELEVISION, SCHOOLING, AND PERCEPTIONS OF PRINCIPALS

Television is ubiquitous. As Allen put it, television is "undeniably, unavoidably, 'there.' And, it seems, everywhere" (1992, p. 1) while Todd Gitlin states, "The obvious but hard-to-grasp truth is that living with the media is today one of the main things Americans and many other human beings do" (2002, p. 4). Another ubiquitous entity in America is schooling. Starting in the 1950s, public schooling achieved one of "[i]ts greatest achievement[s], enrolling nearly everyone" (Reese, 2005, p. 287) with enrollment at 5.7 million. By 1970, it had reached 13 million (Reese, 2005, p. 288). Naturally, these two, nearly inescapable cultural sites—television and schools—become "the stories that make us who we are" because of their power and presence in our lives (Dalton & Linder, 2019, p. 4). In "Images of Principals on Television and in the Movies," Jeffrey Glanz explains: "A cultural studies approach examines the dynamic interaction between cultural images of principals … and the perception we have of them" leading to a collection of "culturally shared cognitive models" that eventually overlap in ways that create then replicate dominant patterns of representation (1997, p. 295). Glanz found that three images of principals are most common—the "autocrat," "bureaucrat," and "numbskull" (1997, pp. 5–6). He also found that perceptions of students, school professionals, and the general public about principals in schools and on screen were negative (1997, pp. 11–12). These pervasively negative images and reactions led Glanz to ask questions about how to reverse the opinions. Ultimately, he advocates for "an ethic of caring" that would focus on "[r]ecruiting, hiring, and retaining principals who, first and foremost, demonstrate that individual needs supersede organizational requirements and bureaucratic regulations" (1997, p. 18).

As Dalton has found, an ethic of caring, combined with effective pragmatism, has begun to surface in popular media (*Hollywood Curriculum*, 2017, pp. 180, 186–89). Principal Belinda Brown, as portrayed on *Vice Principals*, is a new and notable example. Her inclusion at North Jackson High School is a non-stereotypical and honest representation of a school administrator. If this characterization were not so completely overshadowed and undermined by the toxic masculinity, childishness, and vindictiveness, of Principal Brown's direct reports at the office, *Vice Principals* might have gone a long way toward creating a space on television for counteracting more common, and negative, principal archetypes. Dalton describes the caring pragmatist as an "emerging set of positive images of principals" concerned about the budget, supervisors, teachers and students who still manage to do the job (*Hollywood Curriculum*, 2017, p. 186). The most compelling example of the caring pragmatist in the movies, according to Dalton, is Janet Williams (Angela Bassett) in the 1999 film *Music of the Heart* (*Hollywood Curriculum*, 2017, pp. 187–189). Belinda Brown has much more in common with Janet Williams than she does with the other administrators in her office, Neal and Lee, who take the buffoonery often seen among administrators in the movies to new lows.

Overlapping Stories in Life and Onscreen

Even before the onslaught of chaos that Neal and Lee inflict upon her life, Belinda faces challenges that are indicative of what real-life, African-American, female principals face. There are, indeed, "leaky boundaries" here among media texts and real-life narratives, from the underrepresentation of female, African-American principals to the experiences they have at work if they do obtain a position. According to the United States Department of Education, in 2012 women occupied 51.6% of the principalships in public schools ("Number and Percentage Distribution of Principals in Public and Private," n.d.), but on the high school level, that percentage fell to 30% (*Characteristics*, 2013, p. 8). African-American women made up almost 12% of female public-school principals and only 6% of all public school principals ("Number and Percentage Distribution of Public School Principals," n.d.). In *Vice Principals*, North Jackson High School is a suburban school located in South Carolina. It is predominately White, and the only African-American character at North Jackson High who has a substantial speaking role other than Belinda is Dayshawn (Sheaun McKinney), a cafeteria employee.

Armentress D. Robinson followed ten African-American, female school leaders serving as assistant principals, principals, and central office administrators in four

C. E. HARRIS

suburban school districts in the southeast region of the United States (2014, p. 1). When Robinson asked about their challenges, participants recounted stories of racism and sexism they encountered while pursuing positions as school leaders (2014, p. 2). One participant became her school's first African-American principal but did not commemorate her achievement because she was unsure how others would react to her appointment while another was repeatedly denied a promotion to principal, a job that "subsequently went to male colleagues with less experience and less education" (2014, pp. 5–6). Belinda faces this double challenge as well. In "The Principal," soon after she arrives to start her new job, Martin Seychelles (James M. Connor) makes a comment that the new principal received her master's degree from Berkeley to which Neal responds, "I bet she went to Berkeley. And I'm pretty *affirmative* about how she got in," suggesting that Belinda's achievements are due to affirmative action rather than success through a process traditionally understood as meritocracy. Belinda flees Philadelphia for South Carolina to get away from her unfaithful ex-husband, and she brings her young sons, Luke (RJ Cyler) and Mario (Deshawn Rivers), with her. Belinda is battling stressors at work (that are ramped up by Neal and Lee), and her two sons "act out" because they did not want to move. Belinda decides to allow her ex-husband to spend time with Luke and Mario, and she even joins them. While it is clear she is still attracted to her ex-husband and is still susceptible to his charm, Belinda remembers what is best for her own well-being and does not rekindle the romantic relationship. In response to Luke and Mario's pleas in "Gin," she allows the boys to move back to Philadelphia with their father while she stays in South Carolina to pursue her career. She recognizes she has given it enough time and can no longer allow her children to remain unhappy.

Vulnerability and Strength

As part of Belinda's commitment to "restorative justice" (a concept introduced in "Circles" when Belinda establishes a "nonjudgmental space" for discussing underlying issues), the principal shares with a group of students that she has struggled with alcohol addiction and is now sober. This scene shows Belinda to be a leader who holds herself to the same standards she expects of others. Neal chooses hegemonic masculinity over his conscience and takes part in Lee's plan to get Belinda drunk, record her in a drunken state, and use the footage to force her to resign. What transpires is presented as something Belinda will have to face as a person with an addiction, not as a woman facing "punishment" for transgressing a double standard based on what is not "acceptable" for women to do in public. Despite Belinda's presence as a successful woman who openly displays her competence, *Vice Principals* is hardly a bastion of feminist messages or female perspectives. The creators are both men, and no woman is credited with directing or writing an episode. Because this is farce rather than satire, which would make fun of culture to urge a corrective, *Vice Principals* is about over-the-top men who accept and reinforce patriarchy and hegemonic masculinity. Instead of serving a loftier purpose, the series regularly demonstrates that asserting sexual dominance is an integral part of supporting and replicating such ideologies.

When thinking of Belinda as a caring pragmatist, it is easy to question why she does not have the awareness to take definitive action against Neal and Lee. Dramatic irony persists so that viewers see what she does not, which makes it misguided to hold her accountable for what she does not know. There are instances when she does suspect she has been "led to a trap" ("The Foundation of Learning"), but the men dead set on ruining her are masterful manipulators who feed off of one another's anger and sense of entitlement denied. When Neal is violent and deceitful, he gains Lee's respect. After they burn down Belinda's house, Lee praises his accomplice: "I saw your potential." This validation satisfies Neal's insecurities ("A Trusty Steed"). When a neighbor, Jackie (Owen Harn), bullies Lee, Neal comes to his aid ("Circles"). Later, when Neal's conscience prevents him from investing fully in the plan to take advantage of Belinda's taste for and vulnerability to gin, Lee takes the lead ("Gin"). Neal struggles to keep his emotions hidden while Lee is an expert at hiding his. Lee is incapable of asserting himself interpersonally while Neal does this regularly and to his own detriment. This is a destructive, toxic combination, and the two vice principals are more dangerous together than either one would be individually. It is no wonder that Belinda does not see a clear picture of what is happening to her because together these deeply flawed and childish men manage to create the perfect storm of bumbling malevolence. How she reacts to what she *does* see, however, may be the most pragmatic move this caring leader makes.

Power and Pragmatism

At the end of the episode "The Foundation of Learning" when Belinda suspects that she was set up in the textbook scandal, she does not yell at Lee or dismiss him but simply walks away. The implication is that she will fire Lee, but she has not yet acted or even let him know how she feels. She is being pragmatic, and as a school leader, her method, both "strategic" and "subversive" (Mirza, 2005, p. 202), is motivated by her "desire to do well within the system" (Mizra, 2005, p. 207). As an African-American, female school leader working with men who resist her presence on grounds of patriarchal and racial power structures, and specifically with a man like Lee, whose way of securing his power is through the most deliberate treachery, she understands that her smartest move is to allow Lee to be his *own* undoing. This allows her to focus on running her school with less disruption. Unlike the men challenging her, Belinda cares about students and introduces the "Circle Room" to North Jackson High. The beautifully colorful space with beanbag chairs and a popcorn machine gives students, as she puts it, a "nonjudgmental space" to discuss the infraction that led them there. She focuses on the underlying issues that cause students to transgress school rules. This progressive practice recognizes that most discipline problems are students acting out to avoid the embarrassment or humiliation they fear will result if they express the truth about their emotional pain.

C. E. HARRIS

Belinda knows that her efforts will not eliminate all discipline problems. She does not want to create a school culture in which students feel there are no consequences, yet she wants to make a marked difference by helping students improve their emotional intelligence. She has to assert her authority to convince Neal to adopt the restorative justice method, but above all, she listens to him and guides him through the process: "Talk to them with some respect, like equals. You set the tone here." This is an invaluable reminder that all leaders should convey when developing leadership skills in others and another example of how Belinda is depicted in sharp contrast to her vice principals, who do not share these values. This demonstration echoes Robinson's subjects' identification of "mentoring aspiring school leaders" as a key responsibility of a principal (7). Because of his hunger for power, Neal chooses Lee over Belinda after first expressing some vulnerability in the Circle Room. This is yet another missed opportunity in the series to develop more complex characters and to adopt narrative devices that challenge hegemonic toxic masculinity. In the context of this television series, which has many damaging faults, Belinda Brown is a positive image worth our time and consideration. We need more figures like her to inspire real educators because media texts and lived experience inform one another as intertextual narratives.

AN OTHERWISE DAMAGING AND REDUCTIVE
DEPICTION OF SCHOOL LEADERS

Neal Gamby's eagerness to assign in- and out-of-school suspension and to verbally humiliate and harass students, Lee Russell's complete disengagement from students altogether, and both men's desperate desire to be promoted to control the school solely for power's sake may lead many to assign them the label "principal-as-autocrat" (Glanz, "Images of Principals," 1998, pp. 8–11). It is true that Neal and Lee attempt to assert their power "[r]uling by fiat and relying on intimidation … based on hierarchal and patriarchal sources of authority" (Glanz qtd. in Dalton, *Hollywood Curriculum*, 2017, p. 137), but these traits take a backseat to the juvenility that colors them. They are not autocratic in a way that commands respect, not even out of fear. Because these characters mainly display "perpetual adolescence," they come closer as administrators to representing Glanz's "principal-as-numbskull" (1998, p. 11) and Dalton's "principal as buffoon" (*Hollywood Curriculum*, 2017, pp. 180–82). Neal and Lee are indeed stupid and bumbling vice principals (Dalton 180) who are ineffective leaders, but instead of being "easily cajoled by outlandish schemes conceived by presumably far brighter and more creative students, and even teachers" (Glanz, 1997, p. 5), they stand in their *own* way. While they are spitting in her cup, burning down her house, and spray-painting derogatory messages about her on the school walls, Belinda Brown is focused on learning from her mistakes and using the wisdom she gains to deliver an inspirational speech to the student body. In "Run for the Money," after the vice principals accidentally douse themselves with the contaminated water Lee laces with "liquid acid LSD" and see the final failure of their plan when North Jackson wins the football game against Percival for the first time in nine years, Lee laments, "We made her a martyr." Instead of focusing on doing their jobs, Neal and Lee are one-dimensional buffoons; they fool themselves into thinking they can gain power through outlandish schemes rather than through hard work and actual leadership.

CONCLUSION

Administrators in *Vice Principals* demonstrate three archetypes Dalton and Glanz outline, but the most dominant depiction, Neal and Lee in the role of "principal as buffoon," is the most dangerous because it remains uncontested in any significant way. In addition to displaying hypermasculinity through an uncritical lens, it paints careers in secondary education as disreputable, reinforcing the dominant trope in popular culture. In the *Vice Principals: Extra Credit* supplement to "The Field Trip," Walton Goggins offers backstory for the main characters, commenting that Neal and Lee are "bullies who were bullied" and that they "never fit in" (2016). This explains their behavior as men who experienced pain earlier in their lives and deal with it in the present through buffoonish, toxic behavior because they never progressed beyond the childhood and adolescent stages when their traumas occurred. Their default mode of retaliation is to embody and employ sexist, hypermasculine, and violent behavior, and they bring this energy into the school and into their positions of authority, further damaging the image of education in the American psyche.

The problem in *Vice Principals* is not its portrayal of adults who happen to be school administrators still battling insecurities rooted in the often-traumatic years of young adulthood; the problem is that the series is disturbingly similar to Bulman's theory of suburban high school films where *teenagers* rebel with near impunity "to express their emerging adult identities" (2015, p. 98). *Vice Principals* features men who wield power in a school while they are *still trying to find* their adult identities. We need screen representations of men who embody caring, pragmatic leadership, but we must start with representations that deal honestly and critically with the crises boys and men are facing. In *The Mask You Live In*, Michael Kimmel notes, "We've constructed an idea of masculinity in the United States that doesn't give young boys a way to feel secure in their masculinity, so we make them go prove it all the time" (2015). *Vice Principals* is an example of the endless desperation men are trapped in, as Neal and Lee devote themselves to proving their masculinity by taking the position of power they feel entitled to as White, suburban men. To many viewers, this series is "just" a sitcom, but the portrayal represents deep disturbances in boys and men, many of whom attain powerful positions for which they are not prepared, and that lead them to take extreme measures to undermine and sabotage the qualified and competent woman hired to lead them. In the case of educational leadership, we need men who are prepared to help each successive generation develop a dedication to empathy and diversity while supporting colleagues regardless of their identities.

C. E. HARRIS

Like their bad teacher counterparts on big and small screens, both Lee and Neal are "bored by students, afraid of students [Lee], [and] eager to dominate students [Neal]" (Dalton, *Hollywood Curriculum*, 2017, p. 61). Despite indications that he is taking to heart lessons of how to be a principal who is a caring pragmatist, the Season 1 finale ("End of the Line") confirms that Neal's loyalties lie with what he can gain from hegemonic masculinity. He and Lee inform the faculty that Belinda has resigned, citing "family problems," "legal issues," and "more than likely, substance abuse." Later, they walk out of Superintendent Hass's (Brian Howe) office triumphantly after he names them co-interim principals. The deceit, destructiveness, and violence that the men engage in as they "prove" that they exemplify America's dominant definition of masculinity are the deeds that unite them in their maleness. They have little else in common. In "Gin," an exasperated Lee remarks, "I'm just at a loss here. Every single thing we throw at this woman fails." Of course, Neal and Lee do not actually fail, do they?

In the second and final season, we see that Lee has not only succeeded, but he has been named principal permanently. He runs the school as more of an autocrat than a buffoon, as Neal's sometimes-seen *potential* as a caring pragmatist is not present to counteract his treatment of his colleagues as inferiors. Lee refers to himself as "the king" in the season opener, "Tiger Town," and in the episode ironically called "The King." He desires an assistant but not an equal, as he says to Neal, who is home recovering from a gunshot wound he has suffered after his promotion to co-interim principal. Former co-vice principal Nash (Dale Dickey) is introduced in "Tiger Town" and provides a counterbalance to Neal and Lee that becomes stronger as she becomes more comfortable in her role. By the end of the series, Lee is no longer a school administrator, and Neal is the new principal of Forest Hills Middle School. Two women take over as principal and vice principal of North Jackson High. The implicit message is that these two women, unlike the men, have the ability to lead young adults as caring pragmatists. The key difference across seasons has to do with race, however, and that is where *Vice Principals* is even more disappointing than in the first season.

Belinda Brown, the rare principal as caring pragmatist who provides the ultimate opposition to the toxic, White, masculine incompetence of Neal and Lee, appears in only two of the season's nine episodes: the premiere ("Tiger Town") and the finale ("The Union of the Wizard and the Warrior"). The focus of the second season is Neal's quest to find out who tried to kill him and exact revenge. In "Tiger Town," Belinda's appearance serves to explore Neal's belief that she is the culprit. She appears in the finale as the object of Lee's pleas for help—Neal now believes Lee is the shooter. These tactics seem to back up Danny McBride's assertion: "I don't see this as a story about race" (D'Addario). Yet, Belinda's absence, when combined with the second season's *complete* relegation of African-American characters to the periphery, makes race an issue even if McBride chooses not to see it as such. Dayshawn continues his role as Neal's sounding board, and two other African-American characters are added: school resource officer Terrance Willows (Marcuis

Harris) and cafeteria worker Reggie (Diva Taylor). (Jay DeVon Johnson also returns as history teacher Bruce Carter, but he has no lines.) In "Slaughter," Neal invites Dayshawn to dinner, but only so Dayshawn can help find his shooter. In the process, Dayshawn explains that when he told Neal the shooter has "black hair," he did not mean the shooter is an African American. McBride would have a stronger case claiming that race is purely "incidental" if these "jokes" did not accompany the relegation of all Black characters to the sidelines without any context for their lives beyond serving the White characters. If *Vice Principals* were a satire rather than a farce, it would be reflexive, strive to show viewers what they don't naturally see, and take responsibility for the ideologies it contests (instead of those it perpetuates). Unfortunately it does not.

In "Film Gives Teachers Credit They're Due," Dalton imparts a reality we all must face: "The media reinforces the idea that teaching is a dead-end job." The same can be said of school administration (2017). I return to Goggins's comment that discounts the job as "not worth" the energy Neal and Lee put forth. Goggins's perspective on the character he plays represents a textual "leaky boundary." Dalton and Linder note that "media texts never exist separately from contexts" (2019, p. 3). Therefore, there is little doubt that his own experiences and the media he has consumed have shaped his view of school leaders. Now he is part of the entertainment industry that perpetuates the damaging notion that there is no need to try to advance in a career in high school administration because even that will result in a dead end unless you have the prestige of a direct pipeline to Harvard. Goggins, as well as McBride (who is also a *Vice Principals* creator, producer, writer, and director), hold power in their platforms. They can help to improve perceptions if they choose to and bolster support for public education, which can only benefit from a more robust and authentic set of representations. In addition to the artists who create television and films, it is also important for the *viewers* to realize that: "It is never just a movie or a TV show" (Dalton, "Film Gives Teachers," 2017); those who watch have a part to play as *critical* viewers. Fiske's "leaky boundaries" among texts are there regardless (2010). It will take all of us to rethink how we define masculinity, how we practice empathy, and how we value and encourage diversity; and, it will take Hollywood to reflect new attitudes that show more powerful and positive images of school leaders because they are essential to two of the most ubiquitous aspects of American life—schooling and popular media.

REFERENCES

Allen, Robert C. (1992). *Channels of discourse, reassembled* (2nd ed.). Chapel Hill, NC: University of North Carolina Press.

Anyon, Jean. (1980). Social class and the hidden curriculum of work. *Journal of Education, 162*(1), n.p.

Bulman, Robert C. (2015). *Hollywood goes to high school: Cinema, schools, and American culture* (2nd ed.). New York, NY: Worth-Macmillan Education.

Characteristics of Public and Private Elementary and Secondary School Principals in the United States: Results from the 2011–12 Schools and Staffing Survey, First Look. (2013, August). Washington,

C. E. HARRIS

DC: National Center for Education Statistics, Institute of Educational Sciences U.S. Department of Education.

Connell, R. W., & James W. Messerschmidt. (2005). Hegemonic masculinity: Rethinking the concept. *Gender and Society, 19*(6), 829–859.

D'Addario, Daniel. (2017, August 1). Danny McBride on Vice Principals: 'I don't see this as a story about race.' *Time*.

Dalton, Mary. (2017, February 21). Mary Dalton: Film gives teachers credit they're due. *Winston-Salem Journal*. BH Media Group.

Dalton, Mary M. (2017). *The Hollywood curriculum: Teachers in the movies* (3rd rev. ed.). New York, NY: Peter Lang.

Dalton, Mary M., & Laura R. Linder. (2019). *Teacher TV: Seventy years of teachers on television.* New York, NY: Peter Lang.

Eisler, Richard M., Jay R. Skidmore, & Clay H. Ward. (1988). Masculine gender-role stress: Predictor of anger, anxiety, and health-risk behaviors. *Journal of Personality Assessment, 52*(1), 133–41.

Fiske, John. (2010). *Understanding popular culture* (2nd ed.). London: Routledge.

Gitlin, Todd. (2002). *Media unlimited: How the torrent of images and sounds overwhelms our lives.* New York, NY: Henry Holt and Company, LLC.

Glanz, Jeffrey. (1997 March 25). *From Mr. Wameke to Mr. Rivelle to Mr. Woodman: Images of principals in film and television.* Chicago, IL: American Educational Research Association.

Glanz, Jeffrey. (1997). Images of principals on television and in the movies. *The Clearing House, 70*(6), 295–297.

Glanz, Jeffrey. (1998). Images of principals in film and television: From Mr. Wameke to Mr. Rivelle to Mr. Woodman. *Educational Leadership and Administration, 10*, 7–24.

Heldman, Caroline. (2015). *Mask you live in.* Jennifer Siebel Newsom, dir.

Kupers, Terry A. (2005). Toxic masculinity as a barrier to mental health treatment in prison. *Journal of Clinical Psychology, 61*(6), 713–724.

Mirza, Heidi Safia. (2005). Black women in education: A collective movement for social change. In Gloria Ladson-Billings & David Gillborn (Eds.), *The RoutledgeFalmer reader in multicultural education* (pp. 201–208). London: RoutledgeFalmer.

Number and Percentage Distribution of Principals in Public and Private Elementary and Secondary Schools, by Selected Characteristics: Selected years, 1993–94 through 2011–12. (n.d.). *Digest of Education Statistics*. National Center for Education Statistics, Schools and Staffing Survey. United States. Department of Education.

Number and Percentage Distribution of Public School Principals by Gender, Race, and Selected Principal Characteristics: 2011–12. (n.d.). *Schools and Staffing Survey.* United States. Department of Education. National Center for Education Statistics. US Department of Education.

Reese, William J. (2005). *America's public schools: From the common school to "No Child Left Behind."* Baltimore, MD: Johns Hopkins University Press.

Robinson, Armentress D. (2014). Personal, professional, and sociocultural experiences of African American female school leaders. *Alabama Journal of Educational Leadership, 1*(1), 1–11.

Smith, Rachel M., Dominic J. Parrot, Kevin M. Swartout, & Andra Teten Tharp. (2015). Deconstructing hegemonic masculinity: The roles of antifemininity, subordination to women, and sexual dominance in men's perpetration of sexual aggression. *Psychology of Men & Masculinity, 16*(2), 160–169.

Vice Principals: Behind-the-Scenes Conversation. (2016, July 17). "The Principal." HBO.

Vice Principals: Extra Credit. (2016, July 31). "The Field Trip." HBO. 31 July 2016.

Vice Principals: Extra Credit. (2016, August 28). "The Good Book." HBO.

NAEEMAH CLARK

9. THE *INSECURE* TEACHER

How Issa Rae Has Normalized the Black Woman to Create TV Magic

ABSTRACT

In its premier season, Issa, the lead character of HBO's dramedy *Insecure* works for a non-profit organization that goes into Los Angeles schools in hopes of inspiring Black students. The non-profit We Got Y'all's staff of well-meaning, but tone-deaf do-gooders continually frustrate her while the students hone in on her insecurities, forcing her to reexamine her life. This chapter is a discussion of how Issa works to defy the patronizing norms of the non-profit to empower her students, as she works to discover how she can live her best life. Ultimately, the discussion will focus on how she navigates being a professional Black woman, educator, an undercover rapper, a best friend, and a conflicted partner while seeking her authentic self. Ultimately, this series depicts that work of educators is not only edifying for the students but also for the teacher.

Keywords: Issa Rae, Black, women, authenticity, *Insecure*

***

We all know the scene. The hip and/or rich and/or tough and always naïve White educator bravely enters a classroom to find Black students staring back from their desks. Music comes from a boom box while gum-chewing girls cuddle up with bad boys who have their feet on desks or are using worn textbooks as pillows. Of course, there is always a quiet girl in the front of the class who is eager to learn—the teacher needs to have some reason to stay after the first day, right? Popular television programs such as *White Shadow* (CBS 1978–1981) and iconic films such as *Dangerous Minds* (1996) and *Freedom Writers* (2007) feature White teachers figuring out how to cure what ills the troubled students.

Insecure (HBO 2016–) is Issa Rae's first episodic program to air on television, but she had previously created a strong following among online viewers with her comedy series *Misadventures of an Awkward Black Girl* (YouTube 2011–13). In both series, Rae uses rap as a way of expressing her inner thoughts, particularly when it comes to venting about the difficulties educated Black women face while trying to prove their worth in predominately White workplaces. After ABC passed on a pitch from Rae and Shonda Rhimes, Rae and co-producer Larry Wilmore got a

© KONINKLIJKE BRILL NV, LEIDEN, 2019 | DOI:10.1163/9789004398092_009

greenlight to produce their comedy series on HBO. The program features rarely seen sites in downtown LA, frequent affectionate use of the n-word, and eclectic hip-hop music selected by music supervisor Solange Knowles. *Insecure* is HBO's first foray into an urban comedy designed for young, Black viewers.

The lead character of the series is Issa Dee (played by Rae). She works for We Got Y'all, a fictionalized version of thousands of non-profit programs around the country designed to bridge the achievement gap in low performing schools. For example, California has over 4,000 programs that are meant to increase learning for disadvantaged students (My Philanthropedia). We Got Y'all's director Joanne (Catherine Curtin) is a middle-aged, White woman who believes she knows how to reach the disadvantaged Black child because she's read about it in books. This chapter argues that Rae rejects the image of the heroic "White savior" character by valuing the struggles of the professional Black woman. Rae weaves together a character's attempts to be successful in a world full of artifice with the same character's struggle to find authenticity. In the end, the series creates a realistic picture of the concerns that many young, Black professionals have of being fraudulent, real, authoritative, and relatable in the workplace. Issa's fears are made even more complex because they are being negotiated in front of a classroom of students in need. The successful solution—magic—happens when she allows her authentic self to the lead the way.

To understand the original and complex content offered in the program, it is necessary to assess how improving the lives of students of color and other marginalized groups has been portrayed in film. Frequently, these disenfranchised groups are saved by a White outsider who enters the world of the "others" with all of the tools needed to help them. This trope, known as the "White savior," has shown up in recent films such as *The Last Samurai* (2003), *The Blind Side* (2009), and *Grand Torino* (2008), films—not insignificantly—representing a variety of genres (Hughey 2010 and Hughey 2014). Films with White savior characters often feature that character in a new or off-putting setting. Then, after coming to an epiphany about their own strength, these White characters discover something about their newfound talents that enables them to save a group of people from difficult circumstances in their own neighborhoods.

Matthew W. Hughey contends that films with White savior plotlines are reflections of the culture that is present when a film is released. These cultures are not built upon capitalism but on "a 'neoliberal' service economy" where Whites are in service of the downtrodden non-Whites (Bonilla-Silva, n.d.) terms. The production and distribution of these films signals that White viewers find comfort in stories where Whites cross racial lines and help others better themselves. The creation of stories in which Whites help other races/ethnicities is problematic, however. As Eduardo Bonilla-Silva found in his study of the language of racism, this trope posits that the White race is paramount and must be relied upon to fix the ills of society. Moreover, this notion promotes the idea of the "white racial frame" where what is White is what is correct and appropriate for the greater good of society (Feagin, 2009, p. 1, 89).

The White savior is found in a variety of settings. For example, Jaime Schultz discusses historically-based films such as *Cool Runnings* (1993), *The Jackie*

THE *INSECURE* TEACHER

Figure 9.1. We Got Y'all logo on Insecure *(HBO 2016–)*

Robinson Story (1950)*,* and *Glory Road* (2006) that create, ignore, or embellish fact to make a White character the hero of a story when factually the character of color succeeds without the savior figure. The White savior has been particularly prevalent in films featuring classroom settings. While I'm not arguing that good teachers don't improve the lives of their students, it is striking to me how many of these films are biopics that celebrate a scripted version of a real teacher. In films such as *Conrack* (1974), *Dangerous Minds* (1995), *Music of the Heart* (1999), *The Ron Clark Story* (2006), and *Freedom Writers* (2007), White teachers save Black and Latinx students, and both the students and the teacher are generally triumphant. (*Conrack* is more complex and a bit of mixed bag in terms of results, though the general pattern holds.) The authority of these White teachers is challenged until their true talent is revealed, which leads the children to learn and to become obedient.

The dynamic of the White savior is highlighted in Issa's interactions with her colleagues in the We Got Y'all offices. Through voiceover narration, Issa tells viewers We Got Y'all is an organization that is supposed to help kids from the 'hood even though it hasn't hired anyone from the 'hood. Issa, by virtue of the color of her skin, is seen as the purveyor of Black knowledge in the office. She—and by extension viewers—is frequently reminded that she is the only Black person working for the nonprofit. For example, during one scene in the breakroom, a White colleague asks, "Issa, what's on fleek?" Issa responds that she doesn't know what that means, but her voiceover reveals that she does "know what that shit means" but is being "aggressively passive" by feigning ignorance. To provide another example, Issa's White boss Joanne appears wearing a dashiki in her office, which is covered in

99

posters preaching Black pride and empowerment. In one scene, Joanne tells Issa that she is torn by the vastly different teaching philosophies of Booker T. Washington and W.E.B. Dubois, indicating that she really does not understand either. Issa questions, "In 2016?"

We Got Y'all is an example of the "neoliberal" services Bonilla-Silva references in his research about color blind racist language. First, the organization's name is a misguided attempt to conform with slang used by young African Americans to make the kids comfortable with the organization. The choice of the organizational name and of her wardrobe make it seem as if Joanne has taken workshops designed to introduce the culture and language of the kids being served without making an effort to truly connect with their identity. Second, and more problematic for Issa, the organization was started by a do-gooder who assumes she knows the right path to helping the kids while acknowledging that she does not understand their needs. As social entrepreneurs and others recognized the altruistic and financial benefits in the educational sector, non-profit organizations are being formed to support students' curricular and co-curricular development. These organizations, funded through charitable foundations, government grants, or angel investors are plentiful. In some cases, their work is duplicative, and the success generated is difficult to measure accurately, which makes them fertile ground for critique (Callahan, 2015). Issa Dee is the conduit for challenging the notion of the White savior because she is on a soul-searching mission throughout the first season of the series. She questions the intentions of the organization while reconsidering her place in the non-profit and in the world.

QUIZZING THE *INSECURE* TEACHER

The series opens with Issa Dee standing in front of a classroom at Thomas Jefferson Middle School in Los Angeles where the seats are filled with African-American and Latinx tweens. She introduces herself and the non-profit organization she represents as a youth liaison. She tells them We Got Y'all is there to help the kids with test prep, career development, tutoring, and "filling in the gaps" before she invites their questions. The kids eagerly pepper her with queries such as, "Why you talk like a White girl?" and "What's up with your hair?" Issa tries to respond to their questions jovially: "You got me. I'm rockin' Blackface." Then, even though the students' regular classroom teacher tells her to ignore their questions, Issa opts to tell them the truths about her life. She tells the students that it is her 29th birthday, she's worked for the nonprofit since graduating from college, and she's been with her boyfriend for five years. This response prompts another flurry of student retorts: "Why ain't you married?" to which another replies, "My dad says nobody's looking for bitter-ass Black women." Issa says, "That's OK. And tell your dad that Black women aren't bitter. They're just tired of being expected to settle for less." Her response is rehearsed, robotic, and her eyes reveal that not even she truly believes

Figure 9.2. Issa Dee (Issa Rae) on Insecure *(HBO 2016–)*

what she is saying. It is here that the viewers learn of Issa's true ambivalence about her romantic life.

This moment between Issa and her students is designed to be jarring and unsettling to those who have seen students question teachers. After all, the power structure of the classroom is built around students asking questions and teachers responding. The process of questioning in the classroom is "student-centered," a practice in which both the teachers and students ask questions in order to help students learn (Ryan & Townsend, 2010, p. 44). As she stands before the students, Issa fields questions that are more substantive than the procedural inquiries about homework or instructions for a class assignment; they are interrogations that are personal and intimate. The students are extremely engaged but also invasive, which forces Issa to dig deep into her mind and soul for the responses. Clearly, this moment is unlike past question-answer sessions mediated between teacher and students, and Issa's interaction is pivotal to the core of the series.

The psychic remnants of her time in front of the classroom remain with her. In a work meeting about the right way to approach the kids the program serves, Issa daydreams about her fears that Black women are not satisfied with their unmarried lives or with unfulfilling work lives, which renders them purposeless. Once she snaps back to reality, she blurts a solution to her own life and, coincidentally, to the problems with their We Got Y'all initiatives: "Stop treating them like they are one type of person. Nothing is going to change for them if they are stuck in the same place. Build a program outside of the school." And, as if on cue, Issa receives a text message from rap producer Daniel (Y'lan Noel), the "what if" guy she's been pining for since she was 16 years old.

N. CLARK

HEARING THE TEACHER'S VOICE

To create a change for the kids, Issa rejects the suggestions from her co-workers that the kids should be taken to hip-hop *Othello* or to lunch at an LA health food restaurant called Lemonade where they could watch Beyoncé's long-form video *Lemonade*. Even more galling to Issa is the suggestion that she take her students to a sporting event. Issa quickly replies that it is limiting to confine Black kids' entertainment options, she says, "It's crippling for inner-city kids to rely on sports." She knows she doesn't want to fall back on the same activities the We Got Y'all team believes will save the inner-city kids. Ultimately, Issa settles on a beach clean-up day for the kids. To Issa, this outing for the students does not have to be elaborate, but it has to show the kids "what else is out there."

At the same time that Issa wrestles with what to do to connect with the kids, she also considers "what else is out there" for herself. Issa tells her best friend Molly (Yvonne Orji) she's ready to be "the brave me, the no fucks me. I just want to be not scared to not do shit anymore." Initially, Issa tries the new philosophy with various lipstick shades, but those personas are far more superficial than what she has in mind. Instead, she tells her longtime boyfriend Lawrence (Jay Ellis) that she is tired of his unemployment, lack of initiative, and moping. Then, to explore further this new philosophy, she takes the stage at an open mic night in response to prodding from Daniel (now a burgeoning music producer) and freestyles about Molly's constant heartbreak with "broken pussy" as the oft-repeated refrain.

The idea for the kids to breathe the fresh air and touch the sand at the beach that is merely a few miles away—but largely out of reach for the kids—is as rejuvenating as driving down the freeway to see Daniel at the hardcore rap club. The freedom of being on the stage creates a reinvigorated, new version of Issa. The thrill of "no fucks" Issa quickly wears off, however, once the kids at Thomas Jefferson Middle School find the open mic performance on YouTube. In the moment when Issa sees the kids rapping her raunchy lyrics back to her, the conflicts between her creative work and her job collide. She is a Black woman trying to reach Black kids in an authentic way, but her efforts to find her authentic self puts her credibility and career in jeopardy. She asks the students to move on from the video, but it is too late. They have turned the song into a meme, translated it into Spanish, and have made the refrain the response to any question they are asked in school.

Ironically, the "Broken Pussy" incident is reminiscent of a slew of movies that feature teachers in an inner-city classroom. The White teacher figures out how to adapt lessons about Shakespeare, calculus, and other college prep lessons using the language the students prefer—rap. The rap gives the White teacher credibility in the eyes of the students. This dynamic falls into the neoliberal racist category because the assumptions of the White teacher convert what is actually a complex and historical form into "simple" street language; in fact, the White teacher falls far short of understanding the language and culture of the Black students, but the films suggest just the opposite. Furthermore, by discovering this Rosetta Stone, the

THE *INSECURE* TEACHER

teachers in these films find a magical key to communicating with Black students, which oversimplifies the constructive dialogue and compresses the amount of time required for a lasting and transforming connection to develop.

To Issa, the presence of rap in the classroom is tied to a loss of authority and—ultimately—to her job. She does not readily embrace her rhyming prowess because she views it as being inappropriate and embarrassing. Yet, the students warm to Issa once they discover the rap. It's not because she's using it to teach Shakespeare but because it reveals an authentic part of herself, a facet with which they can relate. After the success of the beach trip and the excitement of the video, the students begin to see Issa as a star instead of the insecure youth liaison who stood before them a few weeks before. She forms a connection with them in ways that their regular classroom teacher and rest of the We Got Y'all staff cannot. These students relish finding a real space separate from the social regulations imposed on them about how the Black woman and Black children are supposed to act.

SWITCHING THE CODES

Even though there is eventual comfort in the communication between Issa and her students, *Insecure* does well to demonstrate the balancing act people of color have to perform when communicating with non-African Americans. Issa herself tries to control how the kids present themselves in an effort to maintain her credibility with her White coworkers. On the day the group goes to the beach, the ride is hot and long. Behind her back, her colleagues critique Issa's decision to go to the beach while the kids audibly complain about their discomfort. Still, Issa remains resolute. She tells the kids, "We're in mixed company" with a nod toward the concerned We Got Y'all staffers, who are all White. She is asking the Black kids to code switch in a way that she knows they understand.

This simpatico relationship is echoed in a series subplot when Issa's best friend Molly struggles with her role as the sole Black woman at her law firm. When intern Rasheeda (Gail Bean) comes to work at the firm, Molly sees an opportunity to mentor the young Black woman. Those expectations sour, however, after Molly becomes dismayed at how loud, sassy, and braggadocios Rasheeda is in the breakroom. Molly pulls Rasheeda into a private meeting to tell her: "If you want to be successful here, you've got to know when to switch it up a little bit." An offended Rasheeda replies, "I didn't switch it up in my interview with the senior partners, and I didn't switch it up when I was named editor of the law review. So, I don't think I need to switch it up now." As presented in the series, the expectations of code switching are a double-edged sword in the student-teacher relationship. The expectation that both Issa and Molly have of their charges is based on the ways they have learned to navigate in their respective workplaces. The women have learned when to pick up and when to drop the mannerisms, symbols, and words that they have grown up with in order to be viewed as acceptable to others.

N. CLARK

Black America has long had its own lexicon of coded language and symbols. Sociologist Chandra Waring noted that the ability to code switch can be an asset for Black Americans (2013, p. 4). It is part of how many Blacks navigate American society: yielding to the expectations of the dominant culture while still retaining credibility with other Blacks. Conversely, the notion that Blacks would have to demur to the standards of White America is unpalatable to others. The code switching allows Issa and Molly to negotiate social acceptance in different groups, but it removes them from the Blacks they come into contact with in their workplaces.

For Issa's part, the rap video serves as an antidote to the code switch and the trope of the White savior, which is obliterated once the code shift is shown to be ineffective with the middle school students. The idea that what is "White" is the norm and acceptable is faulty. Actually, reaching the students where they are is the key to connecting with them in a meaningful way. The kids no longer see her as "talking like a White girl" because the need for pretense is over when the students recognize that they share the same code. Once that artifice is erased, Issa can truly serve the students because she has gained their trust. Moreover, instead of complying with the socially accepted norms of We Got Y'all that were created by Joanne, Issa digs into her need to find genuine ways of serving the students. While code switching can aid in the world of work, these characters also challenge its effectiveness by juxtaposing the frustration of conformity and the success of authenticity.

FINDING COMFORT IN THE FAMILIAR

The White savior is often a stranger in a strange land. While Issa is not from the same neighborhood as her students attending Thomas Jefferson Middle School, she knows the value of that space. Her celebration of the students' community is revealed when We Got Y'all plans its annual fundraiser. The nonprofit's staff excitedly talks about a Malibu location that offers free chair rental but does not allow children. Issa reminds the team that the organization is about the children, and they should be present at the event. She suggests the event take place at a home in Baldwin Hills, an upper-class, Black neighborhood near the middle school. In previous years, the event was held without regard to the needs of the students, and Issa invariably went along with the plan. This year, however, she objects because now she sees the world differently. First, she is more engaged with and invested in the students than in previous years. The allegiance she feels with the students encourages her to find ways to celebrate their homes and to see "the beauty in their own backyard." In another subplot, *Insecure* deftly parallels situations in Issa's personal life with situations experienced by the students. At the beginning of the series, she is frustrated with her longtime, unemployed boyfriend, Lawrence. Much like the daydreaming she does at work, Issa is going through the motions of her relationship, ignoring Lawrence's obvious depression. She cheats on him with her teenage crush then tries to heal her relationship with Lawrence by creating a home with him based around the purchase of a new sofa and designer lotion dispenser. To Issa, the need to adhere to the possibilities represented by her apartment is parallel to her desire to have the students see the possibilities available to them in their own neighborhood.

When the students arrive at the multimillion-dollar home in Baldwin Hills, they are impressed. One student notes that the owner of the house has an entire drawer full of batteries. Another announces to the attendees of the fundraiser that he will own a house just like this one day. Overhearing that the kids think the home is owned by a rapper, Issa tells them that the homeowner is a Black dentist. The students marvel that Black people even have dentists, but Issa assures them that Black people believe in good oral hygiene like anyone else. While their awe at the visit to the home initially seems like a humorous fish-out-of-water tale, these moments also defeat the White savior scenario. Here, even though the homeowner is not present, his Blackness is what wins the day. Of course, Issa has anticipated that win. She puts the students in a home similar to the ones she knows. She's introduces them to the possibilities that can come from a college education and from building and maintaining a lovely neighborhood. Even though he is invisible, the homeowner is a powerful tool for teaching the students that they, too, can be successful. The norm here is not what's White; a new norm is established that is built around what is theirs.

CONCLUSION

At the end of the fundraiser, Joanne congratulates Issa on her progress with the students and in the We Got Y'all program. He boss says, "I've been wanting to see this" in reference to Issa's commitment to her work. This exchange is gratifying for Issa, but it seems ironic for the viewer. After all, it is Issa's frustration with the systems that created and programmed We Got Y'all that led to her overall dissatisfaction in the first place. Joanne's false sense of the possibilities presented by White savior-hood stymies most innovations Issa may have had to enhance the program. Joanne does not realize that Issa's disconnection has been due, in part, to Joanne's faux ethnocentricity and her misguided understanding of how to serve the Black child. Issa is faking when she tries to align with the false dynamic set by Joanne and We Got Y'all. In reality, what Joanne believes she has been waiting for is predicated on Issa seeing through the phoniness and embracing her own ethnicity. Issa's success comes from letting the students see her whole and authentic self. In turn, the students can see what's possible from and for someone like them.

Of course, White teachers can have success with non-White students, but the fictionalized White savior stories are disingenuous. In this case, it is Issa's navigation through her life that makes it possible for her to normalize the power of this Black teacher. Taking the kids to the beach and to the elegant house in Baldwin Hills are ways for the kids to recognize what is beautiful within their sphere. The excursions are neither extravagant or elusive. Like the outings, Issa is not a savior, she is just extraordinarily ordinary. Similarly, the raunchy rap, while initially shocking, gives way to a comfortable rapport between the educator and the students. The normalcy

N. CLARK

is not boring; it is liberatingly familiar. The magic happens when a normalized Black woman unleashes and claims her power.

REFERENCES

Bonilla-Silva, Eduardo. (n.d.). The linguistics of color blind racism: How to talk nasty about blacks without sounding 'Racist.' *Critical Sociology, 28*(1–2), 41–64.

Callahan, David. (2015, January 15). Are way too many nonprofits. What are funders going to do about that? *Inside Philanthropy.*

Feagin, Joe. (2009). *The white racial frame: Centuries of framing and counter-framing.* New York, NY: Routledge.

Hughey, Matthew W. (2004). *The white savior film: Content, critics, and consumption.* Philadelphia, PA: Temple University Press.

Hughey, Matthew W. (2009). The white savior film and reviewers' reception. *Symbolic Interaction, 33*(3), 475–496.

My Philanthropedia. (2010). *MyPhilanthropdedia.com.*

Ryan, Patrick A., & Jane S. Townsend. (2010). Representations of teachers' and students' inquity in 1950s television and film. *Educational Studies, 46*(1), 44–66.

Schultz, Jaime. (2014). Glory road and the white savior historical sport film. *Journal of Popular Film & Television, 42*(4), 205–213.

Waring, Chandra D. L. (2013). *"Beyond 'Code-switching:'" The racial capital of black/white biracial Americans* (Doctoral Dissertation). University of Connecticut, Connecticut.

IAN PARKER RENGA AND MARK A. LEWIS

10. CONTRASTING THE ARCHETYPAL SAGE WITH THE MENTOR COACH IN YOUNG ADULT LITERATURE

Insights for Teacher Reflection

ABSTRACT

Fictional stories of teachers convey particular character types like the hero, trickster, or sage that are likely to resonate with many educators. By engaging in archetypal reflectivity while reading young adult literature, teachers can examine these types with respect to their ideals of professional practice and identity. Here we invite readers to consider the teacher as archetypal sage as depicted by Dumbledore in the Harry Potter series as it compares to the mentor coach character of Lionel "Lion" Serbousek in the book *Ironman*. We show how both teacher types forge close mentoring relationships with students, though there are notable differences in how they guide students and to what ends. The contrast, as we discuss, can challenge assumptions about what students are seeking and may ultimately need from their teachers.

Keywords: teacher reflection, young adult literature, archetypes, sage, mentor coach

***

Reflection is vital for good teaching. The notion of a reflective practitioner stems from progressivists like John Dewey, who encourage teachers to consider what they are doing in the classroom, why their instruction is unfolding the way it is, and how their teaching might be different. For reflection to really serve all students, Kenneth M. Zeichner and Daniel P. Liston contend that it must go beyond examining technique and delve into values, assumptions, and the cultural dynamics of one's instructional environment (2013). They observe how this critically oriented conception of a reflective practitioner still struggles to take hold within the teaching profession. A heavy focus on technical mastery and the narrow demands of test-based accountability appears to be blanching the colorful possibilities of teacher reflection.

Our experience as teacher educators suggests that many teachers think deeply about their role in the education of children. They wonder about their relationship to students, how they are perceived by parents, what motivates learning, and the

© KONINKLIJKE BRILL NV, LEIDEN, 2019 | DOI:10.1163/9789004398092_010

I. P. RENGA & M. A. LEWIS

hidden depths in the topics they teach. Sometimes, they question whether or not they are adhering to their values in the classroom. Newer teachers might be surprised by how hard it is to adhere to their instructional ideals while veterans might lament the loss of their ideals, the living tissue of possibility long ago replaced by the hardened minerals of reality. Reflection as expansively framed by Zeichner and Liston (2013), Parker J. Palmer (2003), and others can offer teachers the opportunity to explore teaching's soulful terrain and to reconnect with ideals—to renew commitments to one's self, students, and the world.

Stories are useful for inspiring such reflection. Mark Edmundson argues that the ancient myths have persisted in no small part because of their artful portrayal of ideals that we still find compelling (2015). Contemporary tales—as told through books, movies, podcasts, and other media—repackage old ideals and update them to reflect evolving societal concerns, such as calls for greater inclusivity, equity, and justice. Such narratives present intriguing possibilities for teachers. Indeed, we find that fictional teachers in popular novels offer practitioners an array of character types—archetypes constructed around particular instructional ideals—to study and learn from in their efforts to understand who they are and whom they want to become as teachers. In this chapter, we focus attention on two particular character types common in young adult literature: the sage and the mentor coach.

In many ways the mentor coach character who supports the young athlete, such as the swim coach Lionel Serbousek in Chris Crutcher's *Ironman* (1995), is similar to the archetypal sage who supports the marked adolescent hero, like Dumbledore from J.K. Rowling's Harry Potter series (1997–2007) or the Receiver of Memory in Lois Lowry's *The Giver* (1993). Both mentor coaches and sages are usually portrayed as being invested in their young adult protagonists, forging close relationships and imparting wisdom at crucial moments. Unlike tales of heroic teachers that tend to view teaching from the adult perspective and position students as barriers or obstacles to be overcome for classroom success (see Renga's "Exploring the Heroic Teacher Archetype" [2015]), stories with mentor coaches and sages typically offer the student perspective and position the educator in a supporting role. Despite these similarities, however, there are notable differences between the two character types and the nature of their relationships to students. After briefly establishing our reflective framework, we offer traits of each type and then discuss the tensions and opportunities they pose for teachers.

ARCHETYPAL REFLECTIVITY

We invite educators to engage in what Clifford Mayes refers to as *archetypal reflectivity*, wherein the contents of one's personal story are put into conversation with common story arcs and their familiar character types (1999). The hero is perhaps the best-known archetype, though the sage, trickster, shadow, and crone are recognizable in characters populating a range of stories. Each archetype plays a unique role and can offer helpful insights on intra- and interpersonal dynamics. While

James Rhem has argued that *teacher* is itself an archetype (2015), Mayes's illustrates how educators arguably inhabit different archetypes in response to varying student needs (1999). One students' poor behavior might demand a teacher's inner ogre, for example, while another might require the trickster's humor. In this way, individual archetypes can serve as an accessible heuristic for making sense of complex classroom interactions and relationships. Furthermore, we suggest that reflection aided by archetypes can expand teacher consideration beyond pragmatic concerns over technical improvement to allow for spiritual enrichment as practitioners tap into the larger currents of their work, specifically its emotional, relational, and cultural dimensions. This does not diminish the importance of technique; rather, it situates instructional moves within particular educational narratives and histories, which Zeichner and Liston suggest can inform the efforts of teachers to improve their practice (2013).

Unlike Mayes, we are less inclined to accept the structuralist underpinnings of Jungian archetypal analysis and its assumption of universal psychic energies. Our preference, as we discuss elsewhere, is to view archetypes through a constructivist lens as sociohistorical artifacts, or products of our collective tendency to tell stories and to make sense of them in search of truth and meaning (Renga & Lewis, 2018, p. 29). We agree, however, with Mayes's suggestion of a spiritual component to teaching that is largely undervalued and understudied (1999) (see also Zeichner & Liston, 2013). To this purpose, we think archetypal reflectivity can expose the soul of teaching. Specifically, it can shed light on the ideals feeding our imagination for classroom instruction as well as the desires, revulsions, affections, fears, and many other non-cognitive or pre-cognitive feelings that accompany being a teacher.[1]

Fictional characters in literature can serve as models of particular teacher archetypes and the ideals they exemplify. Comparing these models unearths tensions in the work of teaching and provides insights into the needs of students. As educators, we also find that engaging in archetypal reflectivity with characters in young adult literature (YAL) helps to make sense of the profound attachments we feel toward certain ways of being a teacher and about deeply held beliefs about the best approaches for serving students.

THE ARCHETYPAL SAGE

In myths across cultures, the sage archetype is discernible by several common features. Sages tend to be aloof and live alone as outcasts hidden on the fringes of society often marked by their old appearance, unusual behavior, or notable deformity. Dominique Beth Wilson notes how they are possessors of great and terrible wisdom and a sense of the world's grander narratives (2013). The sage's knowledge risks being dangerously disruptive to a community's status quo. In *The Giver*, for example, we have shown how The Receiver of Memory understands *eros* in a way that threatens to upend the community's social order (Renga & Lewis, 2018, p. 37). Campbell marks the sage as a supporting character who intervenes in the protagonist's tale once she accepts the hero's call (1949). Sages are mysterious, maintaining distance and offering magical objects and some protection though few guarantees. As mentors in YAL, they sometimes form close, one-to-one relationships with students and use more progressive instructional methods (Renga & Lewis, 2015, p. 42). Even so, the care sages offer is limited, and they frequently have a utilitarian interest in their students, treating them as pivotal pieces in a larger game of good versus evil. As such, they are unreliable and typically show little interest in ensuring their charge's physical or emotional wellbeing. Haymitch, for example, offers guidance to Katniss in Suzanne Collins's *The Hunger Games* (2008) but seems to care little about whether or not she survives until she proves herself useful to the greater cause of overthrowing the Capitol.

There are many examples of sages in YAL, including Haymitch, The Receiver of Memory, and Anatov and Sugar Cream in Nnedi Okorafor's lesser-known *Akata Witch*. Here we highlight the wizard Dumbledore, headmaster of Hogwarts School of Witchcraft and Wizardry and mentor to Harry Potter, who provides a helpful illustration of the archetypal sage as depicted in Rowling's *Harry Potter and the Sorcerer's Stone* (1997). In the mold of a typical sage, Dumbledore is more powerful than indicated by his looks or behaviors. He is described as old in appearance with a long, white beard tucked into his belt, and he wears the robes and cloak that we have come to expect of wizards in the mold of Merlin. His ancient visage is deceptive, however, as Rowling reveals suggestive details of wisdom and power in the old man's "light, bright, and sparkling" blue eyes and long nose that looks "as though it had been broken at least twice" (1997, p. 8). He is also quirky with an odd sense of humor that appears to mask, or perhaps soften, his image as a great and powerful wizard. To a colleague fretting about the future, for example, he suddenly offers a lemon drop candy. In another instance, he stands regally to "say a few words" of welcome to the students at the start of the new school year and goes on to proclaim, "Nitwit! Blubber! Oddment! Tweak!" (1997, p. 123).

Similar to sages in other young adult texts, Dumbledore instructs Harry using more of a Socratic approach, making use of riddles or clues to enable thinking and set the stage for the eager learner to forge connections. This is evident as Harry comes across the magical Mirror of Erised and stands transfixed by what it reveals of his family history. Rather than explaining what it does, Dumbledore asks the boy if he has figured out the mirror's enchantment. Harry admits uncertainty, and the wise sage says to him, "Let me explain. The happiest man on earth would be able to use the Mirror of Erised like a normal mirror, that is, he would look into it and see himself exactly as he is. Does that help?" (1997, p. 213). Harry mulls over the riddle and then ventures, "It shows us what we want ... whatever we want ..." Dumbledore affirms the boy's hypothesis but adds that it reflects back the "deepest, most desperate desire of our hearts." He then goes on to explain how such reflections can lead the viewer to insanity as they render her heart's longings visible and seemingly tangible, making imagined futures tantalizingly real. He thus offers candid insight into a source of

*Figure 10.1. Albus Dumbledore (Richard Harris) and Harry Potter
(Daniel Radcliffe) in* Harry Potter and the Sorcerer's Stone *(2001)*

dangerous knowledge, the powerful and intimately human force of desire that can bring joy but also immense pain. In this brief exchange, Dumbledore connects Harry to a larger history by suggesting that the young wizard is only one of many hundreds of wizards who have struggled with the mirror.

The old wizard also withholds direct support for his protégé. Indeed, for such an instrumental character in Harry's story arc, Dumbledore is largely absent through much of the book. He does, however, provide the boy with intermittent support in strange ways. At one point, for example, Harry receives a cloak of invisibility from an unknown benefactor who ends up being Dumbledore, a fact he learns only after using the cloak to confront a terrible danger. Thinking over their perilous adventures, Harry's friend Ron wonders if the sage has knowingly set Harry on the path to confronting his arch nemesis, Voldemort. Appalled by the idea, Hermione exclaims, "*Well* … if he did—I mean to say—that's terrible—you could have been killed" (emphasis in original, 1997, p. 302). Harry responds to her outrage by sharing the following insight:

> He's a funny man, Dumbledore. I think he sort of wanted to give me a chance. I think he knows more or less everything that goes on here, you know. I reckon he had a pretty good idea we were going to try, and instead of stopping us, he just taught us enough to help. I don't think it was an accident he let me find out how the mirror worked. It's almost like he thought I had the right to face Voldemort if I could … (1997, p. 302)

The young wizard thus starts to see himself as beginning a dangerous journey—a journey his sagacious mentor not only condones but understands in ways that will remain a mystery to the protégé. Harry will have to trust Dumbledore, a prospect that is both comforting in the righteousness it bestows his cause but also frightening, as he won't know when or how the sage will support him in confronting the dangers ahead.

I. P. RENGA & M. A. LEWIS

THE MENTOR COACH

We now turn to the mentor coach, a common and inspiring character in young adult literature that advocates for the young protagonist by offering guidance and positive support. Mentors are distinguished from teachers in their tendency to take a vested, long-term interest in the growth and wellbeing of the individual young adults in their care (Rhodes, et al., 2006). Mentors can include extended family members, though the decline in intergenerational households means that youth are more likely to encounter mentors through other community institutions (e.g., school, church, athletics, etc.) and service organizations, such as Boys and Girls Clubs (Taylor, LoSciuto, & Porcellini, 2005). The documented benefits of mentorship are numerous, especially for youth from traditionally underprivileged backgrounds (DuBois, et al., 2002), and include decreased engagement in risky behavior, improved self-esteem, better relationships, and increasing interest in academics (Rhodes, 2009).

As a particular kind of mentor, the archetypal mentor coach is invested in the protégés' athletic talents but also in their development as human beings with lives beyond the arena. Framing an ideal coach-athlete dynamic, a number of scholars have noted how coaches are expected to be role models charged with guiding the personal development of their young protégés (cf. Banwell & Kerr, 2016; Carter & Hart, 2010; Miller, Salmela, & Kerr, 2002). Educationally speaking, they are student-centered practitioners who live what they preach and offer tools for career success and self-fulfillment. Good mentor coaches get to know their athletes' personal dreams and visions of success, show concern for their emotional wellbeing and basic psychological needs (Jowett et al., 2017), and take pains to earn their trust with clear channels of communication. Such coaches avoid unhealthy power dynamics and bossing athletes around, which can impede their reception of vital feedback for improving athlete satisfaction and performance (Kassing & Anderson, 2014). Dean Clark sees parallels between the ideal mentor coach and a professional counselor who forges close, secure relationships with clients so that their strengths can be leveraged and their potential fully developed.

Like the sage, the mentor coach is a popular character in YAL[2] and includes Junior's basketball coach in Sherman Alexie's popular novel *The Absolutely True Diary of a Part-Time Indian* (2009). Here we consider Lionel "Lion" Serbousek, the swim coach and journalism teacher who mentors the angry, aspiring triathlete Bo in Crutcher's *Ironman* (1995). It is evident early on that Lion is looking out for Bo, taking a special interest in his emotional and physical wellbeing. He shields the boy from the bullying of teammates when he can and teaches him how to use it as motivation. When a fellow swimmer, Wyrack, kisses his knuckles and says to Bo, "You're meat, Ironman," Lion whispers to his mentee, "A true Ironman would take that as a challenge" (1995, p. 41).

Exemplifying the idealized, archetypal mentor coach, Lion worries about Bo and whether or not he can really support him. To a colleague he says, "You know how some kids just get under your skin? He seems hungry for something I've got, but I

112

don't know what it is for sure" (1995, p. 54). The colleague tells him he may need to "step up" because "most kids ain't good at tellin' what they need because they don't know." He then advises paying close attention and being ready to act. Lion is unsure of his mentorship or potential value to Bo, and the possibility of falling short causes him concern. To help the young man to develop, he wants to understand him better and get a clearer read on the signals he's getting. Regardless of his progress, however, he will intervene to protect Bo if necessary.

As the story unfolds, Lion works to build a close relationship with Bo. For example, when he notices bruises on his mentee's face, Lion asks if Wryack or perhaps Bo's abusive father caused them. Bo deflects the inquiry, prompting Lion to say, "Look, Bo, I can't help you if you won't tell me what's going on" (1995, p. 70). The mentor coach bides his time and allows the relationship to grow. He encourages Bo in the classroom and in the pool. They spend time together after school, sometimes getting pizza. Lion answers the boy's more personal questions and shares emotional stories about his past in a way that models honesty and trust. The pursuit of such a relationship comes at a cost. Lion's efforts raise suspicions in the small community with Bo's father insinuating that the swim coach is gay and taking an unhealthy interest in the boy. When Lion admits to Bo that he is in fact gay, the boy stays away from his mentor coach for weeks. Bo eventually reconnects with him and apologizes. Demonstrating emotional candor and relational commitment, the coach admits that "it crushes, to have someone as special as [Bo] turn away" for something like sexuality that can't be helped, but it was worth it if the boy learned something about bigotry (1995, p. 186).

Lion works as a mentor to convey important life lessons and ideals to his protégé. When Bo encounters the notion of the *stotan* athlete (a cross between a Stoic and a Spartan) while researching his coach's athletic history, Lion describes the joy and challenges of living a Spartan lifestyle wholly devoted to rigorous training in the pursuit of greatness. Another time, Bo provides an opening to discuss his strained relationship with his father, and Lion shares that his own father sought to control him and could not abide being mocked. Rather than just commiserate over their paternal troubles, though, the coach models empathy by explaining how he had come to appreciate his father's wisdom despite its grating delivery. He advises Bo to see the complexity in any close relationship and to look past the faults and to form a stronger connection with his father. He then reminds the boy that relationships matter and divulges:

> I sit back and watch you now, and know that part of your struggle is developmental—that as an adolescent, you need to separate from your dad to establish who you are. I'm frustrated because I want *you* to learn from *my* experience, and I know that's not going to happen. But it is developmental, Bo. It's a time of life, a time of life that will change. (emphasis in original, 1995, p. 151)

With such comments, the mentor coach exposes his deep investment in Bo's future and concern for the choices he's making. He certainly wants him to succeed as a

I. P. RENGA & M. A. LEWIS

triathlete; but, as an educator, Lion appreciates that athletics is merely a means to an end, a medium through which a committed coach can connect with a young person and provide guidance and support through life's inevitable changes.

COMPARING THE SAGE AND MENTOR COACH

At first glance, the callousness of the archetypal sage would seem to make it a less attractive model for teachers than the more student-centered mentor coach. It can seem odd, and even jarring, for those in a caring profession to imagine being as distanced from their students' wellbeing as Dumbledore is from Harry. Like Hermione, they may find the sage's indifference to the boy's safety inexcusable. We suspect that teachers, especially those who also coach, are more likely to relate to Lion's heartfelt commitment to Bo and his efforts to build a trusting relationship to meet the student's needs better. This is reasonable. A century of child-centered, progressivist sensibility has arguably shaped the understanding educators have of the mentor-student relationship and perceptions of what young people require from their teachers. As the common refrain recommends, we aim to be the *guide-by-the-side* rather than the *sage-on-the-stage*.

Even so, the sage remains a compelling character type in YAL, and we think its appeal rests in part on its alluring image of the wise educator attuned to the world's bigger dilemmas and the heroic possibilities it presents for eager, idealistic young adults. Unlike the mentor coach and other student-centered ways of being a teacher, sagacious educators give students purpose and connection to something greater—mentorship that can help youth to situate seemingly mundane learning and daily drama within history's grander narratives. Dumbledore, for example, brushes aside Harry's petty grievances and invites him into an age-old battle between good and evil. This creates focus for the young initiate but also allows him to frame his education as something bigger than himself, something of vital importance to all that is good in the world. Lion likewise offers Bo some connection to history, such as when he recounts his past experiences as a high school athlete. He also encourages the boy to see how being a teenager is only a single, passing phase of life. Unlike Dumbledore, however, Lion remains preoccupied by an overriding concern for his protégé's immediate needs and does little to connect the boy's journey or its lessons to a greater social cause or purpose for existence.

Indeed, Lion's exemplar of the mentor coach underscores the archetype's focus on cultivating human relationships and promoting personal growth. It could be said that the mentor coach values relationships with students while the sage does not, but this oversimplifies things. Both Dumbledore and Lion arguably build relationships with their young charges that are one-to-one and signal a special investment in the student. Yet, those relationships are constructed around a different understanding of what students need from a mentor. In many respects, the two protagonists face similar challenges. Like Bo, Harry suffers the torment of bullies and experiences a strained relationship with his caregivers—his relatives the Dursleys—who

114

CONTRASTING THE ARCHETYPAL SAGE WITH THE MENTOR COACH

loathe him. He also gets angry and is constantly at risk of expulsion from school. Dumbledore certainly knows that Harry is suffering, though he also knows that the boy will face much worse than wicked relatives and must start hardening himself to emotional challenges. Furthermore, as Harry realizes after facing his first test against Voldemort, his mentor did not intervene because he has faith in the boy's courage and ingenuity. Dumbledore can also see that Harry is not antisocial and is developing valuable friendships; inserting himself into the boy's social and emotional life is thus unnecessary.

This is not so with Bo, whom Lion perceives to be hurting and, in the process, alienating those trying to get close to him as well as those who care for him more than he realizes, like his father. The mentor coach sees potential for greatness in Bo but only if he can repair his emotional wounds and forge stronger relationships. This requires a different kind of mentoring than what the sage offers, an educational approach that builds trust through explicit attempts to intervene and open up dialogue. This kind of personal investment arguably leaves Lion more vulnerable than Dumbledore and able to be wounded by his student. This exposure models for Bo how to discuss one's wounds and how others might be trusted to help repair them. Of course, Dumbledore can also be viewed as modeling how to handle being wounded, though the wound he shares with Harry is seemingly rare—an affliction unique to those possessing tremendous power shrouded in mystery. The great wizard seems to know from experience that harnessing such power for good necessitates learning through painful trial and error rather than through therapeutic counseling.

Examined alongside the mentor coach, the archetypal sage challenges the progressivist assumption that students always require, or even want, an adult's constant presence in their lives. This is not to say that young people's emotional states should be neglected or that interventions are never needed; rather, it affords a richer view of students as having agency and latent power—as individuals who should be trusted and can overcome challenges if given the chance. Bo is perhaps overly convinced that he can face his challenges alone, and Lion reminds him that he is never alone and needs others to be successful. Harry, by comparison, must find confidence in himself and avoid depending on others to shield him from harm. The sage and mentor coach can thus be seen as complementary archetypes with the sage tending to support the project of individuation while the mentor coach supports the project of socialization. Both are important, we argue, and the challenge for teachers is knowing which archetype to channel in a given moment for a given student.

FINAL THOUGHTS

As we demonstrate in this chapter, archetypal reflectivity informed by fiction can be useful for teacher reflection by highlighting ontological possibilities and the strengths and limitations of various instructional ideals. While the archetypal mentor coach is well suited to serve students' psychosocial needs, we believe the sage provides an appealing counterbalance to the de-humanizing forces arrayed against the profession by reminding teachers of their significance in addressing the world's big problems. Seeing teaching in this way can be empowering but also daunting. Referring to the tale of Icarus, Mayes warns teachers against pouring so much of themselves into their work that they risk burning up and burning out, causing their wings to melt in "the unforgiving sun of classroom reality" (1999, p. 13). Instead, he recommends a reflective posture that allows for growth and even retreat when necessary. Ideally, the teacher finds balance as both sage and hero, coach and protégé, thus becoming someone who accepts support from caregivers and wise others. Mayes refers to this as an archetype of cooperative learning, something evident in the efforts of actual teachers to stay open to new possibilities, learn from students, and grow into dynamic ways of being in the classroom. This might sound overly idealistic, but the struggle to achieve our ideals should not lead us to reject them entirely. To this end, fictional educators like Dumbledore, Lion, and other archetypal teachers can provide inspiration, reaffirm ideals, and reinvigorate our imagination of what it means to be a teacher.

NOTES

[1] For more on *eros* in teaching, see Renga's "Unpacking a Liturgical Framing of Desire" (2017).
[2] See also Chris Crowe's summary of the genre (1994).

REFERENCES

Alexie, Sherman. (2007). *The absolutely true diary of a part-time Indian.* New York, NY: Little, Brown and Company.

Banwell, Jenessa, & Gretchen Kerr. (2016). Coaches' perspectives on their roles in facilitating the personal development of student-athletes. *The Canadian Journal of Higher Education, 46*(1), 1–16.

Campbell, Joseph. (1949). *The hero with a thousand faces.* Princeton, NJ: Princeton University Press.

Carter, Akilah R., & Algerian Hart. (2010). Perspectives of mentoring: The Black female student-athlete. *Sport Management Review, 13*(4), 382–394.

Clark, Dean. (2016). From models to moments: Towards an appreciation of coach–athlete AURA. *AI Practitioner, 18*(2), 25–31.

Collins, Suzanne. (2008). *The hunger games.* New York, NY: Scholastic Press.

Crowe, Chris. (1994). The coach in YA literature: Mentor or Dementor. *The ALAN Review, 22*(1), 47–50.

Crutcher, Chris. (1995). *Ironman.* New York, NY: HarperCollins.

DuBois, David L., Bruce E. Holloway, Jeffrey C. Valentine, & Harris Cooper. (2002). Effectiveness of mentoring programs for youth: A meta-analytic review. *American Journal of Community Psychology, 30*(2), 157–197.

Edmundson, Mark. (2015). *Self and soul: A defense of ideals.* Cambridge, MA: Harvard University Press.

Jowett, Sophia, James W. Adie, Kimberley J. Bartholomew, Sophie X. Yang, Henrik Gustafsson, & Alicia Lopez-Jiménez. (2017). Motivational processes in the coach-athlete relationship: A multi-cultural self-determination approach. *Psychology of Sport and Exercise, 32*, 143–152.

Kassing, Jeffrey W., & Rachael L. Anderson. (2014). Contradicting coach or grumbling to teammates: Exploring dissent expression in the coach–athlete relationship. *Communication & Sport, 2*(2), 172–185.

Lowry, Lois. (1993). *The giver.* Boston, MA: Houghton Mifflin Harcourt.

Mayes, Clifford. (1999). Reflecting on the archetypes of teaching. *Teaching Education, 10*(2), 3–16.

CONTRASTING THE ARCHETYPAL SAGE WITH THE MENTOR COACH

Miller, Patricia S., John H. Salmela, & Gretchen Kerr. (2002). Coaches' perceived role in mentoring athletes. *International Journal of Sport Psychology, 33*, 410–430.

Okorafor, Nnedi. (2011). *Akata witch*. New York, NY: Viking.

Palmer, Parker J. (2003). Teaching with heart and soul: Reflections on spirituality in teacher education. *Journal of Teacher Education, 54*(5), 376–385.

Renga, Ian Parker. (2015). Exploring the heroic teacher archetype with help from the trickster. In Daniel P. Liston & Ian Parker Renga (Eds.), *Teaching, learning, and schooling in film: Reel education* (pp. 41–55). New York, NY: Routledge.

Renga, Ian Parker. (2017). Unpacking a liturgical framing of desire for the purposes of educational research. *Educational Studies, 53*(3), 263–284.

Renga, Ian Parker, & Mark Lewis. (2018). Wisdom, mystery, and dangerous knowledge: exploring depictions of the archetypal sage in young adult literature. *Study and scrutiny: Research on Young Adult Literature, 3*(1), 25–50.

Rhem, James. (2015). The teacher archetype in the movies. In Daniel P. Liston & Ian Parker Renga (Eds.), *Teaching, learning, and schooling in film: Reel education* (pp. 9–24). New York, NY: Routledge.

Rhodes, Jean E. (2009). *Stand by me: The risks and rewards of mentoring today's youth.* Cambridge, MA: Harvard University Press.

Rhodes, Jean E., Renée Spencer, Thomas E. Keller, Belle Liang, & Gil Noam. (2006) A model for the influence of mentoring relationships on youth development. *Journal of Community Psychology, 34*(6), 691–707.

Rowling, J. K. (1997). *Harry Potter and the Sorcerer's stone.* New York, NY: Scholastic.

Taylor, A., Leonard LoSciuto, & Lorraine Porcellini. (2005). Intergenerational mentoring. In David L. DuBois and Michael J. Karcher (Eds.), *Handbook of youth mentoring* (pp. 286–299). Thousand Oaks, CA: Sage Publications.

Wilson, Dominique Beth (2013). *Shaman, sage, priest, prophet and magician: Exploring the architecture of the religious wise man* (PhD dissertation). University of Sydney.

Zeichner, Kenneth M., & Daniel P. Liston. (2013). *Reflective teaching: An introduction* (2nd ed.). New York: Routledge.

ELIZABETH CURRIN AND STEPHANIE SCHROEDER

11. *SAVED BY THE BELL*ES

Gender Roles in the Quintessential Teen Comedy

ABSTRACT

Managing an impressive television feat, the classic teen sitcom *Saved by the Bell* delicately evolved over a seven-year span as its young stars grew from pubescent unknowns on *Good Morning, Miss Bliss* to fledgling adults on *Saved by the Bell: The College Years*. An extensive cultural touchstone, steeped in commentary on schools even in its title, *Saved by the Bell* offers ample representative data on American adolescents at the end of the 20th century. Here, we narrow the scope to gender and shift our gaze from students to teachers, taking a critical look at three episodes: "Summer Love," in which a heartbroken Zack seeks extracurricular counsel from Miss Bliss, who happens to be squeezing a romantic date into her busy schedule; "Student-Teacher Week," when Zack and Kelly, as principal and teacher, embody historically gendered roles; and "Kelly and the Professor," when Professor Lasky ultimately encourages the young co-ed's crush. Collectively, these episodes depict varying teacher-student relationships from junior high through post-secondary, and despite the show's trademark campiness, they illustrate the sorts of genuine dilemmas real educators face, albeit neatly resolved in thirty minutes or less.

Keywords: gender, teacher-student relationships, teacher identity, kitsch

***

The classic teen sitcom *Saved by the Bell* (1989–92) evolved over a seven-year span as its young stars grew from pubescent unknowns on *Good Morning, Miss Bliss* (Disney 1987–89) to fledgling adults on *Saved by the Bell: The College Years* (NBC 1993–94). (For everyone's sake, we will leave *Saved by the Bell: The New Class* [NBC 1993–2000] safely ensconced in the recesses of our couch-potato memories.) An extensive cultural touchstone, steeped in commentary on schools even in its hackneyed title, *Saved by the Bell* offers representative data on American adolescents in the 1990s. Robert C. Bulman has examined Hollywood's exaggerated portrayals of students and teachers, though he concedes that even amid blatant simplification, films mirror some bits of reality (2015). We see the same trends in television.

Having ourselves come of age in the *Saved by the Bell* era before launching careers as teachers and teacher educators, we recognize how such shows influence

© KONINKLIJKE BRILL NV, LEIDEN, 2019 | DOI:10.1163/9789004398092_011

the way we think about schools while at the same time bringing our educational experiences to bear on our analysis of the series. In other words, we openly acknowledge the use of "our own perceptual filters" (O'Donnell, 2007, p. 6). Though *Saved by the Bell* is a work of kitschy fiction—and a dated one, at that— we offer a critical look at three episodes: "Summer Love" in which a heartbroken Zack (Mark-Paul Gosselaar) seeks extracurricular counsel from Miss Bliss (Hayley Mills), who happens to be squeezing a romantic date into her busy schedule; "Student-Teacher Week" in which Zack and Kelly (Tiffani-Amber Thiessen), as principal and teacher, embody historically gendered roles; and, "Kelly and the Professor" when Professor Lasky (Patrick Fabian) ultimately encourages the young co-ed's crush. These episodes depict varying teacher-student relationships from junior high through college, and despite the show's trademark campiness, they illustrate the sorts of genuine dilemmas real educators face, albeit these problems are neatly resolved in half an hour.

Figure 11.1. Miss Carrie Bliss (Hayley Mills) on Good Morning, Miss Bliss *(Disney 1987–89)*

Bethonie Butler has argued that the show's original incarnation focuses more on the titular educator than her pupils. Shifting the viewers' gaze teen-ward was an undeniably lucrative decision, but we contend there is value in refocusing on the show's teachers (2016). By re-centering our perspective toward Miss Bliss, Miss Kapowski, Principal Morris, and Professor Lasky, we witness how educators' personal and professional realms often collapse when they give their lives over to their profession. Boundaries between work and home (or dorm) blur, creating and exacerbating profound tensions, conflicts that are sharply visible through a gender lens. Indeed, Madeleine R. Grumet insists that teaching, and any analysis thereof, must be positioned within the feminine, but these complex insights are obscured by the show's shiny exterior (1988). If all eyes are on Zack Morris, the series is a kitschy tale of boy meets girl and girl and girl. We encourage viewers—particularly teachers and teacher educators—to look a little closer.

SITUATING THE SITCOM

On air from 1988 to 1994, *Saved by the Bell* rose to prominence during what Dalton and Linder call a great decade for sitcoms (2019, p. 102), when Americans had a very different relationship to television, though the series has retained a cult following (France, 2014). According to Butler, true fans know the show is a remake of the Disney Channel's *Good Morning, Miss Bliss* (2016). As the comedy morphed and migrated to NBC, *Saved by the Bell* incorporated then-president Brandon Tartikoff's memories of his own teachers, maintaining a decidedly conventional structure (Dalton & Linder, 2019, p. 106). Nat Berman explains how *Saved by the Bell* "was the squeaky clean, utterly hokey, diamond in the rough of an episodic comedy about the ins and outs of high school life," characteristics underscored by its airtime among Saturday morning cartoons (2016). The advent of *The College Years* marked the show's move to primetime where writers began addressing important issues with a light touch according to star Mark-Paul Gosselaar (Mendoza, 1993). As Dalton and Linder note, despite the higher education backdrop, storylines tend to center on the personal lives of students (2019, p. 106).

Like other situation comedies, *Saved by the Bell* certainly provided viewers with a satisfying escape, each episode culminating in "some sentimental reconciliation, a lesson learned, or moral growth" (O'Donnell, 2007, p. 100). Rather than viewing such shows as mere entertainment, however, Marie-Claire Simonetti (1994), Naomi R. Rockler (1999), and other scholars point to the vital role television plays in the transmission of ideology and the social conditioning of youth. For instance, E. Graham McKinley's study of *Beverly Hills, 90210* (Fox 1990–2000)—*Saved by the Bell*'s more dramatic ratings rival—claims the show sought to make its mark by taking young viewers seriously (1997, p. 15). Even without the kitsch of its counterpart, however, *Beverly Hills, 90210* and viewers' responses to it led McKinley to believe "We all delightedly participate in our own enculturation" (1997, p. 241), namely by embracing consumerism, capitalism, and patriarchy. We suspect this is especially true for seemingly innocuous sitcoms like *Saved by the Bell*, given Berman's apt conclusion that "It was cheesy, […] but audiences absolutely ate it up" (2016) Thus, we attempt here to look beyond *Saved by the Bell*'s kitschy common sense with the help of literature related to schools on screen as well as an understanding of gender's historical role in education.

SCHOOLS ON SCREEN

Hollywood's tales of teachers have prompted accusations of oversimplification (Beatty, 2017; Butler, 2016) as well as gross exaggeration (Bodenner, 2017). Not only do these skewed portrayals pose harm for teachers, but we also worry these one-dimensional stories exacerbate misconceptions among the greater public. Dalton and Linder thus urge viewers to evaluate patterns of representations of teachers for the ideological underpinnings that many people tacitly accept without critical attention (2019, p. 2). *Saved by the Bell* offers myriad opportunities, three of which we tackle below.

E. CURRIN & S. SCHROEDER

Bulman's work with full-length feature films is especially useful for our analysis of *Saved by the Bell*. He notes the normalcy of on-screen teachers and students from the middle class, easily understood and seen as "rational, and sensible individuals" (2015, p. 137). Furthermore, he characterizes high school movies as privileging a masculine perspective (2015, p. 27). Though *Saved by the Bell* was small-screen fare, the series essentially operates as the *Zack Morris Show*, reinforced by the character's introductory voice-overs and frequent breaking of the fourth wall. Despite the central focus on Zack, who, along with Slater (Mario Lopez), frequently objectifies women, the show is careful to include alternative perspectives, perhaps as a means to call into question gender norms. Jessie (Elizabeth Berkley), for example, a liberal feminist who is known to call her male friends out on their sexism, offers a counterpoint or balance to their extant misogyny although at times her characterization could be considered patronizing or neurotic. We the viewers are left to unpack the nuance that is made more apparent when viewed against the history of gender in schools.

GENDER IN SCHOOLS

By reducing complexities to sitcom-worthy bites like other on-screen depictions of schools, *Saved by the Bell*, maintains the hierarchical nature of schools, in which women are teachers and men are administrators (Blount, 2005). This practice began in the Common School era when the "feminization of teaching" catalyzed the spread of free public education by relying on "a class of persons too weak to insist on professional honor and impose academic standards" (Sugg, 1978, p. 109). Compounding this condescension, America's earliest schoolmarms embraced self-sacrifice in order to cast schools as sites of moral superiority (Grumet, 1988). To achieve this aim, Grumet argues women had to traverse the "passage between the so-called public and private worlds," teaching children to do the same (1988, p. xv). Lessons thus explicitly and implicitly reinforced gender roles, to the point of "unexamined cliché" (Sugg, 1978, p. 235). Teaching effectively became "an almost pastoral calling for unmarried women," which permeates portrayals of teachers on TV even today (Bodenner, 2017). Women still comprise a majority of teachers, often under the watchful supervision of male principals (Grumet, 1988). When schools on screen reflect these societal structures, critical viewers must identify and interrogate them.

CUTTING THROUGH THE KITSCH

Looking critically at *Saved by the Bell* requires viewers to cut through the kitsch, peeling back the show's campy layers to expose implicit social commentary. In a groundbreaking 1964 essay, Susan Sontag cited "artifice and exaggeration" as the means by which camp "converts the serious into the frivolous." This process, she argues, is depoliticizing, rendering the campy product void of substance and antithetical to tragedy (1964, p. 515). Similarly, kitsch derives its aesthetic with

SAVED BY THE BELLES

the help of "exaggerated sentimentality, banality, superficiality, and triteness" (Botz-Bornstein 306). Functioning as "a kind of perverse idealism" rife with "pseudoappearances" (Wirth, 2015 p. 125), kitsch helps explain why viewers retrospectively regard *Saved by the Bell* with borderline disdain, particularly owing to the show's broad-brush characters (Berman). Prone to "pre-digested formulas for interpreting reality" (McBride, 2005, p. 282), however, kitsch enjoys wide commercial appeal, and camp's ability to unite high and low culture endures even in the current television landscape (Bausells, 2016; Merkin, 2006). While we see kitsch and camp as inherently related, Andrew Ross, like Sontag, distinguishes between the two concepts, arguing that kitsch embodies middle-class aspirations while camp traffics in highbrow tropes. In other words, kitsch and camp persevere, in part, by winking to a rather wide audience.

Though popular sitcoms like *Saved by the Bell* can and do dabble in seriousness, they often make light of problems by virtue of their brevity (Berman, 2016). Dalton and Linder thus fault the "very special episode" approach for ignoring the systemic nature of social problems (2019, p. 153). Indeed, such episodes attract far more lampooning than lauding. One critic, for example, notes how in squeaky-clean *Saved by the Bell*, "all drugs are equal to injecting heroin into a baby" (Morrill, 2016). Teen dramas, by contrast, garner praise for their ability to "deal unflinchingly" with "a litany of social issues" (Simonetti, 1994). Nevertheless, both genres have been guilty of promoting normative gender roles, yet a critical viewer can right that wrong.

Proudly departing from Sontag, Bruce LaBruce views camp as more than capable of being "political, subversive, even revolutionary" (2014, p. 10). Likewise, Thorsten Botz-Bornstein suggests that kitsch cannot entirely obscure reality (2015). We draw on both constructs in our analysis of *Saved by the Bell* below, proposing that depictions of schools on screen are particularly vulnerable to cliché and therefore particularly ripe for critical reflection. Focusing on Zack Morris as protagonist amounts to playing into the show's kitschy hand. Rather, we aim to shift the viewers' attention to other characters and concerns lurking beneath the shiny surfaces of three episodes.

RECENTERING THE SERIES

With this acknowledgement of the kitschy/campy nature of the television series, we have selected three samples of the show from throughout its run to highlight real dilemmas playing out on the screen. As absurd as the situational comedy gets, each episode swirls around an issue relevant beyond the fictional halls of Bayside or generic California University but visible only when we recenter our focus away from the White, male protagonist and put another character's perspective at the center of our focus. Even as the episodes are filtered through Zack's experience—especially when he addresses the audience directly—we must challenge ourselves to see beyond his worldview and critique his perceptions. Here, we place the teacher at the center in order to highlight the distractions that appear in the classroom and the personal drama that seeps into the school. Centering the teacher exposes the collapse of the

123

E, CURRIN & S. SCHROEDER

personal and professional, the simultaneous experience of being student, teacher, lover, and friend. We ultimately suggest that *Saved by the Bell*, despite its campy nature, highlights the deeply moral roots of teaching, particularly as we observe teachers having both personal and professional lives, and we are careful to note the feminization of this experience.

"SUMMER LOVE"

The earliest *Saved by the Bell* episodes, originally appearing as installments of *Good Morning, Miss Bliss*, feature a slightly different cast. Major characters of the later series, Slater, Kelly, and Jessie, have yet to appear, even though the plots in the installments are similar to those of the *Saved by the Bell* series. Zack has a crisis, and the school-based adults help him find resolution while teaching a valuable lesson in the process. Beneath this surface, viewers see the collapse of the personal and professional in the very first episode, "Summer Love." Zack is not the only one with a problem in this episode, and the entangling of teacher and student dilemmas is ultimately where Zack—along with viewers—learns his lessons.

"Summer Love" begins with a voiceover from Miss Bliss. As students and teachers mingle in the hallways, she explains, "There's nothing quite like the first day of school, fresh faces, new clothes, and summer memories. No one is quite ready to give up those memories and get back to the classroom—*especially* the teachers." Indeed, both Miss Bliss and Zack have each found romance on vacation and now must navigate the pitfalls of dating during the school year. Zack admits to his friends that he has met Karen (Carla Gugino), an older girl at camp. He lied about his age, an innocent misstep until she transfers to Zack's school and his lies spin out of control. Karen dumps him: "Get off it, Zack. You're in the 8th grade, aren't you? Give me a break, you must think I'm an idiot." Meanwhile, Miss Bliss has scheduled a date for a school night. The only problem is that Principal Belding (Dennis Haskins) wants her to attend a PTA meeting in his place so he can go on a date with his wife. She refuses, but he begs her throughout the episode to change her plans. Miss Bliss stands firm that she will protect her personal time.

The resolution comes at Miss Bliss's house when Zack shows up unexpectedly to seek advice during her date with a doctor, Brian (Barry Jenner). Lying to her own date by referring to Zack as the paperboy, Miss Bliss faces a dilemma: tell Brian the truth and reveal the extent to which her professional life intrudes on her personal life or keep up the front. She comes clean, and he reveals that he must leave the date because he has been called into work at the hospital. Brian tells Miss Bliss that Zack has a great teacher. She smiles and turns back toward the kitchen where she and Zack share apple pie and realize they are both feeling much better.

While Miss Bliss is the protagonist in this and other early episodes, it is clear that the focus of her attention is on Zack, her student and professional responsibility. Miss Bliss centers Zack, thereby urging the viewer to do so as well. Zoom out a bit and recentering Miss Bliss, viewers see how her professional life envelops her

SAVED BY THE BELLES

personal life, even as she tries to protect the personal. For example, Miss Bliss, while retrieving documents from the school office, tries her hardest to keep her social life from Mr. Belding, who crosses a line by first referring to her as Miss Bliss and then, more personally, as Carrie. Cornered and prodded in the school office and later at her desk, she is ultimately forced to reveal her personal plans. After school, Tina (Joan Ryan), the music and arts teacher, races through the front door. Again, the professional world intrudes on the personal, as Miss Bliss cannot seem to shake her day job even as she transitions into her date night persona, "Carrie." At dinner with Brian, viewers once again see Carrie's inability to escape her professional responsibilities. Brian invites her to dinner for the following week for Cajun food, but a dinner hour faculty meeting would prevent her from attending. Miss Bliss goes into the kitchen for coffee and dessert when Zack appears at the door needing her wise counsel regarding his own dating life. Each of these events showcases the collapse of the personal and professional worlds of the teacher, albeit a bit unrealistically. Do students really just show up at their teachers' homes?

Grumet explains that these encroachments on a teacher's personal life have been a feature of schools for quite some time, particularly as teachers' personal and sexual lives have been ignored or erased by the males overseeing them (1988). The familiar trope of fatherly administrator to daughterly teacher viewers see in *Saved by the Bell* works "to deny [a teacher's] eroticism and extend her infantilization" (1988, p. 53). Historically, encroachments on teachers' personal lives could not be seen as imposing or improper because teachers were not afforded personal lives for their professional lives to encroach upon in the first place.

We see this in "Summer Love" when Miss Bliss ultimately expresses to Brian, "When the bell rings for the start of the school year, my life is not my own anymore." The dilemma, it appears, is not so much that the professional invades the personal, as Miss Bliss *makes* her professional world personal. The dilemma she faces is the decision to reveal to others just how much she has given of herself to her work. To her, the moral lessons of teaching go beyond an academic setting (which is good because we see no academic instruction in the episode), as she teaches her students lessons about personal responsibility and the importance of telling the truth. Indeed, these lessons occur outside of the classroom: in the kitchen, in the cafeteria, and in the hallways. Zack literally seeks out guidance in the places where Miss Bliss lives, eats, and takes professional breaks, showcasing that the professional lives of teachers are often intertwined with the personal lives of both teachers and students and in a manner that does not necessarily resolve itself in thirty minutes or less.

"STUDENT-TEACHER WEEK"

As the series continues and the setting inexplicably shifts from Indiana to California, new characters appear, and Zack becomes protagonist and part-time narrator. These episodes at Bayside High School comprise the core of the *Saved by the Bell* canon. "Student-Teacher Week," in which Bayside students switch roles with the teachers and principal, also showcases the collapse of the personal and professional in education and in so doing emphasizes the moral nature of such work. The *Saved by the Bell* gang is decidedly older in this episode and, as a result, given more responsibility. It is also the week leading up to the "big game against Valley," which sets the stage for comedic drama to ensue. Kelly, chosen to replace Mr. McGee as history teacher, and Zack, chosen to replace Mr. Belding as principal, grapple with a moral dilemma.

Figure 11.2. Kelly as "Miss Kapowski" (Tiffani-Amber Thiessen), Zack as "Principal Morris" (Mark-Paul Gosselaar), and Slater (Mario Lopez) on Good Morning, Miss Bliss *(Disney 1987–89)*

In her assumed role as the history teacher "Miss Kapowski," Kelly must give her class a test. Slater, ostensibly concerned about the lack of time he and the other football players will have to study, heads to "Principal Morris" (who is eating popcorn, playing basketball, and calling "hot" girls to his office) to complain. In his assumed role as "Principal Morris," Zack tells Slater he will handle the problem. Slater leaves, appreciative: "Thanks, pal. It's good to know low people in high places." "Principal Morris" then calls "Miss Kapowski" to his office to explain his new "no test policy," all in service of making learning "fun." Kelly, pleased that Zack is taking his job as principal seriously, agrees, but after sharing the news with Jessie, "Miss Kapowski" realizes "Principal Morris" is just trying to help Slater and the football team and actually has no moral stake in the "no test policy." She tells the players that the test is back on, much to their chagrin.

On the day of the test, the football players fail to show up, encouraging the rest of the class to leave. "Miss Kapowski" is left alone in the classroom feeling like a failure when Mr. Belding shows up to offer some advice, claiming, "A good teacher can always find a way to get through to anyone." In the next scene, "Miss Kapowski" and Slater head to Principal Morris's office in the throes of an argument. "Principal Morris" tells her she is on probation for violating his "no test policy," and Slater adds, "You're taking this teaching thing way too seriously." Kelly exposes Zack's questionable ethics, confessing, "I bet a lot on you. As a boyfriend and as a friend and now as a principal. I always thought you were special. I guess I lost that bet." "Principal Morris," finding his moral compass, helps the friends concoct a compromise, and "Miss Kapowski" hastily gives the test to the football players so the episode can end on a campy note with a Bayside victory—never mind any consequences for the non-athletes.

While this episode is arguably meant to teach Zack a lesson about responsibility and the important role of the principal in handling school-wide problems, viewers can also shift the focus to see more clearly how gender might operate in everyday classrooms. "Principal Morris" and Slater enact a common "good old boy" narrative, one that combines entrenched systems of gendered power and a love of sports and brute masculinity. In this narrative, men unite to silence female teachers and reinforce the status quo (Datnow, 1997). As historians of education have pointed out, gendered features and normative functions are not new phenomena in school hierarchies (Blount, 2005). Thus, we not only see stark contrasts between students and teachers in this episode, but we see clear contrasts between genders. Zack and Slater, united around a masculine love of sports, combine forces to marginalize Kelly in her role as a teacher. As students "ditch" her class in protest, Zack sits idly by in his office either flirting with cute girls, ordering pizzas on Mr. Belding's account, or playing imaginary basketball. Zack acts irresponsibly in the face of power and ultimately saves the day while Kelly acts responsibly, performs her duties as instructed, and must be saved by Zack—although, arguably, it is her morality that ultimately changes his mind.

In this episode, viewers see Kelly internalize her role as a teacher by taking the position seriously and acknowledging her moral obligation to meet the demands of the classroom. She explains early in the episode that she has "been thinking about teaching a lot lately. Teachers help people. They can make a difference." She wants to "do well" and continues throughout the episode to take the job seriously. On the other hand, Zack is woefully underprepared to be principal and needs Kelly to teach him the requisite moral lessons. By calling on both their professional and personal relationship—reminding him of his roles as her boyfriend, friend, and principal—she convinces him to find a compromise. Zack learns his lessons and manages to make everyone happy only when he finds the moral compass that Kelly has possessed all along, thus highlighting the collapse of the personal and professional, as well as the moral sensibilities of teachers.

"KELLY AND THE PROFESSOR"

When Zack and friends graduate from Bayside and conveniently enroll in California University, sans Jessie and Lisa (Lark Voorhies), they also graduate to a new theme song that proudly proclaims, "I'm standing at the edge of tomorrow, and it's all up to me how far I go." This individualistic anthem further promotes a Zack-centric storyline, even in an episode entitled "Kelly and the Professor." The second of a two-part narrative arc, it begins with Zack's recollection of a scene with Kelly, when, copping to his kitsch, he had said, "I was kinda hoping you might want to … well, as corny as this may sound, go steady?" The answer, of course, is no, for as the title indicates, Kelly is in love—or squeaky-clean sitcom lust—with her professor. As the episode proceeds, he and Kelly discuss the "delicate situation" of the affair. Though Kelly finds "Jeremiah" to be "a mature man," Zack maintains "He's ancient." Primed to focus on these two student perspectives, viewers lack a sense of how the professor feels.

Kelly's subsequent visit to the Professor's office provides some insight. The professor's forced ease betrays his underlying discomfort: "You're my student. I'm your teacher. This is my office. No reason in the world that we should feel uncomfortable." Struggling with the merger of personal and professional, Professor Lasky is unsure how to handle the situation. Kelly enthusiastically announces she has removed the obstacle to their relationship: she dropped his class. He then drops his coffee cup and succumbs to her embrace. Centering the teacher in this episode, viewers should contemplate the dizzying experience of being called "Jeremiah" by one student and "Lasky" by Zack, who confronts the professor, passive-aggressively threatening to write a term paper on "the mating rituals of teachers and students."

Arguably, it is the mating rituals of students themselves that generally preoccupies the show. True to that norm, this episode devotes a great deal of time to various kitschy subplots involving the secondary characters, but Lasky's appearance in the dorm—reinforcing the entanglement of personal and professional spheres—provides another opportunity to recenter when Zack asks, "What are you trying to prove? [...] You just don't seem very comfortable about it. Slinking around school together, huddling in corners ...." Though Professor Lasky claims to be "perfectly fine" with the affair, Zack has effectively charged his teacher with violating an unspoken moral code, viewing the professor's apparent discomfort as symptomatic of that breach. Though we might view this merely as the jealous Zack staking his claim on Kelly, we would do better to consider how, in the grand scheme of the *Saved by the Bell* universe, Zack is operating from prior conceptions of what teachers should be and do. Whether or not the professor is "trying to prove" anything, he is, by virtue of his trade, teaching around the clock. Ironically, since Zack has been saved time and again saved by the belles, this time he helps Professor Lasky learn a lesson.

The episode delves into campier territory before Kelly and the professor are no more. Highlighting their age difference, and perhaps reflecting on professional ethics, he shamefully confesses, "You're a terrific girl, but this is not going to work out. I thought I could handle it, but I can't." The collapse of the personal and professional proves too much for the professor to bear. Characteristic of *The College Years*, the plot revels in soap opera theatrics, culminating in a near-rekindling of the Zack-Kelly romance to entice fans to tune in for the next episode.

Patrick Fabian stayed on as Professor Lasky throughout the show's lone season. In fact, in the particularly slapstick episode "Bedside Manner," he plays romantic rival to Zack again, the prospect of a teacher-student relationship evidently still titillating to viewers, albeit lacking deep consideration in the scholarly literature. Tara S. Johnson cites a dearth of research on "sexual dynamics in the classroom"

SAVED BY THE BELLES

as justification for her interest in understanding how "embodiment, desire, and sexuality" function in education (2008, p. 213). We deem it no accident that a teacher-student affair never appeared in the show's earlier seasons, nor that when such a plot finally became palatable to writers and viewers, it was a male professor and a female undergrad. *Saved by the Bell* may handle the topic with its characteristic kitsch, but at least it addresses the topic at all. In so doing, the show provides viewers with an opportunity to consider a very real and very serious issue.

LOOKING ACROSS THE SERIES: LESSONS LEARNED

Though *Saved by the Bell* conforms to Bulman's analysis of suburban school films in that "the school is central to the plot, but primarily as a social space" (2015, p. 75), we readily follow Mark T. Kissling's advice to view curriculum as "personal, storied, and lived" (2012, p. 15). The show's teenage hijinks and hang-ups necessarily intersect with the experiences of on-screen teachers and students, which bear critical semblance to reality. From middle school through higher education, *Saved by the Bell*'s teachers struggle to reconcile their personal and professional lives. The struggle falls most often to women, but *Saved by the Bell: The College Years* also complicates this gender dynamic. From "Summer Love" to "Student-Teacher Week" to "Kelly and the Professor," the series comes full circle to reveal: a guilty and pestered Miss Bliss who must divulge personal details to her principal and professional details to her boyfriend; Kelly and Zack operating at once as teacher/principal, friend, and girlfriend/boyfriend; and, Professor Lasky conspicuously attending a students' party with an undergrad on his arm. In each episode, a teacher must reconcile what would perhaps ideally be considered mutually exclusive spheres of life.

Yet, one wonders if this is truly ideal. Schools on screen—and schools in real life—should reflect reality. As John Dewey has reminded us, the school has a powerful place in advancing social progress, a vision best grounded in reality (1959), or, in Kissling's words, "the social contours of students' lives in the present and not solely in the future" (2012, p. 13). If we agree with this assessment, teachers and students alike should not set aside their personal lives to be merely professional or academic. Honoring William Ayers's vision of "a seamless web between teaching and being, between teacher and person" requires that the personal lives of teachers and students be interwoven into the fabric of schools (1989, p. 130).

Consequently, we view the collapse of identity in these episodes as educative, as the students become teachers themselves in both formal and informal ways. Zack causes Miss Bliss to confess her lie to Brian, student Belding prompts teacher Kapowski's thinking, and Zack gives Professor Lasky a much-needed reality check. If teachers and students bring to the classroom their full humanity, as they often do in *Saved by the Bell*, we as viewers see the school as a site for learning and growing as people beyond the roles of teachers and students. Through this narrative twist, we also see Dewey's progressive ideal, whereby "the authority figures—the teachers—do not possess all of the knowledge and the power" (Dalton & Linder, 2019, p. 12).

129

E, CURRIN & S. SCHROEDER

Saved by the Bell teaches us that all of us in a school have something to offer, and if we collapse our identities—student, teacher, personal, professional, lover, friend, colleague—we, too, might ultimately be saved by the bell.

CONCLUSION

Challenging Botz-Bornstein's belief that kitsch's silliness automatically precludes any substance (2015), as well as Berman's assertion that *Saved by the Bell* serves merely as a reminder of a "less sophisticated" time (2016), we choose to view the show as a product of its era with profound implications for ours, cognizant of the strong but subtle ideological power of popular culture in any decade. Having taken a critical look at *Saved by the Bell* from our vantage as 21st century teachers and teacher educators, we maintain the show provides opportunities to contemplate and complicate real issues facing the nation's teachers and students.

Though television's teachers have been plagued by saccharine stereotypes, Dalton and Linder welcome the current century's willingness to "blur the line between the public and private spheres" (2019, p. 213). As education continues to provide fodder for entertainment, we, too, hope to see teachers—both real and imagined—striving "to bridge the gap that divides the public from the private in our culture and in our consciousness," a process that requires us to reimagine schools as the site of mediation between those separate spheres (Grumet, 1988, p. 33). A kitschy comedy like *Saved by the Bell*, easily passed off as mindless or trivial, may not always achieve that aim, yet the show reminds us that our lives, both public and private, are lived in schools.

REFERENCES

Ayers, William. (1989). *The good preschool teacher: Six teachers reflect on their lives.* New York, NY: Teachers College Press.

Bausells, Marta. (2015, December 14). Slaughterhouse 90210: Where literature meets pop culture. *The Guardian.*

Beatty, Anne. (2017, May 30). Hollywood's reductive narratives about school. *The Atlantic.*

Berman, Nat. (2016, December 13). Why there will never be a show like *Saved by the Bell* again. *TV over Mind.*

Blount, Jackie M. (2005). *Fit to teach: Same-sex desire, gender, and school work in the twentieth century.* Albany, NY: SUNY Press.

Bodenner, Chris. (2017, January 23) Some lessons on teaching. *The Atlantic.*

Botz-Bornstein, Thorsten. (2015). Kitsch and Bullshit. *Philosophy and Literature, 39*(2), 305–321.

Bulman, Robert C. (2015). *Hollywood goes to high school: Cinema, schools, and American culture.* New York, NY: Worth Publishers.

Butler, Bethonie. (2016, July 16). Does television have a teacher problem? *Washington Post.*

Dalton, Mary M., & Laura R. Linder. (2019). *Teacher TV: Seventy years of teachers on television.* New York, NY: Peter Lang.

Datnow, Amanda. (1997). Using gender to preserve tracking's status hierarchy: The defensive strategy of entrenched teachers. *Anthropology & Education Quarterly, 28*(2), 204–228.

Dewey, John. (1959). My pedagogic creed. In Martin S. Dworkin (Ed.), *Dewey on education: Selections* (pp. 19–32). New York, NY: Teachers College Press.

France, Lisa Respers. (2014). Happy 25th Anniversary, 'Saved by the Bell.' *CNN Wire*.

Grumet, Madeleine R. (1988). *Bitter milk: Women and teaching*. Amherst, MA: University of Massachusetts Press.

Johnson, Tara S. (2008). Qualitative research in question: A narrative of disciplinary power with/in the IRB. *Qualitative Inquiry, 14*(2), 212–232.

Kissling, Mark T. (2012). *Teaching where (and who) we are: Emplacing curriculum through stories of living* (PhD dissertation). Michigan State University, Michigan.

LaBruce, Bruce. (2014). Notes on camp and anti-camp. *The Gay & Lesbian Review Worldwide, 21*(2).

McBride, Patrizia. (2005). The value of kitsch: Hermann Broch and Robert Musil on art and morality. *Studies in Twentieth and Twenty-First Century Literature, 29*(2), 201.

McKinley, E. Graham. (1997). *Beverly hills, 90210: Television, gender, and identity*. Philadelphia, PA: University of Pennsylvania Press.

Mendoza, N. F. (1993, September 26). On View: Freshmen, Again: Can 'Saved by the Bell' and 'Beverly Hills, 90210' Pass the Test as they Head off to College? *Los Angeles Times*.

Merkin, Daphne. (2006). *Against lip gloss, or new notes on camp*. New York, NY: New York Times Company.

Morrill, Jenny. (2016). *Saved by the bell: Life lessons from its special episodes*. London: Dennis Publishing Ltd.

O'Donnell, Victoria. (2007). *Television criticism*. Los Angeles, CA: Sage Publications.

Rockler, Naomi R. (1999). From magic bullets to shooting blanks: Reality, criticism, and Beverly Hills, 90210. *Western Journal of Communication, 63*, 72–94.

Ross, Andrew. (1988). Uses of camp. *The Yale Journal of Criticism, 2*(1), 1.

Simonetti, Marie-Claire. (1994). Teenage truths and tribulations across cultures: Degrassi junior high and Beverly Hills, 90210. *Journal of Popular Film and Television, 22*(1), 38.

Sontag, Susan. (1964). Notes on 'Camp.' *Partisan Review, 31*(4), 515–530.

Sugg, Redding S. (1978). *Motherteacher: The feminization of American education*. Charlottesville, VA: University Press of Virginia.

Wirth, Jason. (2015). *Commiserating with devastated things: Milan Kundera and the entitlements of thinking*. New York, NY: Fordham University Press.

CHAD E. HARRIS

12. "GOOD" TEACHER ON HER OWN TERMS

Miss Shaw in ABC's The Wonder Years

ABSTRACT

The term "good teacher" has as many definitions as there are people who experience life as a student—or who watch television to compare their real-life teachers to those they see onscreen. In her work on teachers on film and on television, Mary M. Dalton labels the "Good Teacher" as one who very much resembles recurring attitudes about what makes a teacher "good," but—in Hollywood as in life—such teachers often fulfill stereotypes not unlike the cowboy outsiders who save the day in Westerns. When they do achieve what looks like a substantive impact on students, they often do so in reductive plotlines that make conflict and achievement of their teaching goals too unrealistic to represent real teachers. However, Dalton's model provides endless possibilities to study different combinations of Good Teacher qualities and formulate new interpretations of such an important category. In this essay, I take up the ABC series *The Wonder Years* (1988–93) and Miss Shaw, the favorite teacher of Kevin Arnold—the prototypical American teen with an ambivalent-yet-insightful attitude toward school—and argue for her importance as a Good Teacher on television because of, rather than in spite of, her decision to quit her job on her own terms. Even in leaving her post, she embodies more of what it means to be a Good Teacher than do most teachers deemed "good" and thus memorable for the lessons they teach.

Keywords: Good Teacher, television, The Hollywood Model, episodic television, teachers on television

***

In *Teacher TV: Seventy Years of Teachers on Television*, Dalton and Linder apply The Hollywood Model of the good teacher to television, highlighting TV teacher characters that stand up to authority, personalize the curriculum, implement the "progressive idea of reciprocal education," develop personal relationships with students, and battle administrators who take issue with the very qualities that make Good Teachers good teachers (2019, pp. 9–12). Frequently, they are outsiders from other professions, and generally speaking, they decide to stay put, often sacrificing a more lucrative salary in the process (2019, pp. 10–11; Dalton, 2017, pp. 26, 39). They set up a personalized curriculum in order both to empower and to learn from students.

© KONINKLIJKE BRILL NV, LEIDEN, 2019 | DOI:10.1163/9789004398092_012

C. E. HARRIS

This dynamic results in student-teacher relationships that transcend academics and create opportunities for plotlines outside the classroom that are structured to engage viewers. But, perhaps most importantly, these narratives create teacher heroes in line with endearing Hollywood figures whom viewers celebrate for their courage to question authority and espouse individualism and self-reliance, values prized in America (Dalton & Linder, 2019, p. 10).

As a former high school English teacher who now studies education on the doctoral level, I am always intrigued, sometimes pleased, and often frustrated by the use of the word "good" to describe teachers. The word has been used for *and* against me, so studying the underlying motives behind its use is what attracts me to the concept of the Good Teacher both on a personal level and in my scholarly research on the influence screen representations of teachers have on the reputation of teachers in American culture. Here, I examine these complexities as seen on a television show I adored as a child when it originally aired and that I re-watched as an adult in the thick of life as a high school teacher. Not unexpectedly, the teacher characters have affected me profoundly in new ways.

Because episodic television and film are different in terms of narrative structure, there are differences in how television fulfills The Hollywood Model (Dalton, 2017, pp. 10, 11), and some Good Teachers belonging to a category that Dalton and Linder see emerging on television in the 1990s may not fit the archetypal image (2019, pp. 127–128). Nevertheless, one commonality remains: stories of teachers regularly crossing professional boundaries to sacrifice their personal time and space for students. Few depictions of junior and senior high school deal with these contradictory messages as memorably and realistically as *The Wonder Years* (ABC 1988–93). In voiceover, Kevin Arnold narrates every episode from his perspective as an adult 20 years later, remarking on his life and growth from pre-teen in 1968 to high school junior in 1973. Due to their complexity, Kevin's sophisticated insight concerning his brief relationship with one of his English teachers is a shining example of his development as a character, and the teacher herself is one of the best examples of a multi-valent educator character on television because she does not fit an archetypal image.

At the beginning of the episode "Kodachrome," in the fifth season of *The Wonder Years*, Kevin Arnold (Fred Savage) says about his tenth-grade English teacher Miss Shaw (Lanei Chapman), "Of all the teachers I ever had, I only ever had one who was—a natural." Yet, by the end of the episode, he seems to have a different view: "I guess in the end Miss Shaw did what was best for her. ... The only thing is— she didn't do what was best for us." At the episode's conclusion, Miss Shaw quits her job. She is not fired. She does not get married and move away or leave for another career that is her true passion. She leaves because, in her words, "I'm a teacher, but they [the administrators] don't want me to teach—not the way I can. So I won't." Nevertheless, it is this refusal that makes her stand out in Kevin's life and, consequently, in the landscape of teachers on television.

At least two-dozen actors have speaking roles as teachers during the six seasons of *The Wonder Years*. None are series regulars; they are guest stars or, at most, recurring

134

Figure 12.1. Miss Shaw (Lanei Chapman) and Kevin Arnold (Fred Savage) on
The Wonder Years *(ABC 1988–93)*

characters, appearing according to Kevin's memory. One of the most effective aspects of *The Wonder Years* is how Kevin recounts his relationships with his teachers. As a series, *The Wonder Years* provides us with two layers of character development—Kevin the 12-year-old kid to Kevin the 17-year-old eleventh grader *and* Kevin in the present day, nostalgically retracing the steps he made two decades before through narration. "Kodachrome" deals exclusively with Miss Shaw, providing her only appearance on the series, and resembles a film in narrative structure in that there is no time allotted across an entire season or even several episodes to develop her character further (Dalton and Linder 7). The narrative structure and the seemingly contradictory choice Miss Shaw makes give this episode a unique status among television episodes involving a teacher character. Miss Shaw is a Good Teacher in every aspect of Dalton's framework, but in the end, she puts herself first. While the narrative is limited to Kevin's perspective, "Kodachrome" does show us that Miss Shaw's influence on the other students provides more than they will experience with other teachers.

Carol Black and Neal Marlens, creators of *The Wonder Years*, give us a view of schools and teachers during the late 1960s and early 1970s and communicate directly and indirectly how teachers in real life related to their surroundings as well as how students, while coping with the challenges of being young, related to their teachers. The interplay between what happens in televised life and in real life is important and not entirely discrete. John Fiske writes, "[a]ll popular texts have leaky boundaries; they flow into each other, they flow into everyday life (1989, p. 126). Thus, the perspectives of teachers and students in *The Wonder Years* both reflect and inform us—those who came of age during the time the show is set *and* those who, like me, grew up during the time the show aired. Seeing the period drama each week planted feelings of nostalgia in me that I could not fully understand until twenty years later. Wonder should mature into insight, and we see this in *The Wonder Years*, particularly when it comes to the Good Teacher in "Kodachrome." When Miss Shaw enters Kevin's life and then shortly after walks away from him, she leaves him reflecting on teaching and learning in ways he, the epitome of the "average" teenager, had not before. Kevin's teenage/adult perspectives and Miss Shaw's loyalty (to herself, her students, and her teaching philosophy) make "Kodachrome" an important episode depicting a Good Teacher fulfilling the role on her own terms. There is more than one way to be a Good Teacher, and Miss Shaw's brand is a vital cultural representation.

"Kodachrome" begins with The Narrator (Daniel Stern) giving an overview of his high school teachers, categorizing them by their personalities and teaching styles: "It seemed like my high school teachers came in every conceivable shape, size, and style. There were the hopelessly confused ... the terminally repetitious ... the insufferably boring. ... But of all the teachers I ever had, I only ever had one who was ... [at this point, the tone drastically shifts as we see Miss Shaw's classroom. She is reading *Heart of Darkness* aloud while her students have their eyes closed] a natural." This is the positive break in the mundanity of the school routine, and a teacher is responsible for it. In the midst of social cliques and clubs and sports teams and dances, these teachers remind students of the importance of education. Miss Shaw calls on Kevin to ask him what he thinks Joseph Conrad means by his words, "The horror!" After she continually prompts him with the word "and," he reaches a great answer. She praises him. Her encouraging style of teaching has made the epitome of the average teenager seem like a top student. Miss Shaw's status as a Good Teacher does not stop here. Even though she has a well-developed plan and a rationale for her methods complete with projected outcomes that would prove them effective, she turns out to be too unorthodox for the William McKinley High School of 1972 and, not surprisingly, for most high schools of 1992 when the episode aired and even 25 years after that when this chapter was written.

Dalton sees three of Dwayne Huebner's value frameworks (2017, p. 11) as consistent in her Good Teacher category, and these "aesthetic-ethical-political value frameworks of good teachers" (2017, p. 43) can be applied to *The Wonder Years* and come into play in Miss Shaw's status as an outsider. Miss Shaw is an outsider, but not because she is from a different profession. In fact, she is a young, eager teacher only a year out of graduate school. Kevin explains what makes Miss Shaw unique and why she stands out to him: "She didn't take attendance. ... She let us sit anywhere we wanted. And, she never, ever used the word 'literature.'" This time, age, and philosophy are what establish a Good Teacher as an outsider; Miss Shaw is young, and her teaching philosophy is one usually associated with young teachers. The fresh air she brings comes along with some surprise when she tells the class that she only gives two grades: "Pass and No Pass." Students react to this possible upheaval in everything they know about school. Ricky Halsenbach (Scott Nemes) says, "You mean I'm not gonna get an F?" Randy Mitchell (Michael Tricario) responds out of concern for his wallet, "But my dad gives me a buck for every A." Out of fear for her college prospects, Felicia (Wendy J. Cooke) asks, "But what will happen to my grade point average?" Miss Shaw is adamant that this is the policy she will use. Her rationale is that "[t]his isn't a math class. There are no right or wrong answers here. Only thought. And you can't grade thought. Besides, it doesn't matter what I think about you. It matters what *you* think about you."

"GOOD" TEACHER ON HER OWN TERMS

Literature motivates the thought Miss Shaw values so highly, and she facilitates deep conversations by continually pushing her students with even deeper questions. Miss Shaw, through her commitment to having her students imagine, evaluate, create, and not regurgitate, demonstrates the "aesthetic classroom," a classroom in which teachers help students understand their lives and the world they live in (Dalton, 2017, p. 44). Miss Shaw is encouraging, does not treat her students as young people who enter her classroom "to be acted upon," and believes that "legitimate authority can come only from students and must spring from the relationship between teacher and students," which comprises "the ethical relationship" (Dalton, 2017, p. 49). Her empowering messages ("[I]t doesn't matter what I think about you") and the strong feelings she has about curriculum lead her to defy the board of education and assign *The Catcher in the Rye* on the sly while telling her students to keep the required book (*Ivanhoe*) for show. This duality completes the picture and adds a political language dynamic to the classroom. The linkage confirms what Dalton points out: "The language of curriculum theory, much like the language of Hollywood, tends to intermingle components of the ethical and the political" (2017, p. 52). Miss Shaw serves as an exemplar of both.

It is not difficult to imagine that a young teacher only a year out of graduate school would shun Sir Walter Scott's 1820 romance for a relatively recent, often-banned novel from 1951. Most likely a Baby Boomer who finished college and graduate school in the late 1960s and early 1970s, Miss Shaw represents those in the counter culture who comprised the Civil Rights Movement, the Women's Movement, and the Anti-War Movements, among others. At some point, Miss Shaw chooses to lobby for the cause of emancipating young minds as a schoolteacher. Through her unabashed dismissal of the school board's required reading, she endeavors to embody a strong distrust of traditional politics and serves as the anthesis of traditional ways of teaching and relating to students.

Early in "Kodachrome," the way her students react to her methods shows Miss Shaw to be an outsider in positive and negative ways, as her young pupils are not used to having a teacher like her. The books in the classroom serve as a parallel to reinforce the responses students have to their teacher; *The Catcher in the Rye* functions in this episode as a work pushing new ideas while *Ivanhoe* represents regressive attitudes. Miss Shaw is a product of the 1960s and an African American, an outsider who brings defiance and new philosophies to a school district that is not ready or willing to accept them. Through the methods she employs in the classroom, Miss Shaw fulfills the next three criteria for the Good Teacher—she personalizes the curriculum, learns from students, and is personally involved with students—but when she goes to the extreme (at least according to her current environment), she finds herself having serious problems with the school administration.

When she tells her students about her "Pass and No Pass" grading policy, it is clear, especially through Felicia's reaction, that Miss Shaw has not seen the end of it. In *"Doing School": How We Are Creating a Generation of Stressed Out, Materialistic, and Miseducated Students*, Denise Clark Pope describes Felicia's approach in which

137

C. E. HARRIS

students are trained to care more about getting good grades than actually getting an education (4). This is also in line with Jean Anyon's "middle-class school," in which "[t]here is little excitement in schoolwork" and the "work is getting the right answer. If one accumulates enough right answers, one gets a good grade" (4). Felicia is not interested in an aesthetic-ethical-political classroom. She has been raised to be interested only in the appearance of high standards.

At every turn, Felicia questions Miss Shaw's experimentation. To the *Ivanhoe* scheme, she retorts, "Does the administration know we're doing this?" foreshadowing obstacles that become reality. Tradition is too entrenched. Kevin relishes the praise Miss Shaw gives him after he responds, "He saw the truth," to the question of what is revealed to Kurtz that elicits the reaction, "The horror! The horror!" and The Narrator notes (in voiceover), "But maybe the most remarkable thing about her was she actually liked what she did." On the other hand, Felicia's response is to ask whether or not they will need to know that information for the midterm. She is so uneasy that she appears both eager and nervous. She is only eager for the answer, and the only answer she wants is a concrete one that will let her know how she can secure a good grade. Miss Shaw responds, "No, Felicia. You need to know that for *life*." This concern with "life" is how Miss Shaw personalizes the curriculum. She asks students probing questions hoping that they will seek ways to apply what they learn to their everyday decisions and outlooks. But, she takes it to the extreme. She personalizes the curriculum to the utmost and prioritizes students' views so much so that she literally wants them to grade themselves. This is not before "Pass and No Pass" is dealt with, however.

When Kevin's father, the hardworking, no-nonsense Korean War veteran Jack Arnold (Dan Lauria) sees a "P" on Kevin's report card for English, he immediately wants to know where his tax dollars are going. Meanwhile, Kevin's mother, Norma (Alley Mills), a stay-at-home mom who has recently gone back to college, comments that she knows about this new method because it is in use at the community college she is attending. The tension is palpable, and Jack responds, "Great. When he goes to a university on his own money, he can get a P. As long as I'm paying taxes, I want to see a grade." Kevin unsuccessfully tries out one of Miss Shaw's lines on his father: "Well, besides, it doesn't even matter what you think of me. It only matters what I think of me." This scene in the Arnold kitchen shows how reactions to school issues, especially those that involve radical changes, take place not only inside the school but in households across towns.

Back at school, the principal, Dr. Valenti (Richard Fancy), wants to talk to Miss Shaw about her grading system. He corners her in the hallway and eventually makes her late for her class. He tells her, "We don't do this here." Miss Shaw's response reinforces her experimental, liberal mindset: "You mean we *haven't* done this here." She is cool and calm as Dr. Valenti imparts tradition: "Miss Shaw, students don't respond without grades." When Dr. Valenti sees eavesdropping Kevin smile in response to Miss Shaw's response ("But my students are responding just fine"), he brings the teacher into his office. Dr. Valenti is a blend of Jeffrey Glanz's

"GOOD" TEACHER ON HER OWN TERMS

"principal-as-bureaucrat" and "principal-as-numbskull" (1998, pp. 4–5). He is actively engaged in reining in a Good Teacher because she does not fit the mold despite evidence that she is reaching her students and teaching them how to think. Again, the problem is that she goes to the extreme in personalizing the curriculum (the political element in the aesthetic-ethical-political classroom). Miss Shaw teaches her students to question the system that Dr. Valenti is trying to maintain.

With so many millions enrolled in high school in the 1970s, the education system faced renewed complaints that standards were declining (13 million in 1970 up from 8.4 million in 1960 and 5.7 million in 1950). In fact, high school earned the nickname, sometimes applied ironically, the "people's college" because it was enrolling such vast numbers of students at an unprecedented level under the stated goal of providing the masses with an education (Reese, 2005, pp. 180–87). Skyrocketing enrollment began in the postwar 1950s, as did the complaints (2005, pp. 287–88). The question of how to educate almost everyone—students with enormously varied ability levels and needs, many of whom "went to high school, whether reluctantly, infrequently, or inattentively" (2005, p. 289)—while keeping academic standards high is an impossible one and would be even if schools were not expected to do so while also facing America's most difficult economic and social issues (288). High school students were graduating without being able to read and write, leading to criticism that "social promotion, soft standards, and a creeping progressivism had likely ruined the people's college forever" (2005, pp. 287–88). Middle-class parents, anxious about their children's college readiness, balked at any attempt to alter the traditional academic course requirements (2005, p. 301).

Arthur E. Bestor's *Educational Wastelands* (1953), published at the beginning of one of the movements to elevate standards, attacked the "'interlocking directorate of professional educationists' for weakening the curriculum and fostering 'life adjustment'" (qtd in Reese, 2005, p. 290). While parents faced attacks from teachers who believed that life adjustment was "necessary for effective, democratic living" (2005, p. 301), they remained adamant that nothing get in the way of their own children's college prospects. While "career education"—as it was called in the 1970s, a change from "vocational education" (2005, p. 312)—may be fine for, as James B. Conant writes, "'other people's children' (qtd. in Reese, 2005, p. 313), suburban parents made sure that their schools focused on academics" (2005, p. 313). William J. Reese recalls "As one school administrator aptly wrote in 1971, to attempt to reorganize the curriculum by lessening college preparatory courses always led to trouble. Whatever college admissions required, parents of future collegians demanded" (2005, p. 301). Whatever his personal opinions about Miss Shaw's grading policy, Dr. Valenti is no doubt accountable to the board of education, which has its policies and is under pressure from the public. Off-screen, he gives Miss Shaw an ultimatum that leads to her voluntary exit—an exit that is ironic and important for us because she is still a Good Teacher. As a role model for her students—a Good

C. E. HARRIS

Teacher on her own terms—she embodies the nurturing-yet-independent spirit she wishes to engender in her students.

Miss Shaw's ethical (and certainly political) response to Dr. Valenti's mandate that she give traditional grades to her students is to do exactly that—but to allow the students to give *themselves* whatever grade they think they have earned. Her mantra, "Besides, it doesn't matter what I think about you. It matters what *you* think about you," takes on a new meaning. Early on, there is already no question that this teacher will attempt to circumvent school board policy in order to continue to personalize the curriculum to the extreme. When she reveals to the class that Dr. Valenti has informed her that she has "broken several important school regulations," the camera cuts to Felicia, whose face looks pleased, nervous, guilty, and victorious at the same time. One can say with near certainty that there has been an off-screen conversation at her home over her report card just as there is a discussion in the Arnold household. Only, Felicia's role in it is most likely the opposite of Kevin's, and—given Felicia's implied upbringing and the public stance of the day—it is likely that her parents are on her side. It does not take long for the news of students grading themselves to get back to Dr. Valenti, and he wastes no time letting Miss Shaw know that what she is doing is unacceptable. Felicia, usually the dedicated if unimaginative student afraid to step outside the norm, will allow nothing to get in the way of her grade point average. She does not make eye contact with anyone, but Felicia's expression is no longer ambiguous when the teacher tells the students they will be getting traditional grades. She allows a smile to come over her face, and she does not try to hide it. Meanwhile, there is an audible groan from her classmates, and Kevin is expressionless. Ricky chimes in: "There goes my P." When Miss Shaw finally tells them they will be allowed to choose their own grade for the next report card, Felicia seems neither pleased nor displeased, but she does look down then back up again, as if not totally opposed to the idea. After all, her grade point average will remain intact. When Miss Shaw asks if there are any comments about the policy, the majority of the students celebrate.

The next scene (with Miss Shaw holding her class outdoors for a second time) includes Kevin's favorite memories of class. The students discuss and look empowered to share their views. The Narrator remarks, "Instead of lectures, we actually had discussions. And not just about books. About ideas. About life. It was sort of like riding shotgun with Che Guevara. It was pretty cool." With this atmosphere, Miss Shaw encourages her students to express themselves, thus personalizing the curriculum. She listens to them so that she can learn from them. Even Felicia, who sits right next to Miss Shaw, seems impressed with her teacher. She makes a statement that is certainly not untrue: "Well, personally, I think people thrive on structure," to which Miss Shaw responds, "Unfortunately, I think you're right." A student credited as "Smart Kid" (Elliot Goldman) speaks against "living up to other people's expectations." As Kevin makes his "It was pretty cool"

Figure 12.2. Miss Shaw (Lanei Chapman) on The Wonder Years *(ABC 1988–93)*

comment, Dr. Valenti sees the class sitting on the grass and issues a disapproving look.

In gym class, Kevin's best friend Paul (Josh Saviano) expresses his disgust with what he perceives to be the unfairness of letting immature high school students choose their own grades and reminds Kevin that the administration is not going to let Miss Shaw get away with her policy. He questions whether Miss Shaw even knows what she is doing, something Kevin, in his admiration for her, takes for granted. When Kevin asks her for clarification, she imparts her plan to him: "My guess is, when the time comes, I'm gonna have to beg you guys to break even with Cs." The Narrator then has an epiphany: "And that's when I realized ... she had more than a lesson plan. She had a whole concept." She projects the end result of her teaching—what she is structuring each lesson to achieve—to be students learning lessons about life that they can implement every day from there on out. She verbalizes this to Felicia earlier in the episode during the *Heart of Darkness* discussion. She is happy that her grading system makes them think, and she wants them to embrace that challenge and take the resulting courage with them to face difficult questions beyond the classroom. She is using literature, a miraculous teacher itself, to teach "life adjustment" while maintaining high standards for student engagement and scholarship. She wants students to take true ownership of their learning, which, for her, includes giving them the power over their own grades.

While I have never attempted Miss Shaw's method for a report card grade, I have done so with a project. And, I must admit, students were always more honest than one would expect. Yet, it is imperative that the classroom culture is set to high expectations and that the teacher both personalizes the curriculum and is involved with students. The aesthetic-ethical-political classroom is necessary.

C. E. HARRIS

Once students are taught how to interpret and understand the material and students see how the material relates to their lives and the outside world, and once they feel safe to do so, they can make strides in feeling empowered to continue to develop their skills. Seeing the value in learning and understanding the process of learning, students will begin to see how much they do *not* know, which, combined with a humble respect for knowledge and feelings of resiliency stemming from empowerment, fosters a space in which they can honestly evaluate their own work. They revere the Good Teacher who leads them, so that what they expect from themselves comes to exceed what the teacher expects. In such an environment, the teacher can learn from students in a more genuine manner without the pressure of an impending grade.

In an outdoor scene during which he reflects on his favorite memories of Miss Shaw's class, The Narrator remarks, with passionate pride, "Over the next few weeks, Miss Shaw's class took on a life of its own. The word was out. Things were different here." But, in the end, Miss Shaw is not allowed to do what she feels is best in her classroom. Through her methods of allowing free expression of ideas without the anxiety of obtaining a specific teacher-determined grade, she attempts to create the land of opportunity that Reese describes, but the public does not really want that (2005, p. 287). As British sociologist Michael Young puts it, "there is a fundamental conflict between a general desire to give all the children in a community an equal chance and the special desire of each parent to do the best he can for his own offspring. ... They desire equal opportunity for everyone else's children, extra for their own" (qtd. in Reese, 2005, pp. 294, 225). In attempts to break down the hierarchies that stifle self-expression, Miss Shaw pushes against institutional structures built and stabilized by hierarchies that use standardization to force students to fit into predefined frameworks instead of liberating thought.

Miss Shaw is not allowed a chance to break the status quo and try a new way of providing students opportunity because, traditionally, lower-performing students may not be able to handle it (Reese, 2005, p. 304). By conventional thinking (represented by Dr. Valenti), students do not respond without grades. Felicia seems to be responding well in Miss Shaw's outdoor class, but she feels she needs a *measure* of her merit (and colleges need to see a grade point average). Miss Shaw plans for students to give themselves their own grades (personalizing the curriculum to the "extreme"), but is that a credible measure? What if standards fall when students have the final say or the measure is not deemed credible by the appropriate authorities? Where does Miss Shaw's philosophy of learning for life fit here? Breaking with tradition—attempting to redefine course objectives and evaluation methods—meets with resistance from both ends of the spectrum. Caught in the middle, the nearly-forty-year-old narrator does not know if he should be angry at Miss Shaw for leaving or at the system that drove her away. One of the most frustrating and demoralizing situations Good Teachers go through is being told they are not doing what's best for kids or, even worse, being told what is best is not politically or financially expedient.

"GOOD" TEACHER ON HER OWN TERMS

We will never know what grades her English 2A students would have given themselves because outside concerns ultimately drive Miss Shaw out of McKinley High School.

Miss Shaw's short time as Kevin's teacher brings up how "Kodachrome's" treatment of the identities of social class and race compare to how they function in 1960s and 1970s television series in which differences are either overlooked or easily solved. Miss Shaw seems to be operating from a place of privilege when it comes to social class, although all we know about her life is that she has a graduate degree, that she has a father who supported her reading and repaired books she read over and over again, and that she quits her job willingly and abruptly. She does not have to stay in a job that doesn't satisfy her because of her reliance on the paycheck or, presumably, her obligations to support other people. Social class in this episode is addressed only indirectly with the type of middle-class school Kevin attends and the nature of the complaints about Miss Shaw. Her race is not treated as a factor. She is one of a very small number of African-American teachers on the series and is certainly the only one given this much screen time and status. She does not represent mainstream views on education, and her students are exclusively White. The problems she does face in the episode come from how her teaching philosophy generates opposition from the administration and, presumably, a disapproving student.

While unrest in the 1970s, which developed out of the 1960s, is featured in *The Wonder Years* in other ways, social class and race are largely ignored (and they are not on Kevin's mind). "Kodachrome" fits Dalton and Linder's findings concerning 1970s television. Functioning according to Kevin's suburban memory, it does not directly address—with Miss Shaw, the school, or students—social class, how ideologies surrounding it reflect Miss Shaw's choices, or the reaction to her teaching methods (2019, pp. 56–75). Of the three socially relevant shows from the 1960s that feature teachers, only two of them[1] "provide any ongoing references to race and neither addresses race directly, either on a societal or on a personal level" (Dalton & Linder, 2019, p. 53). *The Wonder Years*, set partially in this decade, is no exception. Despite these limitations, it is nonetheless important (both then and now) to see a teacher stand up for herself and her principles. This episode speaks profoundly to me as a teacher (now teaching college undergraduates) in the current climate of mandated curricula, overreliance on standardized testing, and (in some cases) lower limits on grades teachers are allowed to give students—one in which teachers are increasingly treated less like professional educators and more like customer service representatives. Due to *The Wonder Years*'s overall premise as a series, this episode provides viewers with a narrative structure to build the tension that leads to Miss Shaw's departure—her all-important moment of self-assertion—in a way that contests negative elements that have come to typify the current crisis in education. These negative elements are predicated on de-professionalizing teaching, upholding "standards," and using perceived "failures" in the public schools to undermine them in favor of private non-profit and for-profit alternatives.

143

C. E. HARRIS

Episodic television is not confined by a limited amount of time in the same way that films are and has the luxury of developing characters across multiple episodes throughout a season (Dalton & Linder, 2019, pp. 7–8). Thus, there are more opportunities for Good Teachers to personalize the curriculum, to learn from students, and to become personally involved with students (Dalton & Linder, 2019, pp. 7–8). Yet, a Good Teacher's outsider status and disagreements with administrators are what provide the conflict that produces entertainment value (Dalton & Linder, 2019, pp. 12–13). This is where films have the advantage because their runtime is the perfect amount of time to encapsulate one narrative arc that includes, in one fell swoop, all that is entertaining, intense, and touching. "Kodachrome" is more like a film in narrative structure because all of the conflict involving Miss Shaw is condensed into a single episode. This is owing to *The Wonder Years*'s basic premise: Kevin's memory recalls what it recalls, and the purpose of this episode is for Kevin to tell viewers about the teacher who had the most profound impact on him and for him to describe the bewilderment he felt when she quit so suddenly. The effect of "Kodachrome" would not be the same if it had not been Miss Shaw's only appearance. Packed with non-sentimental life lessons, this story leaves viewers inspired but wistful and also questioning what it means to be a Good Teacher. These effects would be diluted if carried out over several episodes or an entire season. Yet, as we see with Kevin, the impact can stay with you for decades.

The Wonder Years is a show that is not neatly contained. Kevin spends the better part of six seasons totally confused about most of life. He has epiphanies and setbacks, and the series does not resolve anything ethically or practically at the end of an episode. A single-camera series categorized as a comedy by the Television Academy (and winning the Outstanding Comedy Series Emmy in 1988), the show is better described as a dramedy. It is characterized, more than anything, by a sense of nostalgia. While the show may emphasize the average-teenager-in-the-average-suburb angle for promotional purposes, it cannot be reduced to that alone; often, even in the simplest stories, there are layers of contradictory meanings. For example, what happens when Miss Shaw, Kevin's favorite teacher for all the right reasons, drives off never to come back?

Miss Shaw does not seem to fit The Hollywood Model because she "chooses to leave … rather than compromise" (Dalton & Linder, 2019, p. 53), but the long-lasting impact she has on Kevin makes her a Good Teacher on her own terms. This story is not tidy, but it is characteristic of real situations that are complicated and revealing. The Narrator remembers her and still respects her two decades later and says of her, "The thing is, I'd never met anyone who was so right for what she did. A woman with a gift. A natural." If the teacher who replaces Miss Shaw is any indication, Miss Shaw's class may have been the last time in high school that Kevin and his classmates were allowed to express themselves freely in an academic, nurturing, and empowering environment. The new teacher is the same teacher whom Kevin describes earlier in the episode as his example of an "insufferably boring" teacher—he has the desks arranged in meticulous rows (in stark contrast

144

"GOOD" TEACHER ON HER OWN TERMS

to Miss Shaw's relaxed arrangement), and he walks over and closes the blinds the instant he sees a lethargic Kevin gaze out the window. The tone of Miss Shaw's former classroom has been transformed, and while Kevin says Miss Shaw did not do what was best for them—the students—he also questions the system. Miss Shaw is not given the chance to test her teaching philosophy, so she leaves, still a Good Teacher. This representation is important for sending the message that teachers, as professionals, can be good at what they do and also assert their own sense of self-worth in the most challenging circumstances. We need these depictions alongside teacher characters who find a way to stay in their current teaching posts while performing as Good Teachers on their own terms.

In *Up the Down Staircase* (1967), Sylvia Barrett (Sandy Dennis) faces critics who think she is too naïve to teach diverse, inner-city students. Like Miss Shaw, she listens to her students and gives them a voice. Miss Barrett does give traditional grades, but she also has to persevere against challenges to her methods and against demoralizing days. Unlike Miss Shaw, however, she is given a chance. The administration allows her to teach, and she elects to stay because she sees her impact (Harris, 2017, p. 142). In *Teachers* (1984), Alex Jurrell (Nick Nolte) has every intention of quitting amid attacks from the administration and parents who accuse him of not doing what is best for kids although he does exactly that when he encourages a student to master reading and writing and not allow himself to be passed along despite his deficiencies. He even faces false accusations from a school board anxious to silence his activism (Dalton, 2017, pp. 50–51). Yet, he decides to fight to stay when his students support him (2017, p. 51). In both films, while the landscape is still portrayed as complicated, Good Teachers are able to see long-term results or secure valued support for what it is they believe about education and reaching students. Miss Shaw is not afforded either, and her choice is to walk away.

If teachers do not teach for the money, why do they teach? As young people, we are told to find a career that does not feel like work. It is work—hard work—to do a job that requires that we change who we are, if only for eight hours a day. Miss Shaw chooses not to continue in a place that does not accept her for who she is, but that does not change the lasting impact she has. Twenty years later, she is still making Kevin think. Perhaps she is a major reason he is a little more than average, a spark for the insights he shares with us over six seasons—insights he undoubtedly passes on to the son we learn he has. Henri A. Giroux, describing the magic of films, writes that they "do more than entertain, they offer up subject positions, mobilize desires, influence us unconsciously, and help to construct the landscape of American culture" (2002, p. 2). The same can be said for television and for Good Teachers. Good Teachers indeed entertain us, but they also pose questions that make us push ourselves to broaden our perceptions, help us find what we want out of life, affect us in ways we cannot articulate until we grow wiser, and help us find out how we will play important roles in our own lives and in the lives of others. Seeing representations of teachers who have the courage to stand by their own principles with definitive action is essential if students and viewers are to see we teachers put into action the

145

C. E. HARRIS

values we preach and, consequently, see our guidance as a legitimate path to self-empowerment. Sometimes the outcomes are untidy and contradict expectation, but those challenges teach us the best lessons of all.

NOTE

[1] The three shows are *Mr. Novak* (NBC 1963–65), *The Bill Cosby Show* (NBC 1969–71), and *Room 222* (ABC 1969–74). The latter two provide oblique references to race. See Dalton and Linder for further discussion of the social relevance of 1960s teacher characters.

REFERENCES

Anyon, Jean. (1980). Social class and the hidden curriculum of work. *Journal of Education, 162*(1), 67–92.

Dalton, Mary M. (2017). *The hollywood curriculum: Teachers in the movies* (3rd rev. ed.). New York, NY: Peter Lang.

Dalton, Mary M., & Linder, Laura R. (2019). *Teacher TV: Seventy years of teachers on television*. New York, NY: Peter Lang.

Fiske, John. (1989). *Understanding popular culture*. Boston, MA: Unwin Hyman.

Giroux, Henri A. (2002). *Breaking in to the movies: Film and the culture of politics*. Malden, MA, & Oxford: Blackwell Publishers.

Glanz, Jeffrey. (1998). Images of principals in film and television: From Mr. Wameke to Mr. Rivelle to Mr. Woodman. *The Journal of Educational Leadership and Administration, 10*, 7–24.

Harris, Chad E. (2017). Race up the down staircase: Teacher as savior and other identities. In Mary M. Dalton & Laura R. Linder (Eds.), *Screen lessons: What we have learned from teachers on television and in the movies* (pp. 137–42). New York, NY: Peter Lang.

Pope, Denise Clark. (2001). *"Doing School": How we are creating a generation of stressed out, materialistic, and miseducated students*. New Haven, CT: Yale University Press.

Reese, William J. (2005). *America's public schools: From the common school to "No Child Left Behind."* Baltimore, MD: Johns Hopkins University Press.

KRISTY LILES CRAWLEY

13. LIBERATORY PEDAGOGY IN ACTION

*The Embodied Performance of Community College
Instructors in Film and Television*

ABSTRACT

To analyze the marginal status of community college faculty represented in television and film, the first half of the chapter contrasts stereotypical disembodied representations of university professors with the embodied portrayals of community college faculty. In the second half of the chapter, I argue that community college instructors' embodied performance in television and film adheres to bell hooks's description of liberatory pedagogy, a pedagogy dedicated to close interaction with students in an attempt to cross borders and open lines of communication in a diverse classroom setting. While most embodied portrayals take place within the context of comedies, instructors reveal personal and professional sides of their characters while shedding their authoritative omnipotent image. The decentering of authority sets the stage for comedy as viewers see instructors' faults, struggles, and strengths through their close interactions with students.

Keywords: liberatory pedagogy, embodiment, representation, community college faculty, film, television

***

Over the years, professors represented in television and film have left a lasting impression on viewers' hearts and minds. A quick walk down memory lane allows viewers to travel the world with a range of professor character types: Indiana Jones, eponymous character, adventurer, archaeologist, and heartthrob in front of the blackboard; the brilliant John Nash, based on a real-life person teaching mathematics at MIT in *A Beautiful Mind* (2001); two hilarious "nutty professors," portrayed first by Jerry Lewis then Eddie Murphy, each an indelible depiction; and, Dr. Sheldon Cooper, a socially-awkward, genius physicist in *The Big Bang Theory* (CBS 2007–19), a top-rated sitcom. Each popular movie and television series helps viewers shape their expectations of what it means to be a professor. Although this brief list does not capture the complexity of representations of professors in popular culture—not to mention teachers of younger students and coaches and mentors who serve as informal teachers—educator characters have been a staple in movies and television

© KONINKLIJKE BRILL NV, LEIDEN, 2019 | DOI:10.1163/9789004398092_013

K. L. CRAWLEY

since the earliest days of each medium and in earlier written narratives as discussed by Steve Benton in the first chapter of this collection. Amid the wide spectrum of educators depicted in television and film, only a few results surface for community college educators, which raises the following question: For the few representations that are present, how are community college faculty represented?

My interest in fictional community college faculty representations arises from my personal experiences. As a full-time faculty member at Forsyth Technical Community College in North Carolina and a doctoral candidate in the English Department at the University of North Carolina at Greensboro, I have a vested interest in representations because fictional depictions frame college students' expectations. These representations of college campuses, educators, and students offer future students a misleading and troubling snapshot of college life and promote negative attitudes and behavior toward community colleges. One way this environment and the people in it have been marginalized is the relatively few representations of community colleges in popular culture, the lack of prior attention to those depictions that exist, and the dearth of them in the scholarly literature. The work I do in this chapter to explore the marginalization of community college faculty members, to consider how representations shape students' attitudes, and to recognize ways in which community college faculty members utilize embodied pedagogy and bring to students' attention the value of embodied learning is a starting point.

The marginal status of community college faculty represented in television and film can be analyzed by drawing on examples from the television show *Community* (NBC and Yahoo! Screen 2009–15) and the movie *Larry Crowne* (2011) where representations of community college faculty stand in sharp contrast to portrayals of university professors. For instance, Mercedes Tainot (Julia Roberts), a community college communications instructor in *Larry Crowne*, moves throughout her classroom as she engages individually with the students in her small class. Ms. Tainot's embodied (connected) performance contrasts markedly with Ross Geller's (David Schwimmer) disembodied (formal and distant) performance in episode four of the sixth season of *Friends* (NBC 1994–2004). When teaching a class, Dr. Geller, a White, male university professor and paleontologist dressed in a black suit, naturally centers his body behind a lectern in an auditorium. In contrast, Ms. Tainot moves among her students while her counterpart is the proverbial "sage on the stage." Comically speaking in an awkward British accent, Dr. Geller continually lectures to quiet, faceless students as they silently record his words. Excluding his fake British accent, which is included for comedic purposes, Dr. Geller's disembodied performance as a university professor symbolizes his authority, status, and impersonal approach, which contrasts with the community college instructor's embodied performance, one that decenters her authority as she moves among the students and interacts with them directly. Her performance serves as a border crossing as she interacts with a group of students who are diverse in age, race, class, sex, and intellectual ability. Because most portrayals of community college instructors take place in comedies, their success in the classroom is not guaranteed. In some instances, the community college instructor

LIBERATORY PEDAGOGY IN ACTION

guides students on a bumpy but ultimately successful road to graduation, which is the expected outcome in most mainstream entertainment narratives, but there are other times when community college instructors cannot overcome the challenges posed by (and facing) their diverse student populations.

The embodied performance of community college instructors in television and film adheres to hooks's description of liberatory pedagogy as demanding "that one work in the classroom, and that one work with the limits of the body, work both with and through and against those limits: teachers may insist that it doesn't matter whether you stand behind the podium [sic] or the desk, but it does" (1994, p. 138). Through cinema's portrayal of liberatory pedagogy, viewers enjoy a few laughs while getting to know the personal *and* professional sides of instructors through their interactions, a perspective only sometimes available to students and coworkers. Because of the expanded perspective of viewers, they know the instructor is more than another talking head dispensing knowledge. The humanness of the teacher character coupled with the instructor's placement in a comedy (with its classical set of conventions) prompts viewers to have a limited set of expectations for the transformational possibilities in this teacher-student dynamic. Even though they may not think of the possibilities in terms so concrete or informed as liberatory pedagogy, they nonetheless think of the community college instructor in a work of comic entertainment as inferior to the authoritative and stereotypical portrayal of a university professor. Of course, even seemingly simplistic media texts are actually complex and contextual; in reality, the instructor is performing what many people fail to acknowledge: "being a teacher is being with people" (hooks, 1994, p. 165).

DISEMBODIMENT AND THE UNIVERSITY PROFESSOR

Disembodiment in the classroom does not happen by accident. Elyse Lamm Pineau eloquently describes the disembodied classroom that so many people have experienced in their own lives and have encountered in film and television, popular narratives that frequently depict the disembodied university professor behind the lectern. "Steeped in the tradition of Cartesian duality, students and teachers effectively have been schooled to 'forget' their bodies when they enter the classroom in order that they might give themselves more fully to the life of the mind" (2002, p. 45). While many professors often serve as minor characters in popular media texts, they typically appear behind a lectern lecturing to docile (or similarly disengaged) students in a large classroom or auditorium. The professor's booming voice is accompanied by ambient sound, the occasional rustling of students in their seats, note taking, whispering to one another, or sometimes asking a question.

While the depiction of the professor behind the lectern seems outdated and contrary to scholarly work promoting engaged pedagogy, the disembodied representation persists because of its link to tradition, knowledge, and authority. As early as 1970, Paulo Freire favored a pedagogy involving dialogue over the

149

K. L. CRAWLEY

"'banking' concept of education" that transforms students into "'receptacles' to be 'filled' by the teacher. The more completely he fills the receptacles, the better a teacher he is" (2000, p. 58). Numerous scholars have echoed Freire's sentiment, but the long tradition of disembodied education one experiences early in life becomes difficult to erase simply by knowing about a better way. Pineau notes, "Schooling systematically domesticates our bodies; it incarcerates them in rows of wooden desks, robs them of spontaneity through rigid demarcations of time and space, and in fact devotes a great deal of energy in hiding the fact that we have bodies at all" (2002, p. 45). While Pineau describes the domestication of students' bodies, professors' bodies are placed behind the lectern where generations of professors have stood before them.

Thus, the long-used lectern, sometimes placed on a podium to create another level of separation, is not just a place for lecturing; it is a place for one to display knowledge and authority. The idea is not confined to schooling; a priest's pulpit serves a similar function. In "On Gender and Rhetorical Space," Roxanne Mountford connects knowledge and authority to an enclosed pulpit. She states that "[o]ne of the primary functions of church architecture is to enact the myth of the preacher as messenger from God, chosen and set apart from the people. Traditionally, this myth is played out through the creation of spaces that only the priest and bishop may inhabit ..." (2003, p. 34). Just as priests communicate God's message to the congregation, professors dispense knowledge from canonical texts within their fields. The podium, like the pulpit, separates professors from students. This prominent position is reserved for the person in charge, a space typically reserved for the powerful and knowledgeable. Students often feel uncomfortable and anxious stepping behind the lectern when they are assigned to make presentations.

Along with the lectern, the gender of the body behind the lectern reinforces the connection between disembodiment and authority. Mari Dagaz and Brent Harger's study of depictions of professors in popular film reveals that professors depicted "in films are much more likely to be male and less likely to be over 60 years old" (2011, p. 278). Also, they discovered that "88 percent" of professors in film are White (Dagaz & Harger, 2011, p. 278). Since the majority of professors are White males, the hidden body that can easily be taken for granted or ignored and takes on a special privilege when it is located behind the lectern. As Abby A. Knoblauch suggests, "[a] view from nowhere, a belief that bodies don't matter, seems much easier to imagine if one lives in a body that is not always already marked as other" (2012, p. 59). For a White, male professor, the fact that the lectern hides the body may seem insignificant due to the perceived universality of the White, male body. For a body marked as other by gender or race, however, the denial of the body's significance is problematic, and associations with gender and race make the body impossible to forget or erase. Like everyone else, students read bodies in terms of attractive or unattractive, able-bodied or disabled, authoritative or submissive, motherly or not motherly. In an attempt to escape the gaze that students cast as they read bodies, Grumet observes that "a teacher's inclination to lecture [is] a way of avoiding the gaze, distracting students

150

with verbal stimuli" (2003, p. 250), and this is an inclination that will be determined by the identities possessed by the teacher in question.

In addition to professors' use of verbal stimuli and lecterns in an attempt to place emphasis on the mind rather than the body, their commitment to a life of the mind physically separates them from their students because many professors prefer other activities to teaching, including pursuit of their scholarship. In film, many male professors are depicted as "disinterested in teaching or not adequately capable of fulfilling the nurturing role associated with teaching. The majority of male professors portrayed in film focus on research and may not be shown in front of the classroom. The focus of their work lies in practical applications of the knowledge they generate" (Dagaz & Harger, 2011, p. 282). Like film writers and producers, the creators of television shows make a conscious choice to focus on professors' research or their lives outside of academia. While reasons for writers and producers placing professors outside of the classroom may be discussed in depth in other sources, I will briefly conjecture that they focus on professors' outside interests for the sake of character development and entertainment as well as to showcase accomplishments such as publications and new inventions that supposedly outrank teaching in terms of respect, monetary value, and fame. For instance, in *The Big Bang Theory*, Dr. Sheldon Cooper (Jim Parsons) and his cohort spend most of their time talking about research or working in a science lab away from students. Similar to Dr. Ross Geller (mentioned above), Ted Mosby (Josh Radnor), an architecture professor on *How I Met Your Mother* (CBS 2005–14), rarely appears in the classroom and spends most of his time pursuing love interests.

LINK BETWEEN REPRESENTATION AND SPACE

The connection between space and representation points to and reinforces the differences in how university professors and community college instructors are depicted in film and television. When discussing space, it is important to note that "rhetorical spaces carry the residue of history within them, but also, perhaps, something else: a physical representation of relationships and ideas" (Mountford, 2003, p. 17). In the section above, proxemics was addressed in terms of the physical spaces associated with university professors, such as labs and classrooms with lecterns. The larger amount of space accorded a university professor than allotted to a community college instructor, for example, is a clear marker of hierarchical status. Similarly, the amount of space devoted to students also helps construct the relationships of these characters one to another. The agility of the mind, presentation of research, and enforcement of academic rigor are ideas associated with professors employed at well-established universities, and the space that separates them from others in the frame reinforces their elevation visually.

Community colleges differ from universities because of their history and hybrid identity, and perceptions associated with community college faculty and students influence people who work and study there. Community colleges, known for their open-door policy, offer a wide variety of programs: GED, early college, vocational education, college transfer, developmental education, and continuing education. The diversity of programs offered there and the variety of students they serve (in terms of ages, interests, and academic abilities) are reflected in the representation of faculty onscreen. The hybrid nature of the community college creates a connection between high school teachers and community college instructors because some high school students are enrolled in early college programs. Also, the association of community college with nonacademic subjects related to crafts and trades often colors all community college instructors as nonacademic faculty who teach easy classes.

In the pilot episode of the sitcom *Community*, both students and employees echo the idea of easiness and question the legitimacy of the school, which reinforces the idea that community colleges lack rigor. For instance, Dean Pelton (Jim Rash) gives an opening speech that reinforces the idea that community college is not like a "real college," meaning a university:

> What is community college? … You've heard it's "loser college" for young people who couldn't make the cut at a university. It's "halfway school" for twenty-something dropouts, crawling back to society with unskilled tails between their legs. A tax-funded, self-esteem workshop for newly divorced housewives piecing together shattered identities, and old people hoping to keep their minds active as they circle the drain of eternity.

At this point in the speech, viewers expect Dean Pelton to provide inspirational words and state the true definition of community college, but expectations are frustrated when Pelton loses his notecards containing the remainder of his speech. He concludes by leaving viewers with the impression that community college is, in fact, a "loser college" and that there is no need for a correction. Although he has alienated the entire population of the school with a negative reference about students' ages, marital status, income level, and academic struggles, students listening do not seem offended as they continue walking to their next classes.

Their lack of offense suggests that these students agree with Dean Pelton's comments, and during the same episode, students expand upon Pelton's speech by questioning the legitimacy of their faculty. If the educators at Greendale are not teaching "real" students, it prompts one to question whether Greendale has "real" teachers. Jeff Winger (Joel McHale), a student at the community college who is seeking a real degree after his employer discovers that his purported bachelor's degree is not legitimate, frequently comments on Greendale's lack of rigor. When talking to Professor Ian Duncan (John Oliver), a psychology instructor and former friend, he references his "fake study group" and questions Duncan's legitimacy as a teacher: "Is it possible you're incapable of teaching? It is a community college." Jeff interprets Duncan's employment at the community college as a sign that his teaching experience and degrees are not legitimate. According to Jeff, for Duncan's credentials to be legitimate, he must have ties to a well-respected university or

LIBERATORY PEDAGOGY IN ACTION

college. Greendale's physical (and psychic) space, defined by the unprepared bodies that Pelton references in his speech, evokes an image of unprepared faculty. The broad brushstrokes that Dean Pelton uses to paint a picture of students as university rejects are employed to imply by extension a picture of instructors who are unable to attain the credentials—publications if not degrees—to work at the university level.

THE COMMUNITY COLLEGE PROFESSOR AS OTHER

Similarly, television and film writers include additional parallels between community college faculty and students that enforce a firm line of distinction between university faculty and community college instructors. In Dean Pelton's speech, he captures the diversity of the student body in terms of age, social class, and intellectual ability. Like the diversity among the student population, film and television programming showcases diversity among community college faculty while maintaining stereotypes. The White, male instructors still outnumber female instructors and instructors of color in *Community*, although the creators have generated two memorable female characters: June Bauer, an anthropology professor, and Michelle Slater, a statistics professor. While Bauer and Slater are referred to as "professor" due to their credentials, they are marginalized because they teach at a community college. Professor Bauer, played by Betty White, conforms to the stereotype of the aging professor who has lost touch with reality. At one point, dissatisfied with a student's response to her question, Professor Bauer demonstrates the power of a blowgun by shooting a student in the face, and she later drinks her own urine to show what she had to do for survival when traveling. Professor Bauer's soft voice and gentle

Figure 13.1. Professor Bauer (Betty White) on Community
(NBC and Yahoo! Screen 2009–15)

demeanor coupled with her extreme actions add to the comedy of the show. She casts off the stereotype of women professors being nurturing or motherly toward their students. Also, because Professor Bauer is over the age of sixty, she breaks the age barriers often found in depictions of university professors. As stated earlier, Dagaz and Harger discovered that the majority of university professors depicted in film are White, male, and under the age of sixty (2011, p. 278). The show also includes two male professors over the age of sixty: Noel Cornwallis (Malcolm McDowell), a history professor, and Buzz Hickey (Jonathan Banks), a criminology professor.

Another notable representation of a female educator comes in the form of a young, attractive mathematics professor, Michelle Slater (Lauren Stamile). Professor Slater initially refuses to date Jeff Winger, a Greendale student who is close to her age. Overcome by his persistence, however, she dates Jeff for a short period of time. Professor Slater's representation corresponds to the findings of Donald M. Davis, who concludes that women are often objectified in media portrayals (1990, p. 331). Similar to Professor Slater's role as a love interest in *Community,* Mercedes Tainot, the communications instructor in the movie *Larry Crowne*, eventually falls in love with her student, the eponymous character played by Tom Hanks. Prior to falling in love with these students, Taniot and Slater present "gruff, no nonsense demeanor[s]" that are common in representations of female characters in film (Dagaz & Harger, 2011, p. 281). Their manner is professional and a bit serious to legitimate their authority in the classroom, a place in which a young, attractive professor may be objectified or considered weak.

Race is another means of expressing the diversity of community college instructors in these narratives. In *Community*, Spanish Professor Ben Chang, played by Korean-American actor Ken Jeong, and biology professor Marshall Kane, portrayed by African-American actor Michael Williams, are a few of the faculty members of color. In *Larry Crowne* the few professors of color include, Dr. Matutani, an economics professor played by George Takei, a Japanese American; and Frances, an English professor portrayed by Pam Grier, an African-American. With only a few examples of professors of color from *Larry Crowne* and *Community*, it may seem that the representations of minority community college faculty members are equivalent to university faculty in relative numbers. In Dagaz and Harger's study on university faculty represented in film, however, they conclude that "there is little diversity in popular films beyond the Black/White dichotomy" (285). They also note that "Asian and Pacific Islanders are severely underrepresented" in film (Dagaz & Harger, 2011, p. 278). The inclusion of a Korean American in *Community* and a Japanese American in *Larry Crowne* offers a kind of diversity that has not traditionally been present in the higher education setting depicted in film, which is a positive development.

Besides the relatively small number of minority faculty members presented in film and television, the manner in which their professional identities are questioned also correlates to community college instructors' marginal status. While bodies are often taken for granted, "[b]odies are not objective, static facts. They are seen, appraised and responded to" (Sinclair, 2005, p. 91). In other words, minority professors' colleagues and students closely observe the professors' appearance, reading their bodies in an effort to determine whether they possess the identity of a "real" professor. Therefore, minority professors in film and television must legitimate their scholarly identities in ways that others do not. With marked bodies—those without the "invisibility cloak" of White, male privilege—minority instructors in film and television utilize their bodies in particular ways to legitimize their presence in classrooms. For instance, in film, "African Americans are more likely to have facial hair, wear 'dressy' clothing, wear glasses, and even wear bow ties than their White counterparts" (Dagaz & Harger, 2011, p. 280). With the exception of Ben Chang, female professors as well as professors of color in *Community* and *Larry Crowne* mark their professional identity by wearing suits. Yet, in some cases, the negative representations of minority characters assist in undercutting their legitimacy as professionals. For example, *Community's* Professor Marshall Kane (Michael Kenneth Williams), a former inmate, earned his degree in prison, and Professor Chang, a long-time faculty member at Greendale, lacks a legitimate teaching degree. Although Kane and Chang possess the honorific title of professor, *Community's* use of the title suggests that titles in community colleges are meaningless because both examples send the message that community colleges fail to hire well-qualified educators. Negative representations of minority faculty members force instructors to prove themselves as legitimate professionals who are equally qualified to perform the fundamental duties of an instructor. With that continual demonstration of worthiness as the baseline, any thoughts of these teachers engaging in liberatory praxis are pipe dreams.

EMBODIMENT THROUGH LIBERATORY PEDAGOGY

Before analyzing specific examples of liberatory pedagogy in *Community* and *Larry Crowne*, it is important to define liberatory pedagogy as the terms appear in the literature. bell hooks writes that liberatory pedagogy requires "work with the limits of the body," work that is "with and through and against those limits," and she points to the importance of how teachers position their bodies in the classroom (1994, p. 138). Numerous scholars have echoed hooks's sentiments by utilizing other terms. "Embodied transformative learning" describes a classroom dedicated to the body and mind where "adults co-create the space in which it is safe to participate with their whole selves and become aware of and engage their whole bodies as well as their emotions, intuition, humor, environment, and each other" (Meyer, 2012, p. 29). Betty Smith Franklin refers to embodied learning as a "pleasurable, embodied mix of work and play" (16) while Eric Howden favors embodied learning because "it looks and feels different from what has come to be commonplace in education, learning through lecture and other passive means" (2012, p. 43). As I am using the term in this chapter, liberatory pedagogy refers to the mind and the body being actively engaged in learning. Educators become active participants and facilitators, working side by side with students.

K. L. CRAWLEY

The first example of liberatory pedagogy from the media texts under consideration involves more than a professor stepping out from behind the lectern and moving around the room. Alison Cook-Sather, Catherine Bovill, and Peter Felten recommend that professors "create spaces for students to step into the role of the teacher by leading discussions or presenting their research" (2012, p. 6). In *Larry Crowne*, students assume the role of teacher in Ms. Tainot's communications class when they encounter what she calls hot topics. The instructor sits in the back of the class while students make presentations from the front of the room about a topic they have randomly selected from a hat. By placing students in the teacher's customary position at the front of the class, instructors decenter their authority and offer students an opportunity to research, present, and share information about themselves in order to build a learning community. During Larry Crowne's presentation, he teaches the class about geography and shares some experiences from his time in the Navy. As a middle-aged adult intimidated by the experience of attending college, Larry Crowne discovers his previous knowledge and experiences fit into the classroom setting. He actively makes connections between his academic work and his professional and personal life. While teachers sometimes trade places with their students in embodied learning situations, the instructor does not become a passive listener or just another body in the classroom. When sitting with her students in the rows of desks, Ms. Tainot makes eye contact and interacts in new ways. In other words, effective teachers "listen carefully and watch, providing guidance or asking questions to help students avoid dead-ends and to focus on central issues" (Cook-Sather, Bovill, & Felten, 2012, p. 6).

Figure 13.2. Ms. Mercedes Tainot (Julia Roberts) in Larry Crowne *(2011)*

When acting as an embodied guide or facilitator, teachers often promote teambuilding exercises to engage the body and mind. Howden describes teambuilding

LIBERATORY PEDAGOGY IN ACTION

exercises by explaining that "[d]uring each task, participants are being challenged (physically and mentally), which tends to create mental and social distress. Well managed, this distress creates opportunities to break down barriers and opens the potential for self-discovery by individuals and groups" (2012, p. 48). In *Community*, a group of students work together in Anthropology 101 to decide which tool was the most important for early humans. For the purposes of humor, the scene centers on Professor Bauer's use of age-old weapons. While the group conversations are never heard onscreen, they are implied by the set-up provided by the scene, and viewers can imagine the students touching the tools, considering their uses, and creating their own arguments concerning their selected tools.

Outside of the professor's use of problem-solving and teambuilding exercises, liberatory pedagogy involves just being engaged with students inside and outside of the classroom. In other words, professors cross borders physically as well as emotionally. Prior to presenting examples from television, scholar Amanda Sinclair shares her experience with border crossing as she exits the business classroom and teaches a yoga class with students, faculty, and staff present: "As their yoga teacher, my relationships with some of students and colleagues changed, becoming both more blurred and more spacious. I gain great satisfaction from their increasing flexibility, watching them peel out of their bodily rigidity and supporting them to extend themselves physically and emotionally" (2005, p. 101). In professors' interactions with students outside of the classroom, power and authority are shared as students and professors engage their minds and bodies in activities while learning more about each other. *Community* contains many border crossings as deans, professors, and staff engage in activities along with students. Greendale students and faculty come together for lively interactions and activities engaging their minds and bodies, such as dances, athletic events, debates, aircraft simulations, plays, and social experiments.

FICTIONAL REPRESENTATIONS OF COMMUNITY COLLEGE EDUCATORS IN FILM AND TELEVISION

When taking into consideration the representations of community college educators in film and television, what do viewers learn from fictional representations? How do fictional representations influence the way people view community college educators and their institutions? Dagaz and Harger suggest that "media representations may be particularly strong among students with no access to firsthand information about college life" (2011, p. 276). Students with lower socioeconomic backgrounds may not have access to close friends and family who have attended college, so websites, television, and movies help paint a picture of college life inside and outside of the classroom. The negative representations of community college faculty, specifically, as well as community colleges as institutions, in general, send the message that students cannot possibly receive a quality education in an environment that lacks academic rigor and well-qualified faculty. Sadly, the false message continues

157

to spread until students enter into a community college setting that proves their assumptions false.

Unfortunately, false depictions of community college faculty in television and film shape the beliefs and attitudes of some university educators. In fact, in "Critical Pedagogy: Dreaming of Democracy," Ann George draws attention to Ira Shor's "blistering critique" of the community college system: "Unlike elite liberal arts colleges, which prepare students for roles as future problem-solvers and decision-makers, community colleges with their vocational curricula train students to follow orders and accept subordinate society: 'mass colleges were not to be Ivory Towers or 'the best years of your life' or homecoming parades on crisp autumn afternoons" (2001, p. 95). Shor's critique of the community college system corresponds to the disembodied view of the community college classroom. Although Shor's comment predates *Community* and *Larry Crowne*, his thoughts capture the prevalent misunderstanding about the embodied classroom learning that takes place in community colleges every day. Because of the community college's historical roots in vocational education, many believe that community colleges are a place for memorizing facts and mastering skills. Unfortunately, such attitudes keep university and community college faculty from communicating and collaborating with one another. The hybrid character of the community college muddies the direct ties that exist between faculty teaching community college transferable subjects and university faculty.

In addition to the challenges community colleges face in eliminating negative attitudes, community college educators encounter the challenge of educating current and future students about the benefits of embodied pedagogy. hooks recognizes the obstacles educators struggle to overcome when they practice liberatory pedagogy: "[M]any students confuse a lack of recognizable traditional formality with a lack of seriousness" (1994, p. 143). She also states, "To prove your academic seriousness, students should be almost dead, quiet, asleep, not up, excited, and buzzing, lingering around the classroom" (1994, p. 145). The connection hooks makes between liberatory pedagogy and a mistaken lack of seriousness relates to the disembodied representations of university faculty in film and television. The representation of a professor positioned on a podium and lecturing from behind a lectern in an Ivy League school sends the message that other schools should follow the set example. The movement of bodies, the noise of multiple groups discussing an important issue, and the occasional sound of laughter in an engaged classroom contrasts with the rows of students seated in silence. To an outsider, the busy embodied classroom may appear chaotic while the disembodied classroom seems serious, formal, and disciplined. The fact that many embodied classroom performances take place in comedies further engrains the idea that embodied learning is not serious learning.

The differences in perception of the embodied versus the disembodied classroom have, in some cases, serious consequences for faculty members in both community colleges and universities. In student evaluations of teaching, it is possible that students who believe the disembodied teaching style to be ideal may provide negative feedback for those who employ an embodied approach to teaching. Although scholars have not measured feedback concerning embodied and disembodied teaching styles, other studies suggest that when a professor's performance does not match students' expectations, students often express their dissatisfaction on evaluation forms. For instance, "[f]indings indicate that women who do not follow gendered stereotypical expectations tend to be evaluated lower than those who do" (Dagaz & Harger, 2011, p. 284). Therefore, if expectations tied to gender help determine whether a student provides negative or positive feedback, it makes sense that expectations connected to teaching styles will influence a student's feedback.

CONCLUSION

It is important for all post-secondary educators to engage in discussions about embodied learning with their students. For many years, scholars have touted the benefits of embodied learning in peer-reviewed journals. Students have not been a part of the conversations, however. Their expectations of higher learning have been shaped largely by film and television. A clever quote included in the syllabus concerning embodied learning may generate a conversation about its value on the first day of class. When educators assist students in understanding the reasons behind pedagogical practices, they help dismantle the idealized image of the disembodied professor in film and television.

REFERENCES

Cook-Sather, Alison, Catherine Bovill, & Peter Felten. (2014). *Engaging students as partners in learning and teaching: A guide for faculty.* San Francisco, CA: Jossey-Bass.

Dagaz, Mari, & Brent Harger. (2011). Race, gender, and research: Implications for teaching from depictions of professors in popular film, 1985–2005. *Teaching Sociology, 39*(3), 274–289.

Davis, Donald M. (1990). Portrayals of women in prime-time network television: some demographic characteristics. *Sex Roles, 23*(5–6), 325–332.

Franklin, Betty Smith. (2003). The teacher's body. In Diane P. Freedman & Holmes M. Stoddard (Eds.), *The teacher's body: Embodiment, authority, and identity in the academy* (pp. 15–22). Albany, NY: SUNY Press.

Freire, Paulo. (2000). *Pedagogy of the oppressed.* 1970. New York, NY: Continuum.

George, Ann. (2001). Critical pedagogy: Dreaming of democracy. In Gary Tate, Amy Rupiper Taggart, & Kurt Schick (Eds.), *A guide to composition pedagogies* (pp. 92–112). New York, NY: Oxford University Press.

Grumet, Madeleine R. (2003). Afterword: My teacher's body. In Diane P. Freedman & Holmes M. Stoddard (Eds.), *The teacher's body: Embodiment, authority, and identity in the academy* (pp. 249–258). Albany, NY: SUNY Press.

hooks, bell. (1994). *Teaching to transgress: Education as the practice of freedom.* New York, NY: Routledge.

Howden, Eric. (2012). Outdoor experiential education: Learning through the body. In Randee L. Lawrence (Ed.), *Bodies of knowledge: Embodied learning in adult education* (pp. 43–51). San Francisco, CA: Jossey-Bass.

Knoblauch, Abby A. (2012). Bodies of knowledge: Definitions, delineations, and implications of embodied writing in the academy. *Composition Studies, 40*(2), 50–65.

K. L. CRAWLEY

Meyer, Pamela. (2012). Embodied learning at work: Making the mind-set shift from workplace to playspace. In Randee L. Lawrence (Ed.), *Bodies of knowledge: Embodied learning in adult education* (pp. 25–51). San Francisco, CA: Jossey-Bass.

Mountford, Roxanne. (2003). *The gendered pulpit: Preaching in American protestant spaces.* Carbondale, IL: Southern Illinois University Press.

Pineau, Elyse Lamm. (2002). Critical performative pedagogy: Fleshing out the politics of liberatory education. In Nathan Stucky & Cynthia Wimmer (Eds.), *Teaching performance studies* (pp. 41–54). Carbondale, IL: Southern Illinois University Press.

Sinclair, Amanda. (2005). Body and management pedagogy. *Gender, Work and Organization, 12*(1), 89–104.

ROSLIN SMITH

14. Q THE TEACHER—TV LESSONS FROM THE 24TH CENTURY

You Do Not Have to Be an Omniscient Teacher, But It Helps

ABSTRACT

The character Q from the TV series *Star Trek: The Next Generation,* is an obnoxious and omnipotent male humanoid, often perceived by the crew of the starship Enterprise as an interfering, condescending bully. This chapter examines Q's key characteristics, costumes, absurd shenanigans, and his implementation of egregious exercises with the crew during seven *Star Trek* episodes. Q's persona, proclivity for masquerade, and playground antics are also explored as he evolves over the course of the series from one of malevolence to a fatherly figure. Each of the seven episodes focuses on Q's teaching ingenuity and exemplifies how his lousy behavior is really his stratagem for the illustrious Starfleet officers to learn tough lessons.

Keywords: teachers, students, methodologies, narrative, *Star Trek*, Q, Captain Picard

***

Quintessential big-screen teachers include Mr. Chips (*Goodbye, Mr. Chips* 1939), Yoda (*The Empire Strikes Back* 1980), and Ms. Gruwell (*Freedom Writers* 2007). These movie gods and goddesses and others fitting into the model have mastered the Good Teacher pedagogy, and their names are synonymous with patience, respect, and skilled professionalism. They are all eclipsed, however, by Q (John de Lancie) from *Star Trek: The Next Generation* (Syndicated 1987–94). Relegated to the TV screen, this male, humanoid pedagogue is often perceived as an interfering, condescending bully plaguing the crew of the Starship Enterprise during several intergalactic adventures in the popular science-fiction series, part of the franchise created by Gene Roddenberry. Yet, by examining Q's key characteristics, costumes, and the absurd shenanigans he performs, it becomes clear that the character serves a larger narrative purpose. I will explore how this obnoxious, shape-shifting entity implements surprisingly effective exercises during seven *Star Trek* episodes and, thus, demonstrate that what appears to be Q's lousy behavior is really his stratagem for teaching the illustrious Starfleet officers tough lessons.

© KONINKLIJKE BRILL NV, LEIDEN, 2019 | DOI:10.1163/9789004398092_014

R. SMITH

The pilot for *Star Trek: The Next Generation*, "Encounter at Farpoint," introduces all the main characters, including Captain Jean-Luc Picard (Patrick Stewart). As the new commander of the Starship Enterprise, Picard's diegetic voiceover narration immediately talks of "the mystery of Farpoint" and the "great unexplored mass of the galaxy" that establishes him as a character with the desire to learn, to explore, and to acquire knowledge, a central conceit in the Star Trek series. This is also the first time that Picard and his crew encounter Q. From the outset, the Enterprise bridge crew (and viewers) wonder what the name "Q" symbolizes. Is it just the seventeenth letter of the Roman alphabet or something more meaningful? Does it stand for Question, Quest or uniQue? Since Q can take on other forms, perhaps he is actually a she, and Q stands for Queen? In reality, the creator of the series, Gene Roddenberry, adopted the first character of his friend's surname, Janet Quarton (2), which has no significance to the universe explored in the series.

With an IQ of 2,005, Q's omnipotence and immortality imbue him with godlike qualities that enable him to manipulate time and space, as well as an annoying capability to materialize out of thin air. In this way, Q parallels the Old Testament's malevolent God, whom Oxford ethologist Richard Dawkins scathingly called a "capriciously malevolent bully" (2006, p. 3). Indeed, after the spurious death of Captain Picard in "Tapestry," Q's proclivity for masquerade allows him to don dazzling, white robes as the stereotypical Christian God in the afterlife. All he is missing is the long beard and hair. Throughout the series, Q delivers his own Ten Commandments to our cosmic travelers with instructions to behave and grow up, to work in groups, and to have empathy for everyone. Many teachers try to encourage these ideals in lessons and might even post some iteration of them on classroom walls, but Q is a far, far better teacher than anyone who has gone before. Our Trekkies just don't know that this early in the series.

Creating a good first impression is an instruction that all teachers have heard (and most embrace). Q is no exception. "Encounter at Farpoint" has him materializing onto the bridge from nowhere, dressed as a Conquistador. This denotes that Q, like Captain Picard, is a great explorer, albeit a potentially lethal one. His 15th century costume underscores themes of barbarism, slavery, and exploitation reminiscent of the Age of Discovery and Exploration that, according to Q, parallels the ethos of 24th century travelers on the Enterprise. In this episode, other costume changes—from a WWII marine to a futuristic, drug-dazed soldier—highlight Q's belief that humankind is a savage, childlike race. Throughout the series, subjugators and masculine hegemony persist as the extra-dimensional being impersonates a Napoleonic French Marshall, a Judge from the Spanish Inquisition, and an English Sheriff of Nottingham, though it must also be noted that Q does have a propensity for donning the Starfleet uniform, too.

For teachers entering their very first class, Q's ideas are inspirational (if not aspirational), but classroom teachers can be sure a Mexican poncho, trumpet, and Mariachi singers constitute cultural appropriation. Professors do not always have to dress up to perform an educational role, however. Great teachers know how to

162

command their pupils' attention upon entering the classroom, a skill mastered by Q. In "Déjà Q," he outperforms all of the teachers I know by teleporting onto the bridge and floating in midair completely naked. "I am defrocked. Stripped of my powers," he whines, underscoring a quick lesson that by stripping away all preconceived notions of teaching, fresh ideas can float to the surface. Although innovative thinking is often welcome, it is not recommended that we follow Q by disrobing. Undoubtedly, campus policy would deem this as indecent behavior.

Figure 14.1. Q (John de Lancie) on Star Trek: The Next Generation *(Syndicated 1987–94)*

Encouraging good behavior from students is perennially a worthy goal in class management, and Q is no different from the rest of us in his desire to achieve order. In "Encounter at Farpoint," he uses Lieutenant Torres (Jimmy Ortega) as an example of how bad behavior has consequences when Q freezes the lieutenant into a solid block of ice. By setting strict boundaries, represented by Q's force field that impedes the Enterprise's journey, the foundation for good conduct is established. Similar to boundary-setting efforts in class, parallels with our own students are recognizable in the rebellion of the Enterprise bridge crew. Ever the Klingon warrior, Lieutenant Worf (Michael Dorn) wishes to fight his way out while empath Counselor Deanna Troi (Marina Sirtis) wants to avoid all contact; Picard decides to catch Q by surprise. Good teachers are not thwarted in their quest for obedience, and Q exemplifies this

163

by chastising his novices in a courtroom reminiscent of the Spanish Inquisition. The setting, enhanced by Q's 15th century papal robes, underscores themes of brutality and injustice. Indeed, under the threat of murdering Natasha (Denise Crosby) and Data (Brent Spiner), Picard pleads guilty to Q's charge that humans are a "grievously savage race." The lesson plan is deftly executed, and Q has his novices under control; our campus administrators might harshly criticize his technique.

As with all lesson methodologies, assessment is an indispensable tool, even though our students often lament the dreaded evaluations. Q's lessons have been so effective, however, that Picard is rather different from our typical student of today because he demands a test. It is of no surprise that Q's test is not a standard multiple choice or thousand-word essay. Instead, his is a practical test of skill and endurance. Not unlike some of our students, Picard has no idea what the test is about, where it will take place, or when it will be. Q whisks his students to the experiential testing room, Farpoint Starbase, on the golden planet of Deneb IV. Farpoint's council representative, Groppler Zorn (Michael Bell), gives members of the Enterprise crew everything they desire while Q is opposed to this. After members of the crew explore underground caverns and rescue Zorn, Q asks Picard, "Is it too adult a puzzle?" Q's derision prods the crew to figure things out and, as a byproduct, discover a new life form resembling a giant jellyfish. It is not every day that our students discover

Figure 14.2. Q (John de Lancie) on Star Trek: The Next Generation *(Syndicated 1987–94)*

new life forms, but if they can discover a new and valuable source for citation in their papers, then we can appreciate the wonder this type of knowledge instills. Q acknowledges that "generosity" is his weakness, something we as teachers can all relate to when a student comes to the office unable to fathom the answer to that pesky math equation.

The puzzle is just one example of how Q's love of games finds its way into his lessons and demonstrates his ingenuity as a teacher. In "Hide and Q," pursuant to the pun title, the games he plays are befuddling, even frustrating, but unearth a hidden cache. Q intercepts the USS Enterprise and immediately demands that members of the crew play a game. His first strategy is to take his students out of their comfort zone and onto unfamiliar ground. Despite their protests, Q teleports them to a parched planet, leaving their trusted Captain Picard behind. The desolate landscape proves to be the incubator for imagination. Appropriating from present day educational rhetoric, Q explicitly states that the goal is "the realization of your impossible dream." Continuing with present-day hyperbole, Q says that the game winners will create "the greatest possible future imaginable." Despite imagination as the only rule for playing the game, the novices wail that the penalty box is "completely unfair." What teacher has not heard that refrain before? This childish analogy persists throughout the series and is epitomized by Data practicing his whistling skills through the childish song "Pop Goes the Weasel" in an effort to become human.

Playground antics serve as a fortifying landscape for valuable experiential lessons in "Q Who." Whisked onto the Enterprise shuttlecraft, Captain Picard encounters Q bouncing a ball back and forth. With a deft sleight of thought, they arrive back onboard the Enterprise, which denotes Q's classroom. Displaying a bad example of teacher/student interaction, Q insults Worf by calling him "micro brain." Yet, this may be Q's way of fostering a positive group dynamic, since members of the bridge crew are upset by Q's ridicule of the macro cephalic Klingon. In any case, like a good teacher who navigates the classroom, Q adroitly jumps from Ten Forward (the lounge) to the Bridge, moving between, around, and behind his students and quietly listening to their group discussions. "Where's your adventurous spirit and imagination?" Q demands. "You are not prepared for what awaits," he warns, signifying how ill prepared some of our students can be if they try to do things before they are ready. Just as many of our students struggle with new computer software, Q is instrumental in introducing the challenge of mechanization as embodied by The Borg, the ultimate cybernetic drones within a collective consciousness that Carl Jung would have relished. Eventually, Picard's futile endeavors to overcome The Borg means he has to concede to Q: "I understand. You wanted to frighten us, and you wanted me to say I need you, but could the lesson not have been learned without the loss of 18 crew members?" pleads Picard. Maintaining the playground hectoring, Q retorts, "If you can't take a little bloody nose, maybe you ought to go back home." Q demonstrates his skill as a stern teacher who has given the Enterprise crew members a kick to their complacency. Just like our students, who often slack off work, the crew of the Enterprise need a nudge in the right direction to prepare them for the future.

R. SMITH

As students begin to master new material, mentors often serve as supervisors and gatekeepers of the learning process. Picard tells Commander Riker (Jonathan Frakes) that they are "on probation" in "Q Who?" In "Opid," Picard tells Dianna that he has "done his homework" but still needs to practice. Q takes his time before making his appearance in this episode, highlighting a "hands off" approach to teaching. Under the guise of repaying a debt to Picard, the extra-dimensional being uses a "field trip" to demonstrate Picard's weakness, his love of a woman called Vash (Jennifer Hetrick). In keeping with Q's fondness for medieval history, he transports our merry band to the woods of Sherwood Forest. Once again, childish role-playing and dress up is the name of this game with Picard as Robin Hood, Vash as Maid Marion, and Q as the malevolent Sheriff of Nottingham. Viewers watching the episode can appreciate the chaos, and teachers among them will likely be able to spot ways in which these characters behave similarly to their own students on field trips. Commander William Riker is Little John, the star pupil who does as he is told, which contrasts with Vash, who is frustrating by virtue of insisting on not playing by the rules. Data is the overachieving, smart-but-awkward nerd who ends up getting shot in his positronic chest by hapless Deanna's wayward arrow. Worf is the sullen student who just isn't into this particular history lesson, Geordie (LeVar Burton) is the slacker who just wants to play his cittern, and Dr. Beverly Crusher (Gates McFadden) is conveniently present to bandage up Worf's injuries. Like most great field trips, all involved return home safely, and Picard reflects on the lesson, agreeing that his love for a woman is his Achilles heel but also, paradoxically, his strength. Overall, Q's teaching plan is a do-it-yourself activity featuring instructions on how students can choose their partners with the reassurance that he will be in the background in case the students need any help. Of course, every field trip needs a big payoff, so Q dresses up once again, this time as a Big Game Hunter accompanied by Vash. Remember, every good teacher needs to have fun once in a while.

Episode "Déjà Q" features the unlikely educator being thrown out of the Continuum with his powers revoked. Under the tutelage of Captain Picard and Data, Q reverses his teacher's role and exemplifies how a good teacher can learn from his pupils while demonstrating that a little bit of humility is a good thing. Of course, this realization does not arrive without complications. "These are not my colors," our fashionista laments with regard to his new gray and green uniform. Despite his deposed status, Q can still find time to mock. Attempting to rattle Worf, Q asks, "Eat any good books lately?" Hence, Q's first assignments are designed to curtail his ability to irk and deflate his massive ego, despite his protest that he is "no good in groups." After all, "It is difficult to work in a group if you are omnipotent." Delegated to the engineering crew, Q has to co-operate, albeit petulantly, as he asks Data about Geordie, "Who does he think he is, giving me an order?" "He is the Commander," Data gently reminds him. For Q, Data is the "robot who teaches courses in the Humanities," and the irony is not lost, especially when Data sacrifices himself to save our supreme schoolteacher. Q's pomposity is punctured by his uncharacteristic, selfless act of trying to sacrifice himself for the good of the Enterprise. Working in groups, developing empathy, and forming relationships are the objectives of this lesson.

Over the course of the series, Q's persona has evolved from one of malevolence into a fatherly figure. Although he speaks English, he often addresses Picard in French as a way of recognizing the captain's French ancestry. "Temper, temper, mon capitaine," Q chastises Picard in "Tapestry," signifying a paternal sensitivity toward the Captain of the Enterprise. Christian belief sprinkles many of the lessons taught by Q, and in "Tapestry," Q evokes the paternal, Christian God while Picard connotes Jesus, who—although not nailed to a cross—is actually nailed by a Nausicaan. In the final episode, "All Good Things," Q transports Picard to 3.5 billion years in the past to witness the birth of humankind in a puddle of pond scum. Echoing the Trinity, there are three timelines, three Enterprises, and three crews who have to make a "leap of faith" to save the universe. As Picard and the crew members reach their full potential, Q reveals that his Continuum colleagues "did not think you had it in you, but I did." This is Q's final lesson, believe in yourself and be better than you think you can be. This all-important lesson is the hardest for real-life teachers to emulate and demonstrates Q's intellectual adroitness without diminishing his persona as a bad teacher. Q ends his appearances on the series with a warning: "In any case, I'll be watching. And, if you're very lucky, I'll drop by to say hello from time to time. See you ... out there!" Graduation is within reach for students on the Enterprise and those willing to learn fundamental lessons.

REFERENCES

Alexander, David. (1995). *Star Trek creator. The authorized biography of Gene Roddenberry* (p. 583). New York, NY: Penguin Group.

Dawkins, Richard. (2006). *The god delusion* (p. 31). London: Bantam Press.

MARY M. DALTON

15. SPEECHLESS TO *SPEECHLESS*

Nontraditional Teacher Characters in Recent Sitcoms

ABSTRACT

Television series have featured teachers since the first years of the medium. Connie Brooks, of *Our Miss Brooks* (CBS 1952–56), is among the most popular sitcom educators, and she conforms easily to the pattern of the idealized teacher, which dominated among TV series until the last fifteen years. In keeping with traditional, gendered representations, she was a spinster. In recent years, depictions of TV teachers have become more complex, such as Roland "Prez" Pryzbylewski (HBO 2002–08). At first, this was a positive development as women characters balanced a successful professional life with personal relationships, but the trend has reversed more recently. The "good" teacher on TV has become overshadowed by negative portrayals of educators who: flee in emotional distress (*Mike & Molly*, CBS 2010–16); behave inappropriately (*Teachers*, TV Land 2016–19); straddle the childish and tawdry (*Those Who Can't*, 2016–); and, are generally deplorable (*Vice Principals*, HBO 2016–18). Two of the most promising educator characters on television are not conventional teachers, Kenneth (*Speechless*, ABC 2016–), an aide to a severely disabled student, and Issa (*Insecure*, HBO 2016–) an employee at a non-profit education organization. Kenneth and Issa, both played by African-American actors, are not classroom teachers, and their status as "outsiders" to the institution of education (a concept also explored in terms of race) separates them from the downward spiral of depictions of educators on television, notably the deprofessionalization of teaching during the years since the enactment of No Child Left Behind and Common Core. This chapter examines intersectional approaches to Kenneth's character in *Speechless* ranging from his positioning as a man of color, a caregiver, a "man's man," an honorary member of the family, and a school employee and explores these categories as a basis for the construction and performance of a character that brings more positive than negative attributes into the blighted media landscape featuring educators on television.

Keywords: education, educators teaching, teachers, popular culture, television sitcom, media studies, race, gender, disability studies

© KONINKLIJKE BRILL NV, LEIDEN, 2019 | DOI:10.1163/9789004398092_015

M. M. DALTON

INTRODUCTION

After a storied past in classrooms on the small screen, teacher characters have declined from teaching, mentoring, and inspiring students into a collection of childish, churlish, vulgar, burned out, disturbed incompetents. These depictions reinforce erroneous stereotypes of educators and contribute to the de-professionalizing of teaching. Television series have featured teachers as stock characters since the first years of the medium. Connie Brooks of *Our Miss Brooks* (CBS 1952–56) is among the most popular sitcom educators, and she conforms easily to the pattern of the idealized teacher, which dominated among TV series until the turn of this century. In keeping with traditional, gendered representations, she is a spinster. The many men who followed her in subsequent television series may or may not have been coupled with other characters romantically, but like Miss Brooks, they have been cast in a heroic mold most often (unless they were administrators). Laura R. Linder and I have written about these patterns of representation extensively in our book, *Teacher TV: Seventy Years of Teachers on Television* in which we link the sociohistorical context of the time period to television series across decades. In recent years, depictions of TV teachers have become more complex. At first, this was a positive development as women characters balanced a successful professional life with personal relationships (*Friday Night Lights* NBC 2006–11; see also Dalton, 2017, pp. 29–36) and heroic teachers who transcend the hackneyed "White savior" model in complex and compelling series (Season 4 of *The Wire*, HBO 2002–08; see also Dalton & Linder, 2019, pp. 163–171; Erb, 2017, pp. 165–69), but the trend has reversed more recently. The Good Teacher on TV has become overshadowed by negative portrayals of educators who: flee in emotional distress (*Mike & Molly* CBS 2010–16); behave inappropriately (*Teachers* TV Land 2016–19; see also Regan, 2017); straddle the childish and tawdry (*Those Who Can't* truTV 2016–); and, are generally deplorable (*Vice Principals* HBO 2016–18; see also Harris in this volume). The rare appearance of a caring and competent teacher, the type of depiction that used to be commonplace if not the norm, is mostly relegated to the odd, one-off appearance of a series guest star, such as Professor Grant (Josh Cooke), who appears in the "Crushed" episode of *The Middle* (ABC 2009–18) and is kind but professional with Sue Heck (Eden Sher) when he recognizes that she has a crush on him.

Two of the most promising educator characters on television are not conventional teachers, Kenneth (*Speechless* ABC 2016–), an aide to a severely disabled student, and Issa (*Insecure* HBO 2016–), an employee at a non-profit education organization. This is a notable turn of events because both series situate the characters outside of our traditional understanding of teaching and institutions of education. Kenneth and Issa are both played by African-American actors. Their position as "outsiders"— both in terms of their status with the institution of education and in terms of race— separates them in the media worlds they inhabit from the downward spiral of depictions of educators on television, notably the de-professionalization of teaching that accompanied the adoption of No Child Left Behind and Common Core.

170

SPEECHLESS TO *SPEECHLESS*

Naeemah Clark offers a detailed analysis of Issa Rae's character in the chapter "The *Insecure* Teacher: How Issa Rae Has Normalized the Black Woman to Create TV Magic," whereas this essay explores intersectional approaches to Kenneth's character in *Speechless*—ranging from his positioning as a man of color, a caregiver, a "man's man," an honorary member of the family, and a school employee—as a basis for the construction and performance of a character that brings more positive than negative attributes into the blighted media landscape featuring educators on television.

SPEECHLESS IS ANYTHING BUT

Speechless premiered in September 2016 to positive reviews and ratings that were strong and consistent enough across the 23 episodes in its inaugural season to have the sitcom picked up for a second year on ABC. This domestic sitcom features the DiMeos, a quirky family unit that moves around Orange County, California to find the best schools for the oldest of three siblings, a 16-year-old boy restricted to his wheelchair due to cerebral palsy, a condition that also leaves him unable to speak. So much attention is focused on JJ DiMeo (Micah Fowler), that his younger brother Ray (Mason Cook) and sister Dylan (Kyla Kenedy) are used to accommodating the plans made by fierce advocate mom Maya (Minnie Driver) and easy-going dad Jimmy (John Ross Bowie). When their latest move takes them to a public high school where JJ will be mainstreamed and provided a full-time aide to speak for him (paid for by school funds), the situation pushes Maya out of her role as JJ's primary voice and into the uncomfortable spot of accepting her son's choice of aide in place of the disastrous first hire. In keeping with the broad strokes of The Hollywood Model of the Good Teacher, the character written to fill this role is an outsider, personally involved with his student, engaged in reciprocal learning through his relationship with the DiMeos, personalizes the curriculum to meet JJ's needs, and has a sense of humor. If one considers Maya analogous in role to an administrator, then he has conflict with administration, too (Dalton *Hollywood Curriculum* 21–41). Who is the aide JJ chooses? The job goes to school groundskeeper Kenneth (Cedric Yarbrough), an African-American man with a resonant and soothing voice. This is essential to JJ since the aide will serve as his voice by reading words and letters that JJ points to on a board with a laser strapped to his head.

The DiMeos's first meeting with Kenneth in the "P-I-- PILOT" advances plot and introduces characters (the episode titles are all written to express dialogue readings as if characters are spelling out words from JJ's board by reading aloud several letters before the word is recognized and spoken in whole). JJ has been complaining to Jimmy that he hates the assigned aide's voice when the principal, Dr. Miller (Marin Hinkle), bounces out to meet the family. She acknowledges there is no wheelchair ramp at the front school entrance and takes the DiMeos away to a garbage ramp has been designated "acceptable alternative access." Kenneth walks up with flowers to plant in time to register Maya's disapproval and adds that a "sweet, crippled grandma" used the ramp to get to a sporting event the previous week. The lines

171

of conflict are drawn immediately, and the rest of the DiMeos prepare for retreat from yet another school, as Maya asks that Kenneth be written up for using hate speech. This time, Maya has met her match, however, not in the shrinking violet of a principal but in "*The* Black man in Newport," who says he appreciates her "*Blind Side* energy," shares that he is "pulled over twice before he leaves the school parking lot," and notes that "the irony of being called intolerant is not lost on me." Maya says immediately that she doesn't like Kenneth, and the rest of the family backs off.

Figure 15.1. JJ DiMeo (Micah Fowler) and Kenneth (Cedric Yarbrough) on Speechless *(ABC 2016–19)*

Emotionally healthy 16-year-olds—whether or not they have physical disabilities—reach a point when they must separate from their parents and flex muscles of independence. While the challenges are greater for some children than for others, the time is right for JJ to make a move. JJ uses his board to connect with Kenneth, "You sound cool." Kenneth takes it in stride, "Of course I sound cool. I am cool." They have an immediate rapport, and JJ offers him the job. With that, the premise of the series is established, and the major characters are introduced. The following sections examine Kenneth's character and his intersectional identities as an unconventional educator, during the first season, linking the categories listed above to his relationships with other characters on the series. This essay makes the case that it is, paradoxically, his marginalized status that allows his positive depiction as an educator during this time when other educator characters are almost uniformly depicted in a negative light. As an aide, rather than a teacher or an administrator, his confidence does not undermine the dominant narrative that deprofessionalizes educators in public schools. The following sections will establish a categorization scheme based on discrete tropes that emerge within the first season of the series. Kevin's identity as man of color is linked to his interactions with JJ in the section

SPEECHLESS TO *SPEECHLESS*

"Beyond the 'Magical Negro,'" his identity as a caregiver is linked to his interactions with Maya in "The Keeper of 'JJ's Care Book,'" his masculine identity is linked to Jimmy in "A Man's Man After All," his identity as a member of the family is linked to Ray and Dylan and others in "Honorary DiMeo," and his identity as a school employee is linked to Dr. Miller and other school personnel in "Informal Educator."

BEYOND THE "MAGICAL NEGRO"

The bond JJ and Kenneth share is almost instantaneous and transcends work to become a deep friendship (as examined later, the aide is under-employed and becomes almost a member of the family). Their connection is forged on a shared understanding of their intersectional identities and lack of status due to race and physical disability. This link is made clear in the episode "H-E-R-- HERO." Ray wants to win a speech competition by writing about JJ, which JJ rejects until some student in the school he doesn't even know writes "inspirational porn" about him. When Kenneth asks what that is, Ray recites "It's a portrayal of people with disabilities as one-dimensional saints who only exist to warm the hearts and open the minds of able-bodied people." Ray, whose goal for winning is to secure funds to buy a hoverboard, now has his older brother's permission to win by writing a speech that makes "people cry and give me pity looks and encouraging pats on the arm, the stuff I hate."[1] Ray starts writing, and JJ indicates words on his board with Kenneth reading out loud, "Now, make me happy all the time. All I want is to help the able-bodied learn and grow." Kenneth stops reading the board and speaks for himself. "Hey! This is the magical Negro!" The two boys just look at him. "You know, like in the movies where the Black character's just there to help the White guy on his journey? And, he mainly speaks in folksy sayings, 'and, I don't know much about blah-blah-blah, and I have a blah.'" JJ writes on his board, "We both get clichés." Kenneth responds, "We sure do, buddy."

The relationship that develops between Kenneth and JJ is one of the strongest elements of the series. From it, in very natural ways, there are teachable moments for viewers and opportunities to expand the understanding viewers may have about physical disabilities. At the beginning of the second episode of the series "N-E-- NEW A-I-- AIDE," Maya wants to know why JJ wants Kenneth to be his aide. "I like him," he writes. "Yeah, what else?" asks his mother. "You don't." She goes on to say that he mows grass for a living and that his chief job competition is goats then is unembarrassed to discover that he has heard her. When Kenneth gives Maya a hug, she doesn't hug back. He wears a jacket and tie this first day of work (reinforcing his outsider status because he is overdressed), but when he settles in to talk with JJ, it becomes apparent to viewers (if not yet to Maya) that his basic decency and sense of humor make him a promising aide. "Do I handle bathroom stuff?" JJ nods yes. "Does your dude stuff work?" Another yes. "Is my voice good to speak for you?" Yes. "I can go lower" (demonstrating a much lower vocal range). No! As they settle into a routine at school and Kenneth asks what JJ's interested in, the boy moves his

173

M. M. DALTON

laser across the rear ends of all of the girls in the hallway. As James Schultz argues about the series *Legit*, there are few series that depict people who are not able-bodied and even fewer that legitimize the sexuality of people with physical disabilities. Openly identifying JJ's romantic interest in girls serves as a political project and also provides a link between him and his aide.[2]

The Keeper of JJ's Care Book

Witnessing that connection between Kenneth and JJ is what keeps the aide in this job. Maya wants the principal to fire Kenneth—to do her dirty work so JJ won't be mad at her—and is thrilled to hear that the school district has not approved the request because Kenneth doesn't have the proper training. That is, until she goes to the bathroom door at the school where the aide has taken JJ when he has an urgent need and realizes that her belief that "He needs *me* for that!" is not true. From the door, she can tell Kenneth is helping JJ inside a stall and hears, "No need to thank me. We're boys." JJ laughs, and Maya is reassured by Kenneth's kindness and sensitivity. Back in Dr. Miller's office, Maya demands, "We're keeping Kenneth" then instructs the principal to "play the race card" to keep him. At the DiMeo home, Kenneth is already being integrated into daily life. His first day on the job, Kenneth drives the van off a short distance before realizing that Jimmy has not yet put the boy and his chair into the back. But, by the second day, Maya says, "Yesterday, I didn't like or trust you. Today, I trust you." Dramatic tension and character arcs being what they are in episodic television, the conflicts are not over for these two, but there is a sort of equilibrium unfolding, and Kenneth has *JJ's Care Book* that Maya has put together on "how not to kill my son."

Throughout the season, various situations arise that disrupt the equilibrium. Kenneth, who loves the social aspects of high school and facilitates lots of connections for JJ, takes his charge to a Halloween party ("H-A-L-- HALLOWEEN"). The aide tells him not to drink beer, but other students conspire to give him one through a straw when he sends Kenneth on errands. Kenneth is horrified to discover the truth and feels betrayed by the teenager, who asks, "What's the big deal?" Kenneth says, "The big deal is that I'm trying to earn your parents' trust," and at first Maya wants to fire the aide when she discovers JJ is drunk. After JJ admits that he tricked Kenneth, she and Jimmy ground JJ for three weeks and back off their criticism of the aide. Once alone, the parents are secretly happy because "We just grounded our special needs son for being a normal teenager!" This is an occurrence that would not have happened without Kenneth's presence. Kenneth brings a cold virus into the DiMeo household then extends his nurturance to other members of the family after they catch it—starting with Maya and marking a shift in their relationship when he gives her a manicure and she shows it off to him, "That's the first time I've wanted to show you all five instead of just the middle one"—but the biggest thaw in their relationship occurs in the season finale, "C-A-- CAMP." JJ has become independent enough that he wants to go away for ten weeks of summer camp for kids with special

174

SPEECHLESS TO *SPEECHLESS*

needs. Maya resists, but eventually Kenneth helps her to see that she is wrong and needs to get out of JJ's way to let him explore and grow but also that she will still be his mom. In the process, she states, "You read the book, my *JJ's Care Book*." The aide replies, "Over and over, and it's right ... except the part about the transfers to the bath ... I have a better way to do that." Her response is delivered with a good-natured tone, "Like bloody hell you do." As mother and son argue, Kenneth functions as the voice of reason, and when they need to reconcile, the aide facilitates the rapprochement. By the beginning of the second season, Kenneth is a de facto member of the family and even accompanies the DiMeos on a trip to London to visit Maya's father in the third season.

A "MAN'S MAN" AFTER ALL

Speechless—which, as a series, is anything but—is a well-crafted, single-camera sitcom with a strong ensemble cast. There are typically several storylines per episode, and each of the six primary characters (the DiMeos and Kenneth) is featured regularly. Most of the personal information viewers glean about Kenneth is revealed in throwaway lines. In "D-A-T-E-- DATE?" the aide thinks a cute girl temporarily confined to a wheelchair after a gymnastics injury has asked JJ on a date, but it turns out to be a group study session. "I don't understand," says Kenneth. "All the signs were there. I am never wrong about women ... except for my two ex-wives. Am I always wrong about women?" JJ rolls away from him. In "T-H-A-- THANKSGIVING," he chooses the DiMeos's dysfunctional relationship with Jimmy's brother over his own family drama, which is revealed in snippets when his sister calls and ruins his day by reminding him that "he is the Clements family disappointment." As Kenneth becomes more connected with various members of the DiMeo family, he has storylines that connect him not just with JJ but with other members of the family and, at times, with other characters at the school. It is through Dylan that viewers learn more about Kenneth's past as the Grim Leaper, a champion on the court, who took money from boosters, was dropped from his team, and crashed hard after his success as a forward went to his head. She's a runner, so they connect over athletics and end up on the basketball court then borrow the only thing he misses from that life, a red Corvette, and take the neglected car to get it washed.

Other details emerge over time—he hosts a Jazz Brunch the family doesn't go to, he has a date scheduled for when JJ wants to go to a movie, and most notably he has a part-time job the family doesn't know about—but traditional markers of his masculinity are expressed most clearly in the one episode that connects Kenneth with the patriarch of the DiMeo family. In "S-U-R-- SURPRISE," Maya throws a surprise birthday party for Dylan against her wishes, and Ray watches after JJ as Jimmy and Kenneth struggle to find something in common. They don't agree on music or on any number of other things but decide to explore their mutual love of grilling as a site for male bonding until it is revealed that Jimmy likes gas grills and Kenneth is a charcoal man. In the process of orchestrating a cook-off and taste test,

M. M. DALTON

their banter develops an edge. It turns out the guys do have something in common: talking trash. Earlier in the season, in "I-N-S-- INSPIRATIONS," Kenneth and JJ go to Dodger Stadium and get a bunch of perks for free (which is fun until it becomes more about Kenneth's ego than about them having fun together), and later in the season, Kenneth mediates marital squabbles ("I don't know what to say except Judge Kenneth Court is now in session") between Maya and Jimmy in "P-R-- PROM." Kenneth is depicted as a "man's man" in terms of activities he prefers, the Jeep he drives, his sense of humor, and his innate qualities of leadership,[3] but being situated as an outsider by virtue of race, employment, and family status position him as a Good Teacher (he goes to school to take notes when JJ is absent from class in "R-O-- ROAD T-R-- TRIP" and helps JJ study after realizing he has inadvertently helped him cheat on tests in "C-H-- CHEATER"). While it is refreshing to see a man of color cast in a complex role as a wise nurturer, it is frustrating to see that the traditional educators in the series, Dr. Miller the principal and Mr. Powers (Jonathan Slavin) the history teacher, as a one-dimensional stereotypes.

HONORARY DIMEO

Kenneth is yet another Black man in mass media without a nuclear family of his own, but he quickly becomes absorbed into the DiMeo family. At the beginning of the third episode of the series, "B-O-N-- BONFIRE," Kenneth arrives at the DiMeo house to see Dylan stretching before a run. She has already been established as a track star at the new school. Kenneth muses that her love of running is fitting because she runs for herself and for JJ since he can't walk, which leaves the girl questioning herself and whether or not she actually likes to run. Two episodes later, the Halloween episode ends with the group one step closer to integration: Kenneth wears his Stevie Wonder costume alongside the DiMeos in their family tableau of *Back to the Future* costumes; they wear different costumes, but that is not detectable as they walk down a darkened, neighborhood street away from the camera as a single unit. As noted above, Kenneth has storylines with individual members of the DiMeo family beyond his daily interactions with JJ and altercations with Maya (the grilling competition with Jimmy and basketball connection with Dylan are two previously cited examples), and those provide a foundation for his integration into the family unit. His interactions with the family grow more intimate as he hangs around the kitchen, props his bare feet on the coffee table, and comes by to shower when the family is expected to be away. Maya finally gives Kenneth his own, empty drawer for storing toiletries in "S-L-- SLED H-O-- HOCKEY" after he is the star student in their CPR class, and she grows afraid another family will steal him away from her family.

As the school year begins to wind down and the first season draws near its close, the DiMeos formalize their connection with Kenneth in "P-R-- PROM." All three DiMeo children are at the dance. Kenneth comes back to the house because he forgot something and discovers Maya and Jimmy fighting. It turns out they have so little time alone that they put notes about what makes them angry in a bottle

SPEECHLESS TO *SPEECHLESS*

and save fights until they are alone. After the aide serves as judge in their scenario, things take an emotional turn, and Kenneth wants to know if they are "in it as deep" as he is with their family. The parents lead the aide into the backyard where candles are lit and ask Kenneth to be a part of their family for a really, really long time. They set off fireworks and give him a ring. It is a touching moment. The ring fits, and he says, "I accept." It is only after he is officially one of them that Kenneth has the standing to intercede with Maya in "M-A-- MAY-JAY" and "C-A-- CAMP" to get her to loosen the apron strings enough for JJ to go across the country to camp and, later, to get her to fly there for a proper goodbye after she gets her feelings hurt before he leaves. Her arrival at camp turns out to be dramatic in a way that is commensurate with her character; she helicopters in, which surely makes an important parental metaphor manifest. In the end, however, as mother and child are reunited for a sweet goodbye demonstrating Maya's acceptance of JJ's growing independence, Kenneth pops in the frame between them. This is fitting, since it is the independence the aide has given JJ from his mom that has led the teenager to this point.

INFORMAL EDUCATOR

It is important to note that Kenneth's role at Lafayette High School and in the DiMeo family is as an informal educator. He is kind, wise, and steadfast in these locations, but he is also marginalized in both, not only through his personal identity but also in terms of the status accorded his position. He spends much more time at school with students than other adults. Kenneth is aware of the social lives of the students, especially the popular students, and is the lubricant that greases the wheels of JJ's social interactions. His discomfort with the other grown-ups is apparent in "R-O-- ROAD T-R-- TRIP" when the DiMeo family embarks on an impromptu road trip and leaves Kenneth to go to school and take notes for JJ. Lunch is particularly challenging. The aide quickly discovers that it is uncomfortable talking with students when JJ is not there. Furthermore, he is sent out of the teachers lounge and even ejected from the "chairs room" (storage room filled with chairs) by the housekeeping staff and crossing guard. On his way to eat alone in his car, Kenneth runs into Dr. Miller on her way to eat alone in her office. "It's funny. Without my little guy to hide behind, I don't belong anywhere. I'm not a student. I'm not a teacher," Kenneth says and wonders, "Where do the aides hang out?" Dr. Miller understands, "Hello? Where do the principals hang out?" He joins her and both seem happy for the company. They even make plans to meet after school to share an ice cream in a special place, but Kenneth gets a call from Maya for help and rejoins the DiMeos. At the end of the day, Dr. Miller is at the designated meeting spot holding two snacks and says, "He'll come." Of course, she remains the ultimate outsider, alone again.

As an administrator in a California high school, Dr. Miller earns a living wage while Kenneth has a part-time job as weekend manager at a grocery store that the DiMeos do not know about until near the end of the season ("D-I-- DING"). He

177

M. M. DALTON

tries to avoid detection and hides in the office where he monitors members of the family from multiple security cameras. He is equal parts afraid of the mess they will make in the store and them finding out about his second job. Ultimately, he reveals himself to clear Maya of suspicions that she dinged another vehicle in the parking lot. Once Kenneth comes into the store, he has to explain that he works an extra job so that he can stay with JJ because the aide job doesn't pay well enough on its own. In one breath, Maya calls Kenneth "selfless," and in the next, she asks for the friends and family discount on the old bread. It also turns out that the school system will not pay for Kenneth to work with JJ over the summer. Kenneth knows about the hiatus even though the DiMeo family does not, and accepting the job on those terms, which eliminates pay completely for several months, is more evidence that his work with JJ is a labor of love. As the second season of the series begins, he has sublet his apartment and lives first on a boat then in the family van (unknown to the DiMeos) while JJ is attending camp.

CONCLUSION

For the purposes of this chapter—and in furtherance of locating something beyond the abysmal in depictions of educators on contemporary television series—I have focused on one of the few positive representations of an educator on television, and it is not accidental that Kenneth is neither a traditional teacher nor an administrator. In a period when public policy strips trained educators of professional status and popular culture reinforces the idea that teachers are hacks in dead-end jobs, it is no surprise that these characters have gained traction. That does not make it right. A strong system of public education is more important now than ever before as we watch corporate rights advance at the expense of citizen rights. The surest way to empower citizens, especially in local communities, is to support public schools and give teachers and principals the tools they need to make the next generation more informed, adaptable, and independent. Perhaps the old shows were idealized (see Currin & Schroeder, 2019; Dalton & Linder, 2019; Linder "Finding Comfort," 2019; Schroeder, 2017), even too idealized at times, but the pendulum has swung too far in the other direction, and having the competency and integrity of educators continually eroded in the public sphere undermines their efficacy in actual classrooms and interactions with real-life parents. Screen images are a powerful force with indirect but indelible effects on our understanding of the institutions around us and our human interactions inside and outside of their walls. After all, it is popular narratives that give us cues about who we are and what it means to be human from our earliest years, a sense of the possibilities and limitations that await us. For all of the good that can come from a series like *Speechless* in terms of expanding some viewers' familiarity with and expectations of people with physical disabilities, there is no progress here in multi-dimensional and affirming representations of teachers and administrators. This is not a call for the return of the reductive teacher as hero or White savior teacher still found periodically in what we generally refer to as the movies (sounds

178

a bit quaint now in the age of transmedia and streaming services), but it is a plea at least for balance on the small screen so that there are some affirming examples of teachers bringing joy into the classroom, teachers working for social change, teachers practicing the ethic of care (Illich, 1972), and teachers educating with skill and vigor. These teachers exist in real life as everyday role models for others and inspiring figures for their students, and it is essential to see some characters modeled after them among the teachers on television. The future of our schools—especially restoring support for public schools—and of our students—especially those most in need of resources—may depend on this affirmation of mission and expertise in popular culture.

NOTES

[1] This theme is reiterated during the "J-J'S D-DR-- DREAM" episode in the second season when Ray pretends he has started a charity to impress his girlfriend, and his parents pull off a charade benefit to cover his lie.

[2] This narrative theme becomes more important in the second season of the series as JJ approaches the age of 18 and the end of high school. In various episodes, his family makes it possible for him to share his first kiss with a deaf girl he meets at camp, he tries to function as Kenneth's "wingman" with an attractive Spanish teacher, he has an orchestrated romance with another student who has cerebral palsy, and events come together so that he gets a lot of attention from girls as well as a midnight kiss at a New Year's Eve party. In the third season, JJ does get a girlfriend, a recurring character who appears in multiple episodes.

[3] During the "U-N-- Forgettable P-A-- Pain" episode in the second season, one storyline revolves around Kenneth teaching Jimmy how to become an "alpha male."

REFERENCES

Clark, Naeemah. (2019). The Insecure teacher: How Issa Rae has normalized the black woman to create TV magic. In Mary M. Dalton & Laura R. Linder (Eds.), *Teachers, teaching, and media.* Leiden, The Netherlands: Brill.

Currin, Elizabeth, & Stephanie Schroeder. (2019). Saved by the Belles: Gender roles in the quintessential teen comedy. In Mary M. Dalton & Laura R. Linder (Eds.), *Teachers, teaching, and media.* Leiden, The Netherlands: Brill.

Dalton, Mary M. (2017). I believe in love and friday night lights. In Mary M. Dalton & Laura R. Linder (Eds.), *Screen lessons: What we have learned from teachers on television and in the movies* (pp. 29–36). New York, NY: Peter Lang.

Dalton, Mary M., & Laura R. Linder. (2019). *Teacher TV: Seventy years of teachers on television.* New York, NY: Peter Lang.

Erb, Alexa. (2017). Not everyone's cut out for teaching: Lessons learned from *The Wire*. In Mary M. Dalton & Laura R. Linder (Eds.), *Screen lessons: What we have learned from teachers on television and in the movies* (pp. 165–69). New York, NY: Peter Lang.

Gatto, John Taylor. (1992). *Dumbing us down: The hidden curriculum of compulsory schooling.* Gabriola Island, BC: New Society Publishers.

Harris, Chad. (2019). Promotion to control? School office culture in HBO's *Vice Principals*. In Mary M. Dalton & Laura R. Linder (Eds.), *Teachers, teaching, and media.* Leiden, The Netherlands: Brill.

Illich, Ivan. (1972). *Deschooling society.* New York, NY: Harrow Books/Harper & Row Publishers.

Linder, Laura R. (2017). Finding comfort in Room 222. In Mary M. Dalton & Laura R. Linder (Eds.), *Screen lessons: What we have learned from teachers on television and in the movies* (pp. 149–52). New York, NY: Peter Lang.

M. M. DALTON

Llewellyn, Grace. (1996). Sweet land of liberty. In Matt Hern (Ed.), *Deschooling our lives*. Gabriola Island, BC: New Society Publishers.

Noddings, Nel. (1984). *Caring, a feminine approach to ethics and moral education*. Berkeley, CA: University of California Press.

Regan, Suzanne. (2017). Bad teacher: Bad judgment, bad intentions, or abuse? In Mary M. Dalton & Laura R. Linder (Eds.), *Screen lessons: What we have learned from teachers on television and in the movies* (pp. 123–28). New York, NY: Peter Lang.

Schroeder, Stephanie. (2017). The golden girls: Dorothy Zbornak and lessons about social class. In Mary M. Dalton & Laura R. Linder (Eds.), *Screen lessons: What we have learned from teachers on television and in the movies* (pp. 195–200). New York, NY: Peter Lang.

Schultz, James. (2016). Disability and sitcoms: A legit analysis. In Mary M. Dalton & Laura R. Linder (Eds.), *The sitcom reader: America re-viewed, still skewed* (pp. 295–304). Albany, NY: SUNY Press.

FILM SOURCES

American Pie (1999)
Beautiful Mind, A (2001)
Blackboard Jungle (1955)
Blind Side, The (2009)
Breakfast Club, The (1985)
Conrack (1974)
Cool Runnings (1993)
Dangerous Minds (1995)
Dead Poet's Society (1986)
Detachment (2011)
Empire Strikes Back, The (1980)
English Teacher, The (2013)
Fast Times at Ridgemont High (1982)
Finding Forrester (2000)
Freedom Writers (2007)
Glory Road (2006)
Goodbye, Mr. Chips (1939)
Grand Torino (2008)
A Hard Day's Night (1964)
Jackie Robinson Story, The (1950)
Juno (2007)
Larry Crowne (2011)
Last Samurai (2003)
Lean on Me (1998)
Mr. Holland's Opus (1995)
Music of the Heart (1999)
Rebel without a Cause (1954)
Rock 'n' Roll High School (1979)
Ron Clark Story, The (2006)
Saving Private Ryan (1998)
School of Rock (2003)
Sleepless in Seattle (1993)
Stand and Deliver (1988)
Teachers (1984)
Up the Down Staircase (1967)
Wild One, The (1953)

TELEVISION SOURCES

Arrested Development (Fox 2003–2006, Netflix 2013–)
Beverly Hills 90210 (Fox 1990–2000)
Big Bang Theory, The (CBS 2007–2019)
Bill Cosby Show, The (NBC 1969–1971)
Bob's Burgers (Fox 2011–)
Boy Meets World (ABC 1993–2000)
Buffy the Vampire Slayer (CBS 1996–2003)
Community (NBC and Yahoo! Screen 2009–2015)
Daria (MTV 1997–2002)
Freaks and Geeks (NBC 1999–2000)
Friday Night Lights (NBC 2006–2011)
Friends (NBC 1994–2004)
Glee (Fox 2009–2015)
Good Morning, Miss Bliss (Disney 1987–1989)
How I Met Your Mother (CBS 2005–2014)
King of the Hill (Fox 1997-2010)
Insecure (HBO 2016–)
Mad Men (AMC 2007–2015)
MADtv (Fox 1995–2006, CT 2016)
Mike & Molly (CBS 2010–2016)
Misadventures of an Awkward Black Girl (YouTube 2011–2013)
Mr. Novak (NBC 1963–1965)
New Girl (Fox 2011–2018)
Our Miss Brooks (CBS 1952–1956)
Room 222 (ABC 1969–1974)
Saved by the Bell (NBC 1989–1992)
Saved by the Bell: The College Years (NBC 1993–1994)
Saved by the Bell: The New Class (NBC 1993–2000)
The Simpsons (Fox 1989–)
South Park (Comedy Central 1997–)
Speechless (ABC 2016–)
Star Trek: The Next Generation (Syndicated 1987–1994)
Teachers (TV Land 2016–2019)
Those Who Can't (truTV 2016–)
Vice Principals (HBO 2016–2017)
West Wing, The (NBC 1999–2006)
White Shadow, The (CBS 1978–1981)
Wire, The (HBO 2002–2008)
Wonder Years, The (ABC 1988–1993)

INDEX

A

Absolutely True Diary of a Part-time Indian, The, 112
  Junior, 112
academic(s), academia, 23, 37, 38, 41, 69, 72, 75, 76, 87, 112, 122, 125, 134, 139, 144, 151, 152, 156–158. *See also* educators
  nonacademic, 152
Academy Award, 34
accountability. *See* learning
acculturation, 1, 5
active, 14, 55, 152, 155
  hyperactive, 70
addiction. *See* drugs
administrator(s), administration(s), administrative, ix, 12, 23, 28, 29, 35, 40, 47, 49, 50, 57, 58, 63, 74, 81–96, 122, 125, 133, 134, 137–139, 141, 143–145, 164, 170–172, 177, 178
  assistant principal(s), 89, 94
  department chair, 47, 48, 55, 83
  fatherly, 125
  patriarchal administrative class, 47,
  principal(s), 10, 27, 39, 58, 62, 63, 81–83, 85, 88–90, 92, 94, 119, 120, 122, 124, 126, 127, 129, 138, 171, 172, 174, 176–178
    autocrat, 81, 88, 92, 94
    buffoon, 81, 82, 86, 89, 92–94
    bureaucrat, bureaucratic, 81, 88, 89, 139
    caring pragmatist, 81, 82, 89, 91, 94
    numbskull, 88, 92, 139
    paternal principals, 48
  school bureaucracy, 54
    budget, 89
  superintendent, 54, 94
  supervisors, 10, 89
  vice principal(s), 81–96
adolescent(s), adolescence, 9, 37, 51, 69, 70, 83, 86, 93, 108, 113, 119

delinquents, 73
  perpetual adolescence, 92
  teenage, teenager(s), 26, 30, 69, 70, 87, 93, 104, 114, 129, 135, 136, 144, 174, 177
    anti-social, 69
    rebellion, 69, 73
  young adulthood, 93
advertisers, 48
affection, affectionate, 24, 98
  disaffection, 69, 76
affirmative action. *See* race(s) and ethnicity, racial
African American(s) (noun), African-American (adjective). *See* race(s) and ethnicity, racial
agencies, 68. *See also* government, federal and state agencies
agency, 45, 115. *See also* autonomy
Agnone, Milan, 64. *See also South Park*
Agrarian Ideal, 78
Akata Witch, 110
  Anatov, 110
  Sugar Cream, 110
Albrecht, Robert, 77
Alcott, Louisa May, xiii, 1, 2, 5–10
Alexie, Sherman, 112
Alice Cooper, 73
alienate, alienated, alienating, alienation, 28, 40, 41, 54, 73, 115, 152
altruistic, 50, 100
America, American(s), 1–12, 14, 16, 17, 19, 20, 33, 35, 38, 42, 44, 47, 50, 53, 67, 75–78, 82, 83, 86, 88, 93, 95, 104, 119, 121, 122, 133, 139, 145. *See also* culture, and United States
  American. *See* narrative, identity narrative
  American individualism, 18, 29, 78, 86, 87, 134
  American Republic, 1, 2
  American Revolution, 6

INDEX

non-American, 75
American Pie, 87
Angarano, Michael, 61. *See also The English Teacher*
animated, 47, 49. *See also* cartoons
"Another Brick in the Wall Part 2," 73
antebellum, 47
anthropology. *See* subject areas, subject(s)
anti-elitist. *See* elite, elitist, elitism
anti-intellectual, anti-intellectualism. *See* intellectual, intellectualism
antithesis, 42
Anyon, Jean, 87, 138
Arlington National Cemetery, 43
Arnold, Benedict, 5
Arrested Development, 64
    Rita, 64. *See also* Charlize Theron
art. *See* subject areas, subject(s)
Articles of Confederation, 13
assessment(s). *See* learning
attachment(s), 23–32, 109
athlete(s). *See* sports
attrition, 33, 38, 39
authentic, authenticity, 34, 35, 38, 45, 50, 73, 83, 95, 97, 98, 102–105
    inauthentic, 40, 44
authority, authorities, authoritative, authoritarian, authoritarianism, 5, 14, 30, 35, 40, 41, 62, 69, 77, 78, 92, 93, 98, 99, 103, 129, 133, 134, 137, 142, 147, 148, 149, 150, 154, 156, 157. *See also* educator(s)
    anti-authoritarian, 69
autonomy, 40, 45. *See also* agency
Ayers, William, 23, 24, 129

B
Baby Boom, Baby Boomers, 67, 69–72, 77, 78
Back to the Future, 176
backlash, 70, 77, 78
Banks, Jonathan, 54. *See also Community*
Bartlett, Robin, 83. *See also Vice Principals*
baseball, 36, 42
Bassett, Angela, 89. *See also Music of the Heart*
"Be True to Your School," 76
Beach Boys, The, 76

Beach, Richard, 64
beatniks, 73
Beautiful Mind, A, 64, 147
    John Nash, 147
Bell, Michael, 164. *See also Star Trek: The Next Generation*
belonging, 23, 26, 28
Benjamin, H. Jon, 49, 54. *See also Bob's Burgers*
Berkeley, California, 90
Berkley, Elizabeth, 122. *See also Saved by the Bell*
Berman, Nat, 121
Berlant, Lauren, 23, 24, 25, 26, 27, 30, 31
Berry, Chuck, 70, 71
Bestor, Arthur E., 139
Beverly Hills 90210, 121
B-52's, 77
Bible. *See* Old Testament
Big Bang Theory, The, 147, 151
    Dr. Sheldon Cooper, 147, 151. *See also* Jim Parsons
Biggs, Jason, 87. *See also Vice Principals*
Bill Cosby Show, The, 146
binary, 30. *See also* dichotomy
    bifurcations, 83
Biographical Memoir of Daniel Boone, 2, 8
biography, 7, 31
biology. *See* subject areas, subject(s)
biopic. *See* narrative(s)
bisexual. *See* sexuality and educator(s)
body, bodies, 31, 33, 36, 87, 148, 149, 150, 151, 153, 154, 155, 156, 157, 158. *See also* educator(s), embodied, disembodied
    appearance, 63, 83, 155
    marked bodies, 150, 155
Black(s). *See* race(s) and ethnicity, racial
Black, Carol, 135
Blackboard Jungle, 86
Blind Side, The, 89, 172
Blount, Jackie, 48
Blum, Susan, 35
board of education, 48, 137, 139
Bob's Burgers, 47–56, 62
    Bob Belcher, 49–55. *See also* H. Jon Benjamin

186

Gene Belcher, 47, 49–51, 53, 54. *See also* Eugene Mirman

Linda Belcher, 47, 49–55. *See also* John Roberts

Louise Belcher, 47, 49–54. *See also* Kristen Schaal

Tina Belcher, 47, 49–51, 53, 54. *See also* Dan Mintz

Mr. Frond, 47, 49–55. *See also* David Herman

Bonds, Gary U.S., 71

book(s), 3, 5, 10, 26, 35, 58, 65, 67, 68, 71, 76, 78, 98, 107, 108, 111, 137, 140, 143, 166, 170

literary classics, ix

textbook(s), 91, 97

yearbook, 36

young adult literature, YAL, ix, 107–117

Botz-Bornstein, Thorstein, 123, 130

Bovill, Catherine, 156

Bowie, David, 77

Bowie, John Ross, 171. *See also Speechless*

Boy Meets World, 62

Mr. Feeney, 62. *See also* William Daniels

Boys and Girls Clubs, 112

Boz, Ryan, 85. *See also Vice Principals*

Brambell, Wilfred, 68. *See also A Hard Day's Night*

Brando, Marlon, 69, 71. *See also The Wild One*

Breakfast Club, The, 63

Principal Vernon, 63. *See also* Paul Gleason

Breaks, Suli, 75

Brexit, 48

British, 5, 6, 72, 142, 148

Brody, Adrien, 25, 29. *See also Detachment*

brouhaha, 48

Brown, James, 76

Buffy the Vampire Slayer, 63

bully, bullies, bullied, bullying, 37, 85, 91, 93, 112, 114, 161, 162

Bulman, Robert C., 86, 87, 93, 119, 122, 129

Burns, Ed, 37. *See also Saving Private Ryan*

Burton LeVar, 166. *See also Star Trek: The Next Generation*

Business Roundtable, 19

Butler, Bethonie, 120, 121

C

cable news, 11

calculus. *See* subject areas, subject(s)

canon, canonical, 3, 35, 39, 73, 125, 150

capitalist, capitalism, 77, 98, 121

carpe diem, 42

cartoons, 49, 121. *See also* animated

Catcher in the Rye, 137

category, categories, categorizes, categorization, 18, 23, 24, 64, 69, 81, 82, 102, 133, 134, 136, 144, 169, 172

censorship, 35, 55

cerebral palsy. *See* disabled, disability, disabilities

chaperone, chaperoned, chaperoning, 47, 49, 53, 70

Chapman, Lanei, 134, 135, 141. *See also The Wonder Years*

character. *See* narrative

Charlotte Temple, 2

childhood, 48, 93

children. *See* relationships

Christian, 19, 162, 167

Christian fundamentalist, fundamentalism, 18, 19

Christian Right, 19

church, 7, 9, 75, 112, 150

citizen(s), citizenry, citizenship, 3, 5, 13, 14, 15, 16, 17, 20, 77, 78

city, 58, 63, 102

city councils, 19

civic, 72

engagement, 21

orientation, 67, 78

civilians, 35

civil rights, Civil Rights Movement, 67, 68, 72, 137

civilization, civilizer, civilizing, 3, 4, 35,

Clark, Dean, 112

Clark, Dick. *See The Dick Clark Saturday Night Beechnut Show*

Clark, Naeemah, 171

class. *See* social class

class, classes, classroom(s), ix, xi, 6–8, 10, 11, 15, 25–29, 35, 39, 40, 42, 48, 50–53, 57–66, 72, 75, 86, 97–103, 107–109, 113, 116, 123–129, 134,

INDEX

136–145, 147–160, 162, 163, 165, 169, 170, 176, 178, 179
closed-door classrooms, 2
disembodied, embodied, 147–160
Clementi, Tyler, 30
coach(es). *See* educator(s)
Cochran, Eddie, 71
code, 42, 103–104, 128
Colbert, Stephen, 19
Coleman, James S., 69
collective, collectively, 12, 18, 20, 25, 29, 34, 45, 55, 70, 109, 119, 165
college(s). *See* schools
"College Drop Out," 75
Collins, Suzanne, 110
colonial times, 49, 68
colonizing, 37
Common, 75
Common Core, Common Core State Standards (CCSS), 33, 169, 170
common good, 13, 14,
common sense, 4, 16, 18, 20, 21, 121
communitarian, 67, 78
community, 1–5, 8, 10–12, 18, 61, 64, 68, 104, 112, 113, 156
Community, 148, 152–155, 157, 158
June Bauer, 153, 154. *See also* Betty White
Ben Chang, 154, 155. *See also* Ken Jeong
Noel Cornwallis, 154. *See also* Malcolm McDowell
Professor Ian Duncan, 152. *See also* John Oliver
Frances, 154. *See also* Pam Grier
Buzz Hickey, 154. *See also* Jonathan Banks
Marshall Kane, 154, 155. *See also* Michael Kenneth Williams
Dr. Matutani, 154. *See also* George Takei
Dean Pelton, 152, 153. *See also* Jim Rash
Michelle Slater, 154. *See also* Lauren Stamile
Jeff Winger, 152, 154. *See also* Joel McHale

community college(s). *See* educator(s), and schools, schooling
competition, 18, 20, 54, 84, 86, 173, 176
compromise, 13, 14, 38, 127, 144
Conant, James B., 139
conflict, 5, 6, 23, 27, 64, 81, 133, 142, 144, 171, 172
conform, conformity, 72, 100, 104, 153, 169, 170
non-conformity, 69, 85
Congress, congressional, 13–15, 17, 19
congressman, 17
Connor, James M. 90. *See also Vice Principals*
Conrack, 99
consensus, 34, 68
conservative(s), conservativism, 67
Christian Right, 19
conservative media, 78
neoconservativism, 18
New Right, 18, 19, 20
religious conservatives, 20
Republican Party, 78
right, 69, 78
right-leaning forces, 68
construct, 26, 39, 61, 74, 93, 108, 109, 114, 123, 145, 151, 169, 171
deconstruction, 37
consumerism, 121. *See* also materialism
Cook, Mason, 171. *See also Speechless*
Cook-Sather, Alison, 156
Cooke, Josh, 170. *See also The Middle*
Cooke, Sam, 71
Cooke, Wendy J., 136. *See also The Wonder Years*
Cool Runnings, 98
corporation, 72
cosmopolitanism, 4
educational polish, 4
countercultural, counter-cultural. *See* culture
courage, 115, 134, 141, 145
Cranston, Bryan, 27. *See also Detachment*
creative, creativity, 54, 67, 78, 92, 102
credentials, credentialed, 78, 152, 153
degrees, 75, 152, 153
publications, ix, 151, 153
critical pedagogy. *See* pedagogy

"Critical Pedagogy: Dreaming of Democracy," 158
criticism, critic, 1, 23, 25, 26, 49, 139
   critical acclaim, 49, 55
   critical analysis, 50, 75
Crosby, Denise, 164. *See also Star Trek: The Next Generation*
crossing guard, 177
Crowe, Chris, 116
Crutcher, Chris, 108, 112
cult following, 49, 55
cultural studies. *See* subject area, subject(s)
culture, cultural, 1, 2, 3, 9, 23, 24, 25, 38, 39, 48, 57, 59, 62, 67, 69, 70, 71, 75, 77, 82, 83, 90, 92, 98, 100, 102, 109, 119, 130, 136, 141
   American, 2, 38, 83, 86, 88, 134, 145
   appropriation, 162
   countercultural, counter-cultural, 69, 70, 72, 77, 137
   cultural context, ix
   cultural criticism, 1, 26, 49
   cultural dynamics, 107
   cultural hegemony, 18
   cultural norm, 18
   cultural practices, 4
   dominant culture, 26, 104
   enculturation, 121
   high and low, 123
   political culture, 67, 69
   popular culture, pop culture, ix, xi, 1, 2, 9, 12, 23, 47, 57, 60, 61, 64, 67, 69, 70, 85, 93, 130, 147, 148, 169, 178, 179
   postmodern cultural criticism, 1
   sociocultural. *See* social, socially, socialize, socialization, society, socio-sophistication, 1,
   subculture(s), sub-cultures, 48
   traditionalists, 70
   youth culture, 70
curricula, curricular, curriculum, 24, 35, 39, 42, 72, 75, 76, 87, 100, 129, 137, 139, 143, 158. *See also* subject areas, subject(s)
   co-curricular, 100
   curricular requirements, 52

hidden, 76, 87
personalizing the curriculum, personalized, 23, 133, 137–142, 144, 171
Cyler, RJ, 90. *See also Vice Principals*
cynical, 4, 10

D

Dagaz, Mary, 150, 154, 157
Dalton, Mary M., 20, 23, 24, 27–29, 55, 81, 82, 89, 92, 93, 95, 121, 123, 130, 133–137, 143, 146, 170
Damon, Matt, 35, 41. *See also Saving Private Ryan*
Dangerous Minds, 1, 2, 9, 34, 63, 64, 87, 97, 99
   LouAnne, 64. *See also* Michelle Pfeiffer
Daniels, William, 62. *See also Boy Meets World*
Daria, 49
Davies, Jeremy, 37, 39. *See also Saving Private Ryan*
Davy Crockett's Own Story, 2, 8
Dawkins, Richard, 162
de Lancie, John, 161, 163, 164. *See also Star Trek: The Next Generation*
Dead Poets Society, 1, 2, 9, 34, 42, 45, 54, 60, 62
   John Keating, 42, 45, 60, 62. *See also* Robin Williams
Dean, James, 69, 71. *See also Rebel Without a Cause*
death, die, dying, 17, 30, 38, 41, 44, 46, 162
   slow death, 28, 30
   suicide, 25, 28, 30, 31, 88
debate(s), 2, 21, 157
deliberation(s), deliberative process, 13, 14, 17, 42. *See also* dialogue
democratic, democracy, 5, 6, 11–15, 17, 20, 68, 72, 77, 139
   democrat, 9
   democratic dispositions, 13–15
   democratic education, 1
   democratic system, 17
   liberal democracy, 14
   undemocratic, 1, 2
demographics, 49

189

INDEX

Dennis, Sandy, 145. *See also Up the Down Staircase*
depiction(s). *See* narrative, patterns of representation(s)
deprofessionalize. *See* profession, professional
desegregation. *See* race(s) and ethnicity, racial
Deschanel, Zooey, 62. *See also New Girl*
Detachment, 23–32, 29
    Henry Barthes, 25–32. *See also* Adrien Brody
    Principal Carol Dearden, 27. *See also* Marcia Gay Harden
    Erica, 26, 27. *See also* Sami Gayle
    Grampa, 28, 30. *See also* Louis Zorich
    Sarge Kepler, 27. *See also* William Peterson
    Sarah Madison, 25. *See also* Christina Hendricks
    Meredith, 25, 28–31. *See also* Betty Kaye
    Mr. Dearden, 27. *See also* Bryan Cranston
Dewey, John, 40, 41, 107, 129
dialogue(s), 13, 14, 58, 59, 103, 115, 149. *See also* deliberation
    deliberative process, 13
dichotomy, 26, 154. *See also* binary and spheres
Dick Clark Saturday Night Beechnut Show, 71
Dickens, Charles, 5
Dickey, Dale, 94. *See also Vice Principals*
difference, 38, 58, 127
digital media, 11
director, 28, 33, 60, 95, 98
disabled, disability, disabilities, 53, 150, 169, 170, 172–174, 178
    able-bodied, 150, 173, 174
    cerebral palsy, 171, 179
    disability studies, 169
    wheelchair, 171, 175
discipline, 6, 27, 91, 92. *See also* subject areas, subject(s)
    class management, 163
    conduct violation, 85
    expulsion, 8, 44, 115
    suspension, 8, 85, 92

discourse, 25, 27, 33, 76
    discursive, 35
    dominant discourse, ix
diverse, diversity, 11, 16, 93, 95, 145, 147, 148, 149, 152–154
Dodger Stadium, 176
"Doing School": How We Are Creating a Generation of Stressed Out, Materialistic, and Miseducated Students, 137
dominant, ix, 64, 84, 94
    dominant culture, 26
    dominant depiction(s), patterns of representation, 13, 15, 88, 93
    dominant ideology, 83
    dominant narrative(s), trope, 60, 64, 93, 172. *See also* narrative(s)
"Don't Be a Drop-Out," 76
Dorn, Michael, 163. *See also Star Trek: The Next Generation*
"double focus," 28
Driver, Minnie, 171. *See also Speechless*
dropping out, 38
drugs, 72, 77, 88, 123
    addiction, 90
    alcohol, 90
    heroin, 123
    LSD, 72, 92
    marijuana, 87
    substance abuse, 94
duality, dualism, 26, 137. *See also* spheres
    Cartesian duality, 149

E
Earth, 34
economic, 70, 139
    socioeconomic. *See* social, socially, socialize, socialization, society, socio-
education, educational, 1–9, 13, 18–20, 24, 28, 29, 31, 33, 35, 36, 39, 40, 43, 44, 47, 49, 62, 63, 67, 68, 71, 72, 74–78, 81, 90, 93, 95, 100, 105, 107, 109, 114, 120, 121, 126, 127, 129, 130, 133, 134, 136, 138, 139, 143, 145, 150, 155, 157, 162, 165, 169, 170. *See also* learning, and school, schooling

INDEX

American education, 33, 53
banking concept, 150
career, 41, 74, 100, 112, 139
compulsory education, 70
crisis, 15, 18, 143
democratic education, 1
deschooling, deschoolers, 7
diseducation, dis-education, 67, 76
"educational establishment," 18
educational jargon, 52
factory model, 72, 74, 78
feedback, 40, 61, 112, 159, 160
formal education, 20, 55, 67
liberal, liberating education, 41, 77
linear model, 45
mainstreaming, mainstreamed, 73, 76, 171
meeting(s), 101, 124, 125,
moral education, moral instruction, 5, 7, 9, 16, 17, 121, 122, 124, 126, 127
    implanting "virtues," 4, 7, 16
pragmatic, utilitarian approach, 72, 91, 93
private, private school(s), ix, 20, 34, 69, 74, 143
public, public school(s), ix, 18–21, 35, 39, 44, 67, 68, 69, 74, 78, 79, 88, 89, 95, 122, 143, 171, 172, 178, 179
reform, 28, 74
reformers, 16
thought control, 73
vocational, 139, 152, 158
women's education, 48
Educational Wastelands, 139
educator(s). *See also* administrator(s)
able-bodied, 150
academics, 69, 76
activism, 145
archaeologist, 147
attractive, 11, 150, 154
authoritative, 98, 147, 149, 150
bad teacher, 27, 94, 167
bisexual, 24
caregiver, 116, 169, 171, 173
childless, 49, 55
coach(es), 36, 41, 46, 52, 54, 107, 108, 112–116, 147
    swim coach, 54, 108, 112, 113

community college, 147–160
daughterly, 125
demonized, 13, 15, 18
disabled, 150
disciplinarians, 23
educator as alien, 3–5
educator as noble crusader, 3
embodied, disembodied, 147–160
English teacher, 10, 36, 57, 61, 64, 83, 85, 133–146, 154
ethologist, 162
exemplar, exemplary, 45, 114, 137
faculty, 94, 146–160
gatekeepers, 166
gay, 23, 24, 113
"good," good teacher, 11, 23, 24, 99, 126, 133, 136, 163, 165, 166, 169
Good Teacher, The, ix, 24, 26, 28, 29, 30, 31, 133–146, 161, 170, 171, 176
guidance counselor, 47, 49, 50, 51, 55
guide-by-the-side, 114
gym teacher, 51
hacks, 178
heartthrob, 147
hero, heroes, educator-hero, ix, 1, 2, 5, 7, 9–12, 43, 51, 63, 87, 98, 107, 108, 116, 134, 170, 178
    isolated educator as hero, 5–9
heterosexual, 31
iconic, ix, 9, 34, 42
idealistic, idealized, 10, 51, 63, 64, 108, 112, 158, 159, 169, 170
informal, 129, 147
    Informal Educator, 173, 177, 178
instructor(s), 6, 47, 147–160
    communications, 148
    minority, 155
    psychology, 152
journalism teacher, 112
lesbian, 23, 24
malevolent persona, 91, 161
married, 8, 48
maternal, motherly, 48, 51, 150, 154
    not motherly, 150
"mere drones," 3
minority, 154, 155
moral agents, 13, 15, 16

191

INDEX

multi-valent, 134
nightmare, 62
nontraditional, ix, 169–180
novice, 47, 53
nurturer, 140, 151, 154, 174, 176
ogre, 109
old maid, 47, 48
outlaw, 28
outsider(s), 9, 23, 28, 29, 31, 98, 133,
    136, 137, 144, 169, 170, 171, 173,
    176, 177
paternal, fatherly, 167
pedagogue(s), 3, 4, 48, 51, 52, 53, 54, 161
perfect, 62
preservice teachers, 58, 61, 64
    future educators, 60
    prospective teachers, 59
    teacher candidates, 57, 59, 60
professor(s), 8, 128, 129, 147–160, 162
    aging, 153
    anthropology, 35
    biology, 154
    criminologist, 154
    economics, 154
    English, 154
    history, 154
    mathematics, 154
    paleontologist, 148
    Spanish, 154
progressive, 49
radical threat, 28, 29
role model, 112, 139, 179
sage-on-the-stage, 78, 114, 148
savior, ix, 34, 35, 43, 63, 64, 99, 105
    White savior, 57, 64, 98, 99, 100,
        104, 105, 178
scholar(s), ix, 5, 17, 35, 55, 69, 74, 76,
    78, 112, 121, 150, 155, 157, 159
schoolmarm, 15, 36, 47, 74, 122
schoolmaster, 3, 4
selfless, self-sacrificing, 5, 9, 62, 64,
    166, 178
sexualized, sexy, 63, 64, 74
    seductress, 74
single, 47, 48
social studies teacher, 13, 15, 17
spinster, 48, 169, 170

statistics, 153
submissive, 150
substitute, 25, 28, 47, 49, 53, 63
supervisors, 166
talking head, 149
teacher educators, 33, 107, 119, 120, 130
teacher-parents, 48
transgender, 24,
trickster, 107, 109
tutors, 8
unattractive, 3, 150,
unconventional, ix, 172
unmarried, unwed, 48, 101, 122
elite, elitist, elitism, 9, 19, 77, 158
    anti-elitism, 78
Empire Strikes Back, The, 161
    Yoda, 161
English, English Composition, English
    Language Arts. *See* educator(s) and
    subject areas, subject(s)
English Teacher, The, 61, 62, 64
    Ms. Sinclair, 61, 62. *See also* Julianne
        Moore
    Jason Sherwood, 61. *See also* Michael
        Angarano
episode(s), episodic. *See* narrative(s)
equality, 92, 142
    disparity, 138
    egalitarian, 78
    equity, 108
    inequality, inequity, 42, 94
    parity, 49
    unequal social relations, 87
eras,
    Age of Discovery and Exploration, 162
    centuries
        15th century, 162, 164
        19th century, 72
        20th century, 48, 50, 70, 119
        21st century, 130, 170
        24th century, 161, 162
    Colonial, 49, 68
    Common School, 122
    Jim Crow, 79
    1950s, 69, 70, 73, 74, 77, 78, 88
    1960s, 50, 68, 71–74, 77, 135, 137, 143, 146
    1970s, 68, 74, 78, 135, 137, 139, 143

INDEX

1980s, 74, 77, 78, 87
1990s, ix, 18, 74, 77, 119, 134
post-World War II period, 72
Victorian, 27
World War II. *See* World War II, WWII
establishment, the, 18, 72, 78
anti-establishment, 72
ethos, 70, 162
Europe, European, 5, 9, 27
Everly Brothers, The, 71
exploitation, 24, 162
extracurricular, 3, 37, 119, 120
after-school activities, 70
aircraft simulations, 157
athletic events, 112, 114, 157, 175
Boys and Girls Clubs, 112
clubs, 136
dances, 136, 157
debates, 157
plays, 157
social experiments, 157
sports, 102, 136

F

Fabian, Patrick, 120, 128. *See also Saved by the Bell*
faculty. *See* educator(s)
fail, failure, 6, 11, 18, 27, 29, 38, 44, 55, 61, 63, 64, 75, 92, 94, 126, 143, 155
family, families. *See* relationship(s)
Fancy, Richard, 138. *See also The Wonder Years*
fandom, 69
fascist, fascism, 40, 42, 46, 74
Fast Times at Ridgemont High, 62
father. *See* relationship(s)
Felten, Peter, 156
female. *See* gender
feminism, feminist, 48, 79, 90, 122
proto-feminist, 8
feminine, femininity, feminization. *See* gender
Fiedler, Leslie, 39
field trip, 52, 93, 166
fight(s), 27, 33, 34, 35, 37, 38, 42–46, 71, 88, 145, 163, 176, 177
film(s), ix, 1, 2, 9–12, 23–31, 33–46, 53, 57–64, 69, 73, 84, 86, 87, 89, 93,

95, 97–99, 102, 103, 119, 122, 129, 133–135, 144, 145, 147–151, 153–155, 157–159. *See also* movies
"Film Gives Teachers Credit They're Due," 95
Finding Forrester, 35
Fiske, John, 31, 85, 135
FitzGerald, Frances, 72
Flint, Timothy, 2, 8
Forsyth Technical Community College, 148
Foucault, Michel, 27
Fowler, Micah, 171, 172. *See also Speechless*
Frakes, Jonathan, 166. *See also Star Trek: The Next Generation*
frameworks, 31, 57, 59, 64, 108, 135, 136, 142
France, 36, 42, 43
Franken, Al, 19
Franklin, Betty Smith, 155
Frann, Al, 15, 18. *See also The West Wing*
Freaks and Geeks, 50
free, freedom, 1, 6, 9, 11, 20, 41, 46, 67, 78, 86, 102, 122, 142, 144
free enterprise, 20,
free market, 18,
free will, 46,
freedom of speech, 14,
individual liberty, 14
Freedom Writers, 1, 2, 9, 10–12, 26, 35, 48, 63, 87, 97, 99, 161
Mrs. Campbell, 10, 11. *See also* Imelda Staunton
Mr. Gelford, 10, 11.*See also* John Benjamin Hickey
Erin Gruwell, 1, 10, 11, 26, 63, 161. *See also* Hilary Swank
Freire, Paulo, 40, 41, 58, 149, 150
Friday Night Lights, 170
Friends, 148
Ross Geller, 148, 151. *See also* David Schwimmer
friendship. *See* relationship(s)
Frost, Robert, 60
fundamentalism, fundamentalist, 18, 19, 35
funding, 20
government, 68
tax-funded, 152

193

INDEX

Furnier, Vincent, 73

G

gang(s), 5, 10
Garland, Merrick, 14
gay. *See* sexuality
Gayle, Sami, 26. *See also Detachment*
Gen Xers, 74
gender, 23, 47, 49, 60, 64, 74, 84, 85,
    119–122, 127, 129, 150, 159, 169
  female, 47, 49, 63, 64, 74, 83, 89–91,
    127, 129, 153–155
  feminine, femininity, 83–86, 120
    antifemininity, 88
    feminine subjectivity, 24
    feminization, 47, 48, 122, 124
    slurs,
      bitch, 83
  gender role(s), gendered role(s), gender-
    role, 23, 84–88, 119–131
  gender stereotype(s), gendered
    stereotypes, 47, 63, 64, 159, 169, 170
  identity, 87, 172, 173
    queer, 23, 24, 25, 31
    transgender, 24
  male, 3, 4, 64, 74, 81, 82, 83, 85, 86, 88,
    90, 94, 122, 123, 125, 129, 148, 150,
    151, 153, 154, 155, 161, 175, 179
  masculine, masculinity, 5, 82, 83, 81–96,
    122, 127, 162, 173, 175
    entitlement, 82, 86–88, 91
    hegemonic masculinity, masculine
      hegemony, 83, 84, 88, 90, 92, 94,
      162
    hypermasculinity, 82, 83
    male buffoonery, 82
    "man's man," 169, 171, 173, 175, 176
    nonhegemonic masculinities, 88
    plurality of masculinities, 88
    slurs,
      bitch, 83
      bitch boy, 83
    toxic masculinity, 81, 84, 85, 88, 89,
      92
genre(s). *See* narrative(s)
George, Ann, 158
German(s), 7, 9, 36, 38, 42

Giroux, Henri A., 145
Gitlin, Todd, 88
Giver, The, 108, 109
  The Receiver of Memory, 108–110
Glanz, Jeffrey, 88, 89, 92, 93, 138
Gleason, Paul, 63. *See also The Breakfast
    Club*
Glee, 61, 62
  Mr. Schuester, 61. *See also* Matthew
    Morrison
Glory Road, 99
God, 7, 150, 162
  Christian God, 162, 167
  "G.O.D. (Gaining One's Definition)," 75
Goggins, Walton, 81, 82, 87, 93, 95. *See
    also Vice Principals*
Goldberg, Adam, 37. *See also Saving
    Private Ryan*
Goldman, Elliot, 140. *See also The Wonder
    Years*
Good Morning, Miss Bliss, 119–121, 124,
    126. *See also Saved by the Bell*
  Miss Carrie Bliss, 119, 120, 124–126.
    See also Hayley Mills
Good Teacher, The. *See* educator(s)
Goodbye, Mr. Chips, 161
  Mr. Chips, 161
Google, 35
Gosselaar, Mark-Paul, 120, 121, 126. *See
    also Saved by the Bell*
government, 13, 20
  federal and state agencies, 68
  government funding, grants, 68, 100
graduation, graduate(s), 8, 75–77, 100, 127,
    136, 137, 139, 149, 167
  bachelor's degree, 152
  college degree, 75
  diploma, 70
  graduate degree, 143
"Graduation Day," 75
Grand Torino, 98
Grant, Ulysses S., 15
Great Society, 78
Green, Cee Lo, 75
Greening of America, The, 72
Gregory, Kimberly Hébert, 82, 84. *See also
    Vice Principals*

194

INDEX

Grier, Pam, 154. *See also Community*
Grossberg, Lawrence, 70
Grumet, Madeleine R., 120, 122, 125, 150
Guevara, Che, 140
Gugino, Carla, 124. *See also Saved by the Bell*

H

Hanks, Tom, 34, 41, 154. *See also Larry Crowne* and *Saving Private Ryan*
happiness, 30, 72
Hard Day's Night, A, 68
  Grandfather, 67, 68, 78. *See also* Wilfred Brambell
  Ringo, 67, 68. *See also* Ringo Starr
Harden, Marcia Gay, 27. *See also Detachment*
Harger, Brent, 150, 154, 157
Harn, Owen, 91. *See also Vice Principals*
Harris, Marcuis, 94, 95. *See also Vice Principals*
Harry Potter and the Sorcerer's Stone, 110, 111
  Dumbledore, 107, 108, 110, 111, 114–116
  Harry Potter, 110, 111, 114, 115
  Hermione, 111, 114
  Ron, 111
  Voldemort, 111, 115
Harvard University, 72, 81, 95
Haskins, Dennis, 124. *See also Saved by the Bell*
Hawke, Ethan, 34. *See also Saving Private Ryan*
Heart of Darkness, 136, 141
hegemony, hegemonic, 31, 83, 84, 88, 90, 92, 94, 162
  cultural hegemony, 18
  nonhegemonic, 88
Heldman, Caroline, 83, 86
Hendricks, Christina, 25. *See also Detachment*
Henry, Patrick, 6
Herman, David, 49. *See also Bob's Burgers*
hero, heroes, heroic, ix, 1, 3–5, 10, 38, 51, 63, 72, 87, 98, 99, 107, 108, 110, 114, 116, 134, 170, 173, 178. *See also* educator(s), and narrative(s)

American hero, 1, 2, 5,
educator-hero, educator heroes, 1, 2, 5–12
heroism, 43
superhero(es), 63, 83, 86
Hetrick, Jennifer, 166. *See also Star Trek: The Next Generation*
Hickey, John Benjamin, 10. *See also Freedom Writers*
hierarchy, hierarchies, hierarchical, 9, 85, 92, 122, 127, 142, 151
Hinkle, Marin, 171. *See also Speechless*
hippies, 78
history. *See* subject areas, subject(s)
History of Sexuality, The, 27
Holly, Buddy, 71
Hollywood, ix, 23–27, 29, 30, 87, 95, 119, 121, 133, 134, 137
Hollywood Curriculum, The: Teachers in the Movies, 24, 27, 81
Hollywood Goes to High School, 86
Hollywood Model, The. *See* theory, theorist(s)
Homer, 78
homework, 51, 71, 74, 101, 166
hoodlums, 69
"Hot for Teacher," 74
housekeeping staff, 177
How I Met Your Mother, 151
  Ted Mosby, 151. *See also* Josh Radnor
Howden, Eric, 155, 156
Howe, Brian, 94. *See also Vice Principals*
Huebner, Dwayne, 136
humanity, 28, 36, 37, 62, 129
  personhood(s), 37, 38
Hunger Games, The, 110
  Haymitch, 110
  Katniss, 110
husband. *See* relationship(s)

I

Icarus, 116
icon, iconic, ix, 1, 2, 5, 6, 9, 12, 34, 42, 69, 97
ideal(s), idealism, idealistic, idealized, 5, 9, 10, 14, 25, 48, 51, 63, 64, 107, 108, 109, 112–116, 123, 129, 158, 159, 162, 169, 170, 178
  Agrarian Ideal, 78

195

INDEX

identity, identities, 2, 36–38, 51, 58, 69, 73, 86, 87, 93, 100, 107, 119, 129, 130, 143, 151, 152, 154, 155, 172, 173, 177. *See also* gender, race(s) and ethnicity, racial
American, 1, 8, 11
income level, 143, 152
intersectional, 172, 173
marginalize(d), 19, 59, 62, 64, 83, 98, 127, 147, 148, 153, 154, 172, 177
marital status, 152
ideology, ideologies, ideological, 1, 11, 12, 26, 31, 82, 91, 95, 121, 130, 143
collective ideologies, 18
dominant ideology, 83
New Right ideology, 18
normative ideology, 84
ignorance, ignorant, 3, 17, 77, 99
illiberalism, 14
Illich, Ivan, 74
"I'm With Stupid," 77
immigrant(s), 7, 16, 70
in loco parentis, 47, 48, 51, 55
independence, independent, 7, 8, 69, 70, 172, 174, 177, 178
nurturing-yet-independent, 140
self-sufficiency, 87
Indiana, 125
individual(s), individualism, 13, 14, 18, 29, 62, 63, 64, 67, 74, 78, 86, 87, 127, 134
American, 86, 87
individual liberty, 14
individuation, 115
rugged, 29
industrialization, 77
injustice. *See* justice
Insecure, 97–106
Issa, 97–106. *See also* Issa Rae
institution(s), institutional, 1, 2, 5, 18–20, 25–29, 31, 33, 35, 39, 40, 50, 69, 72, 75, 76, 78, 79, 112, 142, 157, 178
American institutions, 16, 75
educational institutions, 1, 8, 9, 74, 169, 170
instructor(s). *See* educators
insubordination, 39

integration. *See* race(s) and ethnicity, racial
intellectual, intellectualism, 1, 3, 5–7, 9, 11, 12, 72, 77, 148, 167
anti-intellectual, anti-intellectualism, 1, 2, 5, 76, 77, 78
intellectual community, intellectual communties, 1, 2, 5, 10–12
post-intellectualism, 77
intelligence, intelligent, 15, 17, 60, 82
emotional intelligence, 92
unintelligent, 63
Internet, 78
intertextual, ix, 92. *See also* theory, theorist(s)
intimacy, 23–32
Intimacy: A Special Issue, 25
Iowa, 43
Ironman, 107, 108, 112–115
Bo, 112–115
Lionel "Lion" Serbousek, 107, 108, 112–115
Wyrack, 112
Irving, Washington, 1–4, 8, 10
It Gets Better Project, 30
Ivanhoe, 137, 138

J

Jackie Robinson Story, The, 98, 99
Janney, Allison, 19. *See also The West Wing*
Japanese, 42
Jefferson, Thomas, 13, 78, 100
Jenner, Barry, 124. *See also Saved by the Bell*
Jeong, Ken, 154. *See also Community*
Jesus, 167
Jo's Boys, 8
job(s), 7, 25, 26, 28, 36, 39, 53, 55, 75, 81, 82, 87, 90, 93, 95, 102, 103, 125–127, 133, 134, 143, 145, 171–174, 178
dead-end, 95, 178
extra, second, 10, 178
part-time, 175, 177
Jobs, Steve, 75
Johnson, Jay DeVon, 95. *See also Vice Principals*
Johnson, Tara S. 128,
jokes. *See* narrative

INDEX

Jones, Indiana, 147
journals, 26, 159
    practitioner journals, 50
juke box, 71
Jung, Carl, 165. *See also* theory, theorists
Juno, 48
justice, 108
    inclusivity, 108
    injustice, 164
    restorative justice, 90, 92
    social justice, 21, 59

K

Kaestle, Carl F., 47
Kaye, Betty, 25. *See also Detachment*
Kayne, Tony, 28
Keats, 34
Kenedy, Kyla, 171. *See also Speechless*
Kimmel, Michael, 93
Kincheloe, Joe, 58, 59, 62, 63
King, Georgia, 85. *See also Vice Principals*
King of the Hill, 49
Kissling, Mark T., 129
kitsch, kitschy, 119–123, 127–130. *See also*
    narrative(s)
Knoblauch, Abby, 150
Korean War, 138
Kumashiro, Kevin, 18–20
Kupers, Terry A., 84

L

Laats, Adam, 49
LaBruce, Bruce, 123
language, 35, 83, 100, 102, 137
    coded, 104
    lexicon, 104
    of violence, 85
    of racism, 98, 100
    political, 137
    rap, 102
    street, 102
Larry Crowne, 148, 154–156
    Larry Crowne, 156. *See also* Tom Hanks
    Mercedes Tainot, 148, 154, 156. *See also*
        Julia Roberts
Last Samurai, 98
Latin. *See* subject areas, subject(s)

Lauria, Dan, 138. *See also The Wonder*
    Years
law. *See* subject areas, subject(s)
leader(s), leadership, 45, 70, 82, 87, 89–93,
    95, 176
    cheerleader, 79
Leadsom, Andrea, 48
Lean on Me, 34
learning, 1, 9, 11, 23, 24, 40–42, 57, 59, 60,
    63, 65, 87, 92, 98, 107, 114, 115, 126,
    129, 135, 141, 142, 155, 157, 158,
    166. *See also* education, educational
    accountability, 33, 68, 74, 107
    assessment(s), 60, 164
        formative, 40
        summative, 40
    cooperative, 116
    didactic teaching,
    discussion, ix, 2, 7, 11, 58–64, 140, 141,
        156, 159, 165
    embodied, 148, 155, 156, 158, 159
        embodied transformative, 155
    empathy, 113, 162, 167
    essay, 164
    experiential, 33, 35, 40, 164, 165
    experimentation, 138
    feedback, 112, 159
        constructive, 40
        right/wrong, 61
    grades, grading, 138, 140–145
        pass and no pass, 136
    hands-on, 53
    higher, 159
    Initiate-Respond-Evaluate model, 61
    lesson(s), 3, 40, 41, 76, 94, 102, 114,
        121, 122, 124, 125, 127–129, 133,
        141, 146, 161–167
        lesson plan, 39, 141, 164
        life lesson(s), 24, 30, 113, 141, 144
        moral lessons, 125, 127
    objectives, 36, 38, 40, 142, 167
        Student Learning Objectives, SLOs,
        35
        capstone educational objective, 39
    passive, 155
    planning, 60
    positive group dynamic, 165

197

INDEX

problem-based, 40
reciprocal, 133, 137, 171
rote, 72
schoolwork, 71, 138
Socratic approach, 110
standards, 41, 43, 122, 138, 139,
    141–143
student-centered, 40, 45, 101, 112, 114
teachable moments, 173
teaching philosophy, 136, 143, 145
technical mastery, 107
test(s), test-based, testing, 1, 37, 38, 42,
    44, 68, 74, 107, 115, 126, 127, 143,
    164, 176
    multiple choice, 164
    no test policy, 126
    technical mastery, 107
    test prep, 100
Leary, Timothy, 72
"Legend of Sleepy Hollow, The," 1–5, 10,
    12
    Brom Bones, 3–5, 8
    Ichabod Crane, 1–5, 8, 47
    Hans Van Ripper, 3
    Katrina Van Tassel, 3–5, 8
Legit, 174
Lennon, John, 72, 73
lens, 24–26, 28, 31, 34, 29, 57, 58, 120
    constructivist, 109
    critical literacy, 57, 60, 63
    uncritical, 93
lesbian, lesbianism. *See* sexuality
lesson(s). *See* learning
Levin, Robert, 28
Lewis, Jerry, 147
liberal, liberalism, 14, 69, 77, 122, 138. *See
    also* democratic, democracy
    left, 69
    left-leaning communities, 69
    neoliberalism, 18, 98, 100, 102
    progressive, progressivism,
        progressivist(s), 69, 107, 114, 115, 139
liberated, liberating, liberation, liberatory, 8,
    38, 40–42, 142, 147, 149, 155–158
libertarians, 78
liberty. *See* free, freedom
life. *See also* work, working

afterlife, 162
"bad life," 30
"good life," 30, 43
intellectual life, 11
life choices, 9
life lesson(s), 24, 30, 113, 144
life of the mind, 3, 149, 151
private life, personal life, 27, 28, 104,
    125, 129, 156, 169, 170
public life, professional life, 27, 124,
    129, 169, 170
real life, real-life, 39, 40, 63, 81, 89, 129,
    133, 135, 147, 146, 178, 179
Life of Washington, The, 2
Linder, Laura R., 20, 55, 95, 121, 123, 130,
    133, 134, 143, 146, 170
Liston, Daniel P., 107, 108, 109
literacy, 57, 58, 72, 78
    anti-literacy, 72
    critical literacy, 57–65
    media literacy. *See* subject areas,
        subject(s)
    post-literate, 77
literary, ix, 3, 9
Little Men, 8
Little Women, 1, 2, 5–9, 12
    Professor Bhaer, 7–9
    Mr. Davis, 5–8
    Theodore "Laurie" Laurence, 8, 9
    Amy March, 5–8
    Jo March, 7–9
    Marmee, 6–8
Liverpool, England, 73
Lopez, Mario, 122, 126. *See also Saved by
    the Bell*
Los Angeles, LA, 10, 26, 97, 98, 100, 102
    1994 LA riots, 26
love(s), 11, 40, 42, 47, 51, 63, 71, 87, 128,
    151, 154, 166. *See also* relationships
    crush, 62, 104, 119, 120, 170
    eros, 109, 116
    lust, 128
    romance, romantic, 4, 27, 64, 70, 71, 90,
        101, 119, 120, 124, 128, 170, 174,
        179
Love, Maya G. 85. *See also Vice Principals*
Love and Death in the American Novel, 3

198

INDEX

Lowe, Rob, 15, 16. *See also The West Wing*
Lowry, Lois, 108
loyal, loyalty, loyalties, 1, 11, 12, 40, 76, 94, 136
  disloyal, 1, 2, 11
Lu, June Kyoto, 83. *See also Vice Principals*
Lund, Carl, 28
Lynn, Lonnie. *See* Common

M

Madison, James, 14
Madison, Soyini D., 20
Mad Men, 83, 86
  Donald Draper, 83, 86
MADtv, 57, 59
Malcolm X, 75
male. *See* gender
Mallozzi, Christine, 74
Mann, Horace, 72
Marlens, Neal, 135
marriage. *See* relationship(s)
Martin, Linda, 70
Marxist, 77
masculine, masculinity. *See* gender
Mask You Live In, The, 83, 93
Massachusetts, 68
MIT, 147
materialism, 87. *See also* consumerism
maternity leave, 48
math, mathematics. *See* subject areas, subject(s)
May, Theresa, 48
Mayes, Clifford, 108, 109, 116
McBride, Danny, 81, 82, 87, 94, 95. *See also Vice Principals*
McDowell, Malcolm, 154. *See also Community*
McFadden, Gates, 166. *See also Star Trek: The Next Generation*
McHale, Joel, 152. *See also Community*
McKinley, E. Graham, 121
McKinney, Sheaun, 89. *See also Vice Principals*
McLuhan, Marshall, 77, 78
McWilliam, Erica, 74
media literacy. *See* subject areas, subject(s)
mental health issues, 157

nervous breakdown, 11
neurotic, 122
mentor(s), 103, 107, 108, 110–115. *See also* narrative(s), character(s)
meritocracy, 90
Middle, The, 170
  Professor Grant, 170. *See also* Josh Cooke
  Sue Heck, 170. *See also* Eden Sher
middle class, middle-class. *See* social class
Mike & Molly, 169, 170
military, militaristic, 33–46, 72. *See also* war(s), War(s)
  Navy, 156
Millennials, 67, 69, 74, 78
Mills, Alley, 138. *See also The Wonder Years*
Mills, Hayley, 120. *See also Saved by the Bell*
Mirman, Eugene, 49. *See also Bob's Burgers*
Mintz, Dan, 49. *See also Bob's Burgers*
Misadventures of an Awkward Black Girl, 97
Mississippi, 68
Mr. Holland's Opus, 34
Mr. Novak, 146
modernism, 77
modus operandi, 53
money, 10, 64, 75, 138, 145, 175
  financial independence, 70
  funding, 20, 68
Mongeau, Lillian, 48
Moore, Julianne, 61. *See also The English Teacher*
moral(s), morality, morally, 1, 5–7, 9, 12, 13, 15–17, 20, 77, 122, 124, 126–128
  immoral, immorality, 7, 70
  moral education, moral instruction, moral lessons, 7, 8, 121, 125, 127
  moral idealism, 9
mores, 47
Morrison, Matthew, 61. *See also Glee*
mother(s), mom. *See* relationship(s)
motherhood, 48, 55
  motherly, 51, 150, 154
Mountford, Roxanne, 150
movies, ix, 25, 31, 34, 35, 37–39, 42, 44, 57, 58, 60, 61, 64, 69, 82, 87, 89, 102, 108, 122, 147, 157, 173, 178. *See also* film(s)

199

INDEX

Murphy, Eddie, 147
music, ix, 54, 67–80, 97, 98, 102, 125, 175.
    See also subject areas, subject(s)
  anti-rock, 70
  Black, 70
  chorus, 73, 74, 76, 79
  emancipatory, 70
  genres,
    blues, 70, 71
    country, 70
    country & western, 71
    folk, 70
    jazz, 86
    popular music, ix, 69
    rap, 67, 69, 74, 75, 77, 78, 79, 97,
      101, 102, 103, 104, 105
    rhythm and blues, R&B, 70, 71
    rock 'n' roll, rock, 67–80
    Western, 70
  immorality, 70
  jungle beat, 74
  lyrics, 67, 69, 75, 102
  miscegenistic, 70
  musician, 9, 40, 67, 77
  physiological effects, 77
  surrogate, 77
  transgressive, 70
  White, 70
Music of the Heart, 89, 99
  Janet Williams, 89. *See also* Angela
    Bassett
music video(s), 74, 75

N

narrative(s), ix, 1, 2, 4–6, 8, 9, 11–13,
    15–17, 20, 23–27, 29–31, 33, 36–38,
    43, 60, 61, 64, 71, 82, 85, 87, 89, 92,
    108, 109, 114, 127, 129, 134, 135,
    143, 144, 148, 149, 154, 161, 172,
    178, 179
  archetype, archetypal, 35, 50, 62, 83, 86,
    89, 93, 107–117, 134
    archetypal reflectivity, 107–109
    crone, 108
    heroic teacher, 108
    man-child, 83
    shadow, 108

    strong, silent guy, 83
    superhero, superheroes, 63, 83
    thug, 83
    wizard(s), 110, 111, 115
  backstory, 93
  biopic(s), 10, 99
  character(s), ix, 17, 19, 28, 37, 38,
    49–51, 81, 83–86, 92–95, 98, 104,
    108, 109, 123–125, 128, 133–135,
    144–147, 149, 151, 153–155, 162,
    166, 169–172, 175, 178, 179
  caricatures, 5, 6, 50
  coach, coaches, ix, 36, 41, 46, 52, 54,
    107–117, 147
  eponymous, 47, 49, 147
  foil, 51
  hero, heroes, heroine, ix, 1–12, 51,
    63, 72, 86, 87, 99, 107, 108, 110,
    116, 134, 178
  mentor(s), ix, 103, 107–117, 147, 166
  minor, 149
  narrator, 3, 4, 125, 136, 138,
    140–142, 144
  protagonist(s), 3, 38, 74, 78, 108, 110,
    112, 114, 123, 124
  prototypical, 38, 133
  recurring, 134, 135, 179
  stock character(s), 25, 170
    cowboy, 133
    nemesis, 5, 111
    nerd, 74, 166
    outlaw, 28, 69
    rebel, 69
    sage, 107–117
    trickster, 107, 108
    villain, 11
climax, 24, 29
convention(s), 39, 87
counter narrative, 13, 15, 17
dominant, 172
dramatic logic, 4
epic, 34
episode(s), episodic, 15, 17, 19, 50–53,
    61, 62, 64, 81, 83, 87, 88, 90, 91, 94,
    97, 119–121, 123–129, 133–137, 141,
    143, 144, 148, 152, 161, 162, 166,
    167, 170, 171, 173–176, 179

finale, 94, 174
pilot, 15, 152, 162, 171
"very special episode," 123
falling action, 24
flashback(s), 28, 30
foreshadowing, 138
formula(s), formulaic, 1, 2, 9, 71, 87, 123
genre(s), 24, 29, 34, 70, 72, 76, 98, 116, 123
 comedy, comedies, 49, 81, 86, 97, 98, 119, 121, 123, 130, 144, 147–149, 154, 158
 drama, 3, 5, 14, 17, 24, 135
 melodrama, 62
 sitcom(s), 51, 93, 119, 121–123, 128, 147, 152, 169–171, 175
 subgenre, 29, 30
 teen movies, 87
 war film(s), 33, 34, 38, 39
grand narrative(s), 1, 2
hijinks, 53, 55, 129
homage, 53
hyperbole, 165
identity narrative, 1, 2, 8, 11
joke(s), 48, 55, 81, 85, 88, 95
kitsch, kitschy, campiness, 119–123, 127–130
mainstream, 25, 87, 149
metaphor, 33, 35, 39, 41, 88, 177
monologue, 51
myth(s), 108, 109, 150
parody, 57, 76
 spoof(s), 54, 58
patterns of representation(s), ix, 88, 121, 170
 depiction(s), ix, 5, 13–18, 20, 21, 28, 31, 33, 34, 37, 38, 61, 63, 64, 65, 82, 92, 93, 122, 123, 134, 145, 147–150, 154, 158, 169, 170, 172, 178
 negative, 5, 8, 67, 69, 89, 155, 157, 169, 170, 172
 portrayal(s), 26, 34, 35, 37, 39, 49, 51, 55, 57, 59–65, 82, 93, 108, 119, 121, 122, 147–149, 154, 173
personification, 39
plot(s), plotlines, 11, 49, 50, 98, 124, 128, 129, 133, 134, 171

epiphanies and setbacks, 144
 soap opera theatrics, 128
 subplot, 103, 104, 128
radical narratives, 31
revisionist, ix, 24, 30
rising action, 24, 29
satire, satirical, satirized, 7, 55, 58, 62–64, 90, 95
sexualization, 63, 64, 74
story, storyline, ix, 2, 3, 4, 5, 10, 24, 25, 34, 36, 39, 45, 50, 60, 88–90, 94, 98, 99, 105, 107–109, 111, 113, 121, 127, 134, 144, 175, 176, 179
 arcs, 8, 37, 108, 111, 127, 144, 174
structures of texts, 28, 121, 134, 135, 143, 144
suspension of disbelief, 49
temporal convention, 39
theme(s), 38, 39, 49, 54, 75, 78, 127, 162, 164, 179
traditional(s), 16, 17, 29, 38, 61, 150, 169, 170
tropes, ix, 6, 9, 74, 87, 93, 98, 104, 123, 125, 172
ur-text, 3
verisimilitude, 49
vignettes, 55
nation, national, nationalist, 2, 3, 5, 7, 8, 12, 13, 15, 16, 18, 20, 24, 77
 nation building, 16,
National Defense Education Act, 50
National Education Association, 48
Navy. *See* military, militaristic
Nazi(s), 34, 36, 38–40, 42, 46
Nelson, Ricky, 71
Nemes, Scott, 136. *See also The Wonder Years*
neoliberalism. *See* liberal, liberalism
neoconservativism. *See* conservative(s), conservativism
networks,
 ABC, 62, 97, 133–135, 141, 146, 169–172
 CBS, 63, 97, 147, 151, 169, 170
 Comedy Central, 49
 Fox, 47, 49, 52, 54, 57, 61, 62, 64, 78, 121

INDEX

HBO, 81, 82, 84, 87, 97, 98, 99, 101, 169, 170
MTV, 49
NBC, 14, 16, 18, 50, 119, 121, 146, 148, 153, 170
YouTube, 74, 75, 97, 102
New Deal, 78
New Girl, 62
    Miss Day, 62. *See also* Zooey Deschanel
New Hampshire, 15, 19
New Right. *See* conservative, conservativism
"New Romantics," 72
New York City, 7, 8, 48
New York Times, The, 14, 70
news, 11, 59
    fake news,77
    Fox News, 78
No Child Left Behind, 33, 74, 169, 170
Nolte, Nick, 145. *See also Teachers*
norms, normal, normalcy, normalize(d), normative, 1, 2, 14, 18, 24, 30, 49, 62, 63, 69, 84, 85, 97, 104–106, 110, 122, 123, 127, 128, 140, 170, 171, 174. *See also* sexuality, heteronormative
Normandy, 36
North Carolina, 148
nostalgia, 135, 144

O

Obama, President Barack, 14
obedience, obient, 40, 42, 99, 163
O'Gorman, Mike, 86. *See also Vice Principals*
Ohio, 13, 15, 17
Okorafor, Nnedi, 110
Old Testament, 162
    Ten Commandments, 162
Oliver, John, 152. *See also Community*
Omaoko, Darryll Suliman, 75
One Day It'll All Make Sense, 75
101st Airborne, 43
oppression, oppressive, 1, 2, 24, 34, 36, 41–43
Orange County, California, 171
ordinariness, 28, 30, 105

Ortega, Jimmy, 163. *See also Star Trek: The Next Generation*
other, othering, 38, 70, 85, 153–155
Our Miss Brooks, 169, 170
    Connie Brooks, 169, 170
Oxford, England, 162

P

pagan, 67
Palmer, Parker J., 108
paradigm(s), paradigmatic, 5, 7, 35, 37
parent(s). *See* relationship(s)
parenthood, 47, 48, 52
    parental authority, parental engagement, parental involvement, 55, 69
parity. *See* equality
Parker, Walter, 14
Parks, Susan, 88. *See also Vice Principals*
Parrot, Dominic J., 84
Parsons, Jim, 151. *See also The Big Bang Theory*
passion, 28, 134
passive, 14, 99, 155, 156
    passive-aggressively, 128
patriarchal, patriarchy, 47, 86, 90–92, 121
patriot, patriotic, 5, 6
Patterson, Edi, 87. *See also Vice Principals*
Paulding, James K., 2, 8
pedagogy, pedagogical, 2, 5, 7–9, 11, 12, 34, 39, 40, 42, 54, 74, 87, 161
    "banking concept of education," 150
    critical pedagogy, 57–65
    "embodied transformative learning," 155
    experiential, 33, 40, 164, 165
    humility, 7, 166
    immersive, 40
    lesson(s). *See* learning, lesson(s)
    liberatory, 147–160
    methodology, methodologies, 76, 161, 164
    multimedia presentation, 57
    pedagogical fantasy, 2
    pedagogue. *See* educator, pedagogue
    problem-based learning, 40
    problem-solving, 157
    public pedagogy, 33
    reflection(s), 64, 83, 107, 108–110, 115
    teambuilding exercises, 156, 157

INDEX

Pepper, Barry, 37. *See also Saving Private Ryan*
Peterson, William, 27. *See also Detachment*
Pfeiffer, Michelle, 64. *See also Dangerous Minds*
Philanthropy Roundtable, 19
Phillips, Busy, 85. *See also Vice Principals*
philosophy, philosophies, philosopher, philosophic, 7, 81, 100, 102, 136, 137, 142, 143, 145
physical education. *See* subject areas, subject(s)
Pink Floyd, 73
Philadelphia, Pennsylvania, 90
Playboy Magazine, 77
podcast(s), 57, 108
poet, 7
police, 64
policy, policies, ix, 12, 21, 27, 68, 69, 74, 126, 136, 137, 139, 140, 141, 152, 163, 178
politics, political, politician(s), 14, 17–20, 28, 44, 57, 59, 62, 67–69, 72, 77, 78, 123, 136, 137, 138, 139, 140, 141, 174. *See also* culture
 depoliticizing, 122
 political action committees, 18
 sociopolitical. *See* social, socially, socialize, socialization, society,
polling, 19
Pope, Denise Clark, 137
popular culture, pop culture. *See* culture
populist, 49
portrayal(s). *See* narrative(s), patterns of representation(s)
post-intellectualism. *See* intellectual, intellectualism,
postmodern, 1, 2
post-traumatic stress disorder (PTSD), 42
poverty, 3
power(s), 4, 9, 18, 19, 29, 38, 41, 42, 48, 58, 59, 60, 62, 64, 71, 84, 88, 91–93, 101, 105, 106, 110, 112, 115, 127, 129, 130, 141, 153, 157, 163, 166
 empower, empowered, empowering, empowerment, 42, 54, 59, 97, 100, 116, 133, 137, 140, 142, 144, 146, 178
 overpowered, 85

powerful, 2, 43, 55, 70, 93, 105, 110, 111, 129, 150, 178
powerless, 20
powerlessness, 14
practical, practices, praxis, 4, 9, 12, 14, 21, 28–30, 40, 48, 61, 83, 84, 86, 87, 91, 95, 101, 107, 109, 122, 144, 151, 155, 158, 159, 164–166, 179
pragmatic, pragmatism, pragmatist, 33, 42, 72, 81, 82, 89, 91–94, 109
pregnant, 48
prejudice(s), 5, 14, 87
Presley, Elvis, 70
Price, Richard, 13
Prime Minister, 48
principal(s). *See* administrator(s)
print, 77
prison, prisoners, 35, 36, 71, 72, 75, 79, 85, 155
 inmate, 155
Prisoners of War (POWs), 35
private, ix, 6, 18, 20, 26, 27, 28, 103, 122. *See also* education and sphere
 privatized, 20
privilege(s), privileged, 36, 82, 86, 87, 122, 143, 150, 155. *See also* race(s) and ethnicity, racial
 "invisibility cloak," 155
 underprivileged, 112
production practices
 camera angle(s), 60, 64
  male gaze, 64, 74
 camera movement, 63, 140, 176
 costume(s), 60, 161, 162, 176
 editing, 60
  montage, 51, 60
 fourth wall, 122
 lighting, 60
 objectification, 63
 shots, 28, 60, 63
 single-camera, 144, 175
 sound(s), 50, 158
  ambient, 149
  musical montage, 54
  narration, 99, 135
   diegetic voiceover narration, 162
  soundtrack, 51, 69
  voice-over,

203

INDEX

profession, professional, professionalism, professionalization, 3, 15, 25, 33, 35, 36, 38–40, 42, 47–49, 59, 61, 62, 78, 82, 89, 97, 98, 107, 112, 114, 115, 120, 122, 124–130, 133, 134, 136, 139, 143, 145, 147, 149, 154–156, 161, 169, 170, 178
   deprofessionalize(es), ix, 169, 170, 172
   pink profession, 48
   professional development, 33
professor(s). *See* educator(s)
progressive. *See* liberal, liberalism
Puar, Jasbir K., 30
public, publicness, ix, 11, 14, 18, 19, 25–27, 35, 67, 69, 70, 78, 90, 121, 130, 139, 140, 142, 178. *See also* education and sphere
   consciousness, 14, 16, 23
   relations, 43
punk, 73
puritanical, 77

Q

Quarry Bank High School, 73
queer. *See* gender identity

R

race(s) and ethnicity, racial, 18, 24, 49, 58, 63, 64, 68, 82, 86, 87, 91, 94, 95, 98, 105, 143, 146, 148, 150, 154, 162, 164, 169, 170, 173, 174, 176
   affirmative action, 67, 68, 90
   African American(s) (noun), African-American (adjective), 18, 74, 75, 81, 82, 89, 90, 91, 94, 95, 100, 103, 137, 143, 154, 155, 169, 170, 171
   Asian and Pacific Islanders, 154
   Black(s), 35, 70, 74, 75, 95, 97–106, 154, 171, 172, 173, 176, 179
   Blackface, 100
   desegregation, 55, 68
   French, 162, 167
   German(s), 7, 38, 42
   integration, 67, 68, 176
   Japanese, 42
   Japanese-American, 154
   Korean-American, 154

Latinx, 99, 100
magical negro, 173
minority, minorities, 58, 70, 154, 155
people of color, 58, 103
   man of color, 169, 171, 172, 176
   students of color, 58, 98
privilege, 82, 150, 155
segregation, segregationist, 79
   desegregation, 55, 68
   White flight, 74
White, Whiteness, 18, 57–59, 63, 65, 70, 74, 75, 82, 85–89, 93–95, 97–100, 102–105, 123, 143, 148, 150, 153–155, 173
   White savior, 57, 98–100, 104, 105, 170, 178
racism, 58, 74, 83, 85, 90, 98
radical, 18, 28, 29, 31, 74, 138
   "radical openness," 49
radio, 73, 78
Radnor, Josh, 151. *See also How I Met Your Mother*
Rae, Issa, 171, 179. *See also Insecure*
Rakove, Jack N., 14
rap. *See* music
Rash, Jim, 152. *See also Community*
reading. *See* subject areas, subject(s)
reality, 8, 33, 36, 38, 40, 75, 95, 101, 105, 108, 116, 119, 123, 129, 138, 149, 153, 162
Rebel Without a Cause, 69. *See also* James Dean
Reese, William J., 139, 142
Reich, Charles A., 72, 73
Reitman, Jason, 48
relationship(s), 23–32, 38, 49, 60–62, 64, 86, 87, 90, 103, 104, 107–117, 119, 120, 127, 128, 133–135, 151, 157, 167, 169–175. *See also* love(s)
   boyfriend(s), 100, 102, 104, 126, 127, 129
   caregiver(s), 114, 116, 169, 171, 173
   children, 3, 7, 9, 16, 19, 48–50, 52–55, 87, 90, 139, 176
   date, 27, 29, 119, 120, 124, 125, 154, 175
   divorce(d), 11, 152

204

INDEX

family, families, 5–8, 19, 27, 30, 36, 44, 48–50, 51, 64, 68, 69, 94, 110, 112, 157, 169, 171–179
father, 3, 7, 19, 20, 33, 34, 50, 86, 90, 113, 115, 138, 143, 175
  patriarch, 53, 175
friendship(s), 38, 115, 173
girlfriend, 129, 179
grandfather, 30, 67, 68, 78
honorary member of the family, 169, 171
husband, 11, 27
  ex-husband, 90
in-laws, 50
intergenerational households, 112
inter-relational conflict, 27
kinship, 27, 30
marriage, 5, 8, 27, 48
matriarch, 51
mother(s), mom, 6, 16, 28, 48, 51–53, 87, 138, 171, 173, 175, 177
mother-in-law, 83, 88
parent(s), 7, 10, 11, 47–53, 55, 64, 70, 87, 107, 139, 140, 142, 145, 172, 174, 177–179
  estranged parents, 11
  helicopter, 177
  teacher-parents, 48
progeny, 48, 51
wife, 13, 15, 17, 27, 43, 46, 49, 88, 124
  ex-wife, 85
religion, religious, 7, 19, 78
  evangelicals, 78
  religious conservatives, fundamentalism, 18–20, 35
  religious leaders, 70
  religious zealots, 20
remedial, 10
Renga, Ian Parker, 108
representation(s). *See* narrative(s), patterns of representation(s)
revisionist. *See* narrative(s)
Revolutionary War, 5
Rhem, James, 109
Ribisi, Giovanni, 37. *See also Saving Private Ryan*
"Rip Van Winkle," 3
rite of passage, 69

Rivers, Deshawn, 90. *See also Vice Principals*
Roberts, John. *See also Bob's Burgers*
Roberts, Julia, 148, 156. *See also Larry Crowne*
Robinson, Armentress D., 89, 90, 92
rock 'n' roll, rock. *See* music, genres
Rock 'n' Roll High School, 54
Rockler, Naomi R., 121
Roddenberry, Gene, 161, 162
Rolling Stone Magazine, 77
Room 222, 146
Roosevelt, Franklin Delano, 15
Ron Clark Story, The, 99
Rose, Phil, 73
Roth, David Lee, 74
Rowling, J.K., 108, 110
Rowson, Susanna, 2
rubric, 23, 30
rural, 48
Rury, John, 49
Rush, Benjamin, 48
Ryan, Joan, 125. *See also Saved by the Bell*

S

sacrifice(s), 13, 46, 122, 134, 166
satire, satirical, satirized. *See* narrative(s)
Savage, Fred, 134, 141. *See also The Wonder Years*
Saved by the Bell, 119–131. *See also Good Morning, Miss Bliss*
  Principal Belding, 124, 125, 126, 127, 129. *See also* Dennis Haskins
  Miss Carrie Bliss, 119, 120, 124–126, 129. *See also* Hayley Mills
  Brian, 124, 125, 129. *See also* Barry Jenner
  Jessie, 122, 124, 126, 127. *See also* Elizabeth Berkley
  Karen, 124. *See also* Carla Gugino
  Kelly, 119, 120, 124, 126–129. *See also* Tiffani-Amber Thiessen
  Professor Lasky, 119, 120, 128, 129. *See also* Patrick Fabian
  Lisa, 127. *See also* Lark Voorhies
  Zack Morris, 119, 120, 122–129. *See also* Mark-Paul Gosselaar
  Slater, 122, 124, 126, 127. *See also* Mario Lopez

205

INDEX

Tina, 125. *See also* Joan Ryan
Saved by the Bell: The College Years, 119, 121, 128, 129
Saved by the Bell: The New Class, 119
Saviano, Josh, 141. *See also The Wonder Years*
Saving Private Ryan, 33–46
   Todd Anderson, 34. *See also* Ethan Hawke
   Sargeant Horvath, 37, 45. *See also* Tom Sizemore
   Private Jackson, 37. *See also* Barry Pepper
   Private Mellish, 37. *See also* Adam Goldberg
   Captain John Miller, 33–46. *See also* Tom Hanks
   Private Reiben, 37. *See also* Ed Burns
   Private Ryan, 33–36, 39, 41–46
   Corporal Upham, 37, 39. *See also* Jeremy Davies
   Medic Wade, 37. *See also* Giovanni Ribisi
savior(s). *See* educator(s)
   White savior. *See* race(s) and ethnicity, racial
Schaal, Kristen, 49. *See also Bob's Burgers*
Schiff, Richard, 17. *See also The West Wing*
scholar(s). *See* educator(s)
school(s), School, schooling, 1–3, 5, 7–13, 15, 16, 20, 21, 26, 28, 30, 35–57, 59, 62, 63, 67, 69–79, 87–90, 92, 93, 95, 97, 112, 115, 119, 120, 122, 124, 125, 127, 129, 130, 133, 135, 136, 138, 139, 143, 149, 150, 158, 171–174, 176, 177, 179. *See also* education, educational
   anti-school, 73, 74, 76
   "at-risk," low performing, 26, 98
   British public school (fee paying), 72
   charter, 68, 69, 74
   college(s), 8, 11, 41, 75, 76, 79, 100, 102, 105, 120, 136–139, 142, 143, 153, 157, 158
   common, Common School, 16, 47, 122
   community college(s), 138, 147–160
      college transfer courses, 152

continuing education, 152
      developmental education, 152
      early college, 152
      GED, 152
      vocational education, 139, 152, 158
   deschooling movement(s), 74
   elite liberal arts colleges, 158
   for-profit, 68, 143
   graduate, 136, 137
   high, 10, 36, 69–71, 73, 76, 81–83, 86, 87, 89, 121, 125, 134, 136, 139, 143, 144, 171, 174, 177, 179
      "the people's college," 139
   home schooling (noun), home-schooling (adjective), 8, 74
   Ivory Towers, 158
   Ivy League, 158
   junior high, 119, 120
   middle, 94, 100, 102, 104, 129
   middle-class school, 138, 143
   parochial, 74
   primary, 68, 75
   private, privatized, ix, 20, 34, 69, 74, 143
   public, public education, ix, 18–21, 35, 39, 44, 67–69, 74, 78, 79, 88, 89, 95, 122, 143, 171, 172, 178, 179
   school governance, 19
   secondary, 64, 75, 93, 119
   suburban, 89, 90
   violent school environments, 63
   vouchers, 20
   urban, city, 26, 35, 58, 63, 68, 87
school board, 15, 19, 20, 137, 140, 145
school choice, school choice vouchers 15
"School Days," 87
"School is Out," 71
"School's Out," 73
School of Rock, 35
"School Spirit Skit #2," 75
Schultz, Jaime, 98
Schultz, James, 174
Schwimmer, David, 148. *See also Friends*
science. *See* subject areas, subject(s)
Scott, Sir Walter, 137
screenwriter, 28
Segrave, Kerry, 70
Sehr, David T., 14

206

INDEX

self-actualization, 21
self-esteem, 112, 152
sex, 24–27, 31, 72, 77, 82, 86, 87, 125, 148
    boy(s), 4, 5, 8, 9, 34, 41, 45, 60, 63, 85,
        90, 93, 97, 110–115, 120, 171, 173,
        174
    erotic, eroticism, 64, 125
    girl(s), 4, 6, 8, 85, 97, 100, 104, 120,
        124, 126–128, 174–176, 179
    lovemaking, 50
    man, men, 3–7, 9, 17–19, 26, 27, 34,
        36–43, 45, 75, 76, 78, 79, 82–88, 90,
        91, 93, 94, 110, 111, 113, 122, 127,
        128, 169–173, 175, 176
    mating rituals, 128
    one-night stands, 25
    pornographic videos, 87
    sex roles. *See* gender
    sex-worker, 26,
        call girl, 15
    sexual abuse, 28
    sexual assault. *See* violence
    sexual dominance, 91
    sexual dynamics, 128
    sexual intercourse, 70
    sexual relationship(s), 27, 28, 87
    woman, women, 4
sexism, 63, 64, 82–85, 88, 90, 122
    gender bias, 64
    male gaze, 64, 74
    patronizing, 97, 122
    sexist, 83, 88, 93
sexuality, 23, 24, 27, 31, 64, 87, 113, 129,
    174
    bigotry (homophobia), 113
    bisexual, 24
    gay(s), 23, 24, 30, 31, 83–85, 113
    heteronormative, 30
    heterosexual, 31
    homosexual, 83
    lesbian, lesbianism, 23, 24, 31, 48
        dyke, 28
    queer. *See* gender, identity
    straight, 83
sexualized, sexualization, 63, 64, 74
STI, 42
Shakespeare, William, 60, 102, 103

Sheen, Martin, 15. *See also The West Wing*
Sher, Eden, 170. *See also The Middle*
short story, 2, 5
Simonetti, Marie-Claire, 121
Simpsons, The, 49
Sinclair, Amanda, 157
Sirtis, Marina, 163. *See also Star Trek: The*
    Next Generation
sitcom(s). *See* narrative(s), genre(s)
Sizemore, Tom, 37, 45. *See also Saving*
    Private Ryan
Slavin, Jonathan, 176. *See also Speechless*
slavery, 162
Sleepless in Seattle, 34
Smith, Allison, 15, 16. *See also The West*
    Wing
Smith, Rachel M., 84
social, socially, socialize, socialization,
    society, socio-, 11–13, 15, 24–26,
    29, 33, 40, 48–51, 55, 57, 59, 62, 64,
    69–71, 75, 76, 84, 87, 98, 103, 104,
    109, 114, 115, 121, 125, 129, 139,
    143, 147, 157, 152, 158, 174, 177
    alienate(s), alienated, alienating,
        alienation, 28, 40, 41, 54, 73, 115,
        152
    anti-social, antisocial, 69, 70, 115
    cliques, 136
    clubs, 136
    commentary, 24, 28, 47, 49, 55, 119, 122
        pro-social commentator, 75
    dance(s), 136, 157, 176
    isolation, 11, 30, 38, 73, 83
    psychosocial, 115
    social change(s), 59, 77, 179
    social construct, social constructions, 26,
        39, 74, 93, 108, 123, 145, 169
    social division, 26
    social entrepreneurs, 100
    social exclusion, 3
    social issues, problems, 123, 139
    social justice, 21, 59
    social lives, 177
    social norms, custom, 49, 78
    social order, 4, 16, 109
    social progress, 87, 129, 139
    social relevance, 146

INDEX

sociocultural, 49
socioeconomic, 76, 87, 157
sociohistorical, 48, 109, 170
sociopolitical, 77
social class, 64, 87, 143, 153
   administrative class, 47
   class system, 21
   middle class, middle-class, 75, 87, 122,
     123, 138, 139, 143
   professional, credentialed class, 78
   social mobility, 70
   upper-class, 104
   working class, working-class, 47, 49, 70
   blue-collar workers, 78
"Social Class and the Hidden Curriculum of
   Work," 87
social media, 78
social studies. *See* educator(s) and subject
   areas, subject(s)
Socratic approach. *See* learning
soldier(s). *See* war(s), War(s)
Sontag, Susan, 122, 123
Sorokin, P.A., 77
South Carolina, 89, 90
South Park, 49, 64
   Ike, 64. *See also* Milan Agnone
space(s), 25, 26, 27, 30, 42, 45, 50, 59, 90,
   91, 103, 104, 129, 134, 142, 150,
   151–153, 155, 156, 162
   proxemics, 151
Spanish American War, 15
Spanish Inquisition, 19, 162, 164
specialist(s), 50, 51
speech, 11, 14, 38, 39, 92, 152, 153, 173
   freedom of speech, 14
   hate speech, 172
Speechless, 169–180
   Dylan DiMeo, 171, 173, 175, 176. *See
     also* Kyla Kenedy
   JJ DiMeo, 171–179. *See also* Micah
     Fowler
   Jimmy DiMeo, 171, 173–176, 179. *See
     also* John Ross Bowie
   Kenneth, 169–179. *See also* Cedric
     Yarbrough
   Maya DiMeo, 171–178. *See also* Minnie
     Driver

Ray DiMeo, 171, 173, 175, 179. *See also*
   Mason Cook
Dr. Miller, 171, 173, 174, 176, 177. *See
   also* Marin Hinkle
Mr. Powers, 176. *See also* Jonathan
   Slavin
Spencer, John, 15. *See also The West Wing*
sphere(s), 26, 27, 48, 49, 55, 105, 128, 129,
   130
   dualism, 26
   private, 26, 27, 28, 48, 130
     personal, 128
     private-affective, 26
   public, 26, 48, 70, 130, 178
     professional, 128
     public-instrumental, 26
Spiner, Brent, 164. *See also Star Trek: The
   Next Generation*
spiritual, spiritually, 74, 109
sports, 88, 102, 127, 136
   athlete(s), 108, 112, 114
     stotan athlete, 113
     triathlete, 112, 114
   non-athletes, 127
stakeholders, 35
Stamile, Lauren, 154. *See also Community*
Stand and Deliver, 34
Star Trek: The Next Generation, 161–167
   Dr. Beverly Crusher, 166. *See also* Gates
     McFadden
   Data, 164–166. *See also* Brent Spiner
   Geordie, 166. *See also* LeVar Burton
   Natasha, 164. *See also* Denise Crosby
   Captain Picard, 161–167. *See also*
     Patrick Stewart
   Q, 161–167. *See also* John de Lancie
   Commander William Riker, 166. *See
     also* Jonathan Frakes
   Lieutenant Torres, 163. *See also* Jimmy
     Ortega
   Counselor Deanna Troi, 163. *See also*
     Marina Sirtis
   Vash, 166. *See also* Jennifer Hetrick
   Worf, 163, 165, 166. *See also* Michael
     Dorn
   Groppler Zorn, 164. *See also* Michael
     Bell

INDEX

Star Wars, 28
Starr, Ringo, 67, 68. *See also A Hard Day's Night*
status, 5, 87, 135, 136, 143, 148, 151, 170, 176–178
    deposed, lack of, 166, 173
    marginal, marginalized, 147, 148, 154, 172
    marital, 152
    outsider, 144, 169, 173
status quo, 28, 29, 48, 53, 109, 127, 142
Staunton, Imelda, 10. *See also Freedom Writers*
stereotype(s), stereotypical, stereotypically, stereotyping, 47, 53, 58, 63, 64, 88, 162. *See also* gender, race(s) and ethnicity, racial
    domineering administrator, 6
    buffoon(s), buffoonish, buffoonery, 81, 82, 86, 89, 92, 93, 94
    educators, schoolteachers, teachers, teaching, 2, 63, 64, 130, 133, 170, 176
        Ichabod Crane, 5, 8
        professors, 147, 149, 153, 154, 159
    erroneous,
    non-stereotypical, 82, 89
    school, 62
    urban students, 63
Stern, Daniel, 136. *See also The Wonder Years*
Stewart, Jon, 19
Stewart, Kathleen, 30
Stewart, Patrick, 162. *See also Star Trek: The Next Generation*
stigmatization, 84, 85
story, storyline. *See* narrative(s)
Stoic, stoicism, 6, 113
student(s)
    class clown, 52
    co-ed, 119, 120
    colonial-era schoolchildren, 49
    disengaged, 149
    docile, 149
    future problem-solvers and decision-makers, 158
    loner, 25, 29

lost causes, 23
nerdy, 74
nightmare, 62
perfect, 62
prep schoolers, 35
protégé(s), 111–114, 116
receptacles, 150
salvageable, 23
Student-as-Person, 37
students of color, 58, 98
undergraduate(s), 57, 143
visual learners, 52
Student Learning Objectives (SLOs), 35
student-teacher, 23, 25, 31, 103, 134. *See also* teacher-student
subject areas, subject(s), 36, 76, 79, 152, 158
    algebra, 5
    anthropology, 35, 153, 157
    art, 7, 30, 40,
    biology, 71, 154
    calculus, 38, 102
    civics, 14
    criminology, 154
    cultural studies, 26, 67, 88
    economics, 154
    English, English Composition, English Language Arts, 10, 36, 57, 59, 61, 83, 85, 134, 138, 143, 148, 154
    ethology, 162
    French, 71
    geography, 16, 156
    Greek, 5
    history, 14–17, 71, 78, 86, 95, 126, 154, 166, 176
    home economics, 53
    journalism, 112
    Latin, 5
    law, 16
    math, mathematics, 25, 71, 136, 147, 154, 165
        arithmetic, 76
        statistics, 153
    media literacy, 57, 64
    methods courses, 57, 64
    music, 125
    physical education, 51
        swimming, 52

INDEX

psychology, 69, 152
reading, 76, 145
science, 71, 78, 151
shop, 53
social studies, 13, 15, 17
Spanish, 87, 154, 179
transferable, 158
vocational. *See* education, educational
writing, 76, 145
subjugation, 84, 85
suburb, suburban, 34, 86, 87, 89, 90, 93,
124, 139, 143, 144
success(es), successful, 3–5, 7, 8, 24, 25, 38,
39, 40, 45, 62, 64, 68, 74, 75, 86, 90,
98, 100, 103–105, 108, 112, 115, 148,
149, 169, 170, 175
unsuccessfully, 138
suicide. *See* death
summer, 71, 73, 124, 174, 178
Supreme Court, 14
Swank, Hilary, 10, 26. *See also Freedom
Writers*
Swartout, Kevin M., 84
system(s), systemic, 17, 28, 35, 42–44, 91,
105, 123, 127, 139, 142, 145
class system. *See* social class
school, education, community college, 20,
44, 48, 57, 75, 76, 81, 139, 158, 178
grading system, 138, 141

T
taboo,
Takei, George, 154. *See also Community*
talk radio. *See* radio
Tartikoff, Brandon, 121
Taylor, Diva, 95. *See also Vice Principals*
Tea Party, 78
teacher(s). *See* educator(s)
teacher-student, 11, 24–27, 31, 119, 120,
128, 129, 149. *See also* student-
teacher
teachers unions, 18, 35
Teachers (movie), 145
Alex Jurrell, 145. *See also* Nick Nolte
Teacher (television series), 169
*Teacher TV: Seventy Years of Teachers on
Television*, 133, 170

teaching. *See* learning
technology, 57, 77, 78
technocracy, 72
technological state, 72
teenage, teenager(s). *See* adolescent,
adolescence
television, TV, ix, 27, 49, 55, 57, 59–61, 64,
70, 71, 74, 81, 82, 84, 86, 88, 89, 92,
95, 97, 119, 121–123, 130, 133–135,
143–145, 147–149, 151, 153–155,
157–159, 161, 163, 169–171, 174,
178, 179. *See also* narrative(s)
premium channel, 82
remake, 121
Television Academy (Academy of
Television Arts & Sciences), 144
Emmy, 144
terrorist, 14
test(s). *See* learning,
text(s), textual, ix, 1, 2, 24, 28, 31, 42, 57, 59,
60, 62, 64, 69, 83, 86, 89, 92, 95,101,
110, 135, 149, 150, 156
ur-text, 3
Tharp, Andra Teten, 84
theory, theorist(s), 23
border crossing, 148, 157
cognitive models, 82, 88
collective consciousness, 165
constructivist, 109
curriculum, 137
aesthetic classroom, 137
aesthetical-ethical-political
classroom, 136, 138, 139,
141
ethical relationship, 137
developmental psychology, 69
factory model, 72, 74, 78
Hollywood Model, The, 23–28, 30, 31,
133, 134, 144, 171
intersectional, intersectionality, 169,
171–173
intertextuality, "leaky boundaries," 85,
89, 95
intimacy, 23–32
Jungian, 109
"new knowledge" and "old knowledge,"
73

210

INDEX

queer theory, 23, 24, 25, 31
scientific methodology of research, 76
third-space theorists, 50
Theron, Charlize, 64. *See also Arrested Development*
Thiessen, Tiffani-Amber, 120, 126. *See also Saved by the Bell*
think tanks, 18
Thoreau, Henry David, 60
Those Who Can't, 170
titular, 50, 53, 120
tradition, traditional, 6, 9, 84, 138, 142, 149, 150
transcendental, 42
transgender. *See* gender, identity
Trekkies, 162
Tricario, Michael, 136. *See also The Wonder Years*
Trinity. *See* Christian
Trump, President Donald, 78
truth, 88, 91, 109, 124, 125, 138, 174

U

United States, 1–12, 14, 16, 17, 72, 77, 78, 90, 93. *See also* America
United States Constitution, 13
United States Department of Education, 89
"Unpacking a Liturgical Framing of Desire," 116
Up the Down Staircase, 50, 145
    Sylvia Barrett, 145. *See also* Sandy Dennis
urban, 35, 48, 58, 60, 63, 68, 86, 87, 98
utopian, 30

V

values, 26, 31, 38, 86, 92, 107, 108, 114, 137, 146
    American, 1, 2, 11, 134
    family, 78
Van Halen, 74
vice principal(s). *See* administrator(s), administration(s), administrative
Vice Principals, 81–96, 169, 170
    Ms. Abbott, 87. *See also* Edi Patterson
    Dr. Belinda Brown, 81, 82, 84, 89, 92, 94. *See also* Kimberly Hebert Gregory

Bruce Carter, 95. *See also* Jay DeVon Johnson
Christine, 88. *See also* Susan Parks
Dayshawn, 89, 94, 95. *See also* Sheaun McKinney
Gale, 85. *See also* Busy Phillips
Neil Gamby, 81–96. *See also* Danny McBride
Hass, 94. *See also* Brian Howe
Bill Hayden, 86. *See also* Mike O'Gorman
Jackie, 91. *See also* Owen Harn
Janelle, 85, 86. *See also* Maya G. Love
Jim, 87. *See also* Jason Biggs
Ms. LeBlanc, 83. *See also* Robin Bartlett
Ray Liptrapp, 85. *See also* Shea Whigham
Luke, 90. *See also* RJ Cyler
Mario, 90. *See also* Deshawn Rivers
Mi-Cha, 83. *See also* June Kyoto Lu
Nash, 94. *See also* Dale Dickey
Matthew Potter, 85. *See also* Ryan Boz
Reggie, 95. *See also* Diva Taylor
Lee Russell, 81–96. *See also* Walter Goggins
Martin Seychelles, 90. *See also* James M. Connor
Amanda Snodgrass, 85–88. *See also* Georgia King
Terrance Willows, 94. *See also* Marcuis Harris
Vice Principals: Behind-the-Scenes, 81
victim(s), 28, 85
Victorian, 26, 27
victory, 38, 46, 127
Vietnam War, 72
violence, 24, 26, 77, 84, 85, 94
    sexually assaulted, 27
vocational education. *See* school(s), community colleges,
Voorhies, Lark, 127. *See also Saved by the Bell*
vote, voting, 14, 17, 18

W

"Waitin' in School," 71
Walters, Barbara, 19

211

INDEX

war(s), War(s), 6, 10, 33–46. *See also*
    Korean War, Revolutionary War,
    Spanish American War, Vietnam
    War, World War II
  battle(s), 11, 33, 35, 38, 40, 41, 114, 133
  captain, 34–36, 38–46, 161, 162, 165,
    166, 167
  commanding officer, 38, 39
  corporal, 37–39
  fight(s), 17, 27, 33–35, 37, 42–44, 46,
    71, 88, 145, 163, 176, 177
  fronts, 33
  gang wars, 10
  general, 38
  medic, 37, 40
  mission(s), 33, 34, 36, 38, 39, 40, 42,
    43, 45
  munitions expert, 40
  mutiny, 36
  private, 33–39, 41–46
  sniper, 39, 40
  soldier(s), 36–45, 46, 162
  special assignment, 36
  strike, 33
  translator, 39, 40
Warner, Michael, 23, 24
Waters, Roger, 73
weapon, 42. *See also* War
  gun, 58
    blowgun, 153
    gunshot, 94
  knife, 58
Webster, Noah, 14
Weems, Mason Locke, 2, 7
west, West, Western, 9, 69, 70, 153
West Wing, The, 13–21
  President Bartlet, 15, 19, 20. *See also*
    Martin Sheen
  C.J. Cregg, 19. *See also* Allison Janney
  Leo McGarry, 13, 15, 19. *See also* John
    Spencer
  Mallory O'Brien, 15–17, 20. *See also*
    Allison Smith
  Sam Seaborn, 15, 16. *See also* Rob Lowe
  Mr. Willis, 13, 15, 17, 18. *See also* Al
    Frann
  Toby Ziegler, 17. *See also* Richard Schiff

Westward Expansion, 16
Whigham, Shea, 85. *See also Vice*
    Principals
White, Whiteness. *See* race(s) and ethnicity,
    racial
White, Betty, 153. *See also Community*
White House, 13–17, 19
White Shadow, 97
Whitman, Walt, 35, 60
"Why I Hate School but Love Education,"
    75
wife. *See* relationship(s)
Wild One, The, 69. *See also* Marlon
    Brando
Williams, Michael Kenneth, 155. *See also*
    Community
Williams, Robin, 42, 60. *See also Dead*
    Poets Society
Wilson, Dominique Beth, 109
Wire, The, 170
women's rights, 72
Wonder, Stevie, 176
Wonder Years, The, 133–146
  Jack Arnold, 138. *See also* Dan Lauria
  Kevin Arnold, 133–145. *See also* Fred
    Savage
  Norma Arnold, 138. *See also*
    Alley Mills
  Felicia, 136–138, 140–142. *See also*
    Wendy J. Cooke
  Ricky Halsenback, 136, 140. *See also*
    Scott Nemes
  Randy Mitchell, 136. *See also* Michael
    Tricario
  The Narrator, 136, 138, 140–142, 144.
    See also Daniel Stern
  Paul, 141. *See also* Josh Saviano
  Miss Shaw, 133–145. *See also* Lanei
    Chapman
  "Smart Kid," 140. *See also* Elliot
    Goldman
  Dr. Valenti, 138–142. *See also* Richard
    Fancy
"Wonderful World," 71
Wood, Donald, N., 76, 77
World War II, WWII, 33–46, 162
  D-Day, 34

work, working, 26, 27, 30, 49, 50, 52, 55, 59, 60, 62, 64, 76, 81, 87, 89, 90, 97–105, 109, 116, 120, 124–126, 145, 149, 151, 153, 156, 173, 178
work-life balance, 47, 48, 156
work-study situation, 49
workaholic, 47
working class, working-class. *See* social class
"Working Class Hero," 72
writing. *See* subject areas, subject(s)

Y

Yarbrough, Cedric, 171, 172. *See also Speechless*
yoga, 157
young adult literature, YAL, ix, 107–117. *See also* book(s)
Young, Michael, 142

Z

Zeichner, Kenneth M., 107–109
Zorich, Louis, 28. *See also Detachment*

Printed in the United States
By Bookmasters